Richard Hittleman's
YOGA
28 Day Exercise Plan

Now, for the man or woman who has little time and even less inclination for the grueling ordeals of calisthenics, isometrics, and other hardwork routines, here is a single, simple exercise plan which requires a minimum of effort to attain maximum results.

Progressing simply and effortlessly from exercise to exercise, systematically using each new bodily skill to advance to the next more complex movement, this dramatically different plan promises a firmer, fitter body and a happier, more peaceful spirit in only 28 days.

Yet the principles are so sound, the practices so simple, that this four-week program is sure to become a lifetime regimen insuring years of perfect health, lasting beauty and enduring peace of mind.

Bantam Books by Richard Hittleman
Ask your bookseller for the books you have missed

RICHARD HITTLEMAN'S GUIDE TO YOGA MEDITATION
RICHARD HITTLEMAN'S INTRODUCTION TO YOGA
RICHARD HITTLEMAN'S YOGA FOR TOTAL FITNESS
RICHARD HITTLEMAN'S YOGA 28 DAY EXERCISE PLAN
WEIGHT CONTROL THROUGH YOGA

RICHARD HITTLEMAN'S YOGA

28 DAY EXERCISE PLAN

BANTAM BOOKS
TORONTO · NEW YORK · LONDON · SYDNEY

YOGA 28 DAY EXERCISE PLAN

A Bantam Book/published by arrangement with Workman Publishing Co., Inc.

PRINTING HISTORY

Workman edition published September 1969
5 printings through July 1972

Book of the Month Club edition / November 1970

Cosmopolitan Book Club edition / 1970

Bantam edition / February 1973

2nd printing .....August 1973
3rd printing ..December 1973
4th printing ....April 1974
5th printing ...November 1974
6th printing ....April 1975
7th printing ....July 1975
8th printing ....January 1976
9th printing ....May 1976
10th printing ...October 1976
11th printing ......May 1977
12th printing ......May 1978
13th printing ..December 1978
14th printing ..February 1980
15th printing ......June 1980
16th printing ......April 1981
17th printing ..February 1982

Cover and inside photographs by Al Weber
Model: Cheryl Fischer
Book Design: Bernard Springsteel

ISBN 0-553-20999-X

Published simultaneously in the United States and Canada

PRINTED IN THE UNITED STATES OF AMERICA

26 25 24 23 22 21 20 19 18

contents

foreword

Interest in Yoga is at an all time high—and with good reason. During the past decade millions of Americans have come to recognize that the benefits of physical Yoga are very great: Not only do they far surpass those of any system of self-improvement for the body (calisthenics, salon programs, jogging, isometrics, competitive sports) but they extend also to the emotional and mental aspects of the individual. Yoga is concerned with the health and beauty of the organism as a unified **whole.** Weight control, slimming, firming, relief of tension and stiffness, improvement in general health, emergence of hidden beauty, emotional stability and a positive mental outlook will be experienced by all those who apply themselves diligently to the plan of this book. This is true practically regardless of age or present physical condition!

As recently as ten years ago it would have been considered virtually impossible to successfully accomplish, within a 28 day period, the physical techniques presented herein. Formerly, a student who undertook the serious study of Yoga was prepared to devote a minimum of several years to the learning of the major Yoga exercises **(asanas)** and an unknown period of time to the perfecting of them. Human organisms have not changed in the past ten years. But through my personal experience with many thousands of students and in the course of offering more than one thousand "Yoga For Health" television programs, I have evolved an **accelerated** method of instruction that now enables any serious student to learn and practice 38 Yoga exercises within a four week period! It is this unique system that is presented in the following pages.

Our format is simple. Most of the practice days consist of: (1) learning new exercises, (2) adding movements to exercises partially learned, (3) reviewing exercises that have been completed. The titles of each of these reviewed exercises is printed in gray. Every fourth day is devoted entirely to review. The numerous illustrations will always show you exactly how to proceed in new exercises and remind you of the correct movements for review. Days 17-25 list the exercises that are utilized in dealing with special problems.

Each day's exercises are arranged so that the sequence of the movements are performed first in a standing position, then sitting and finally lying. At the end of each day's exercises there is a page of Yogic information that should prove extremely interesting and of real value in your daily life.

Upon completion of the 28 day plan, you will refer to the routines at the end of the book that serve as a lifetime program for practice.

Read the following points carefully before you begin your first day of practice:

- The Yoga exercises are performed on a flat surface with sufficient space to stretch trunk and limbs in all directions. Select a quiet, well-ventilated area where you will not be disturbed.

- Cover your practice surface with a large towel, mat or pad. This cover is put away after exercising and kept only for Yoga.

- Your exercise clothing should allow for complete freedom of movement. Most women prefer leotards. Remove watch, eyeglasses and all confining apparel. Keep watch handy for the timing of certain exercises.

• Plan to devote 20-30 minutes to each day's practice. Anytime of day is satisfactory but always wait at least 90 minutes after eating. (You will find your body more flexible in the afternoons and evenings.)

• Make every effort to complete the program of this book in 28 **consecutive** days. If this does not prove possible, do not allow more than one day to elapse between practice sessions.

• The Yoga exercises are performed in a series of graceful, rhythmic **slow motion** movements with a brief "holding" (completely motionless) period for certain of the positions. Poise and balance are maintained at all times and the attention is fixed unwaveringly on the movements being executed.

• We attempt to approach each practice session in a serene frame of mind, having temporarily put aside all thoughts and activities that might be distracting. Before beginning the day's exercises, assume the cross-legged posture and spend one minute in allowing your body and mind to become quiet. In this way you will derive not only the physical benefits of Yoga but throughout the remainder of the day you will radiate the beauty and peace that are within.

• Remember that our objectives are to become firmly established in the principles of **Hatha** (physical) Yoga and experience major positive changes throughout the organism within the extremely brief period of only 28 days. Therefore, resolve now to proceed exactly as directed and let's begin. . . .

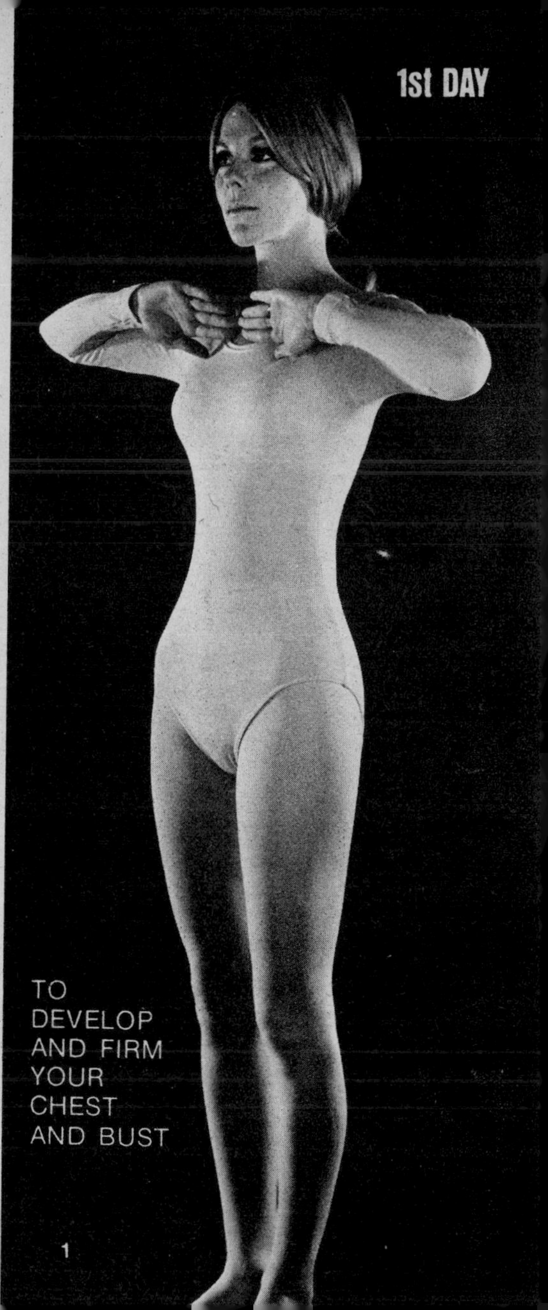

1st DAY

TO DEVELOP AND FIRM YOUR CHEST AND BUST

1st DAY

2

3

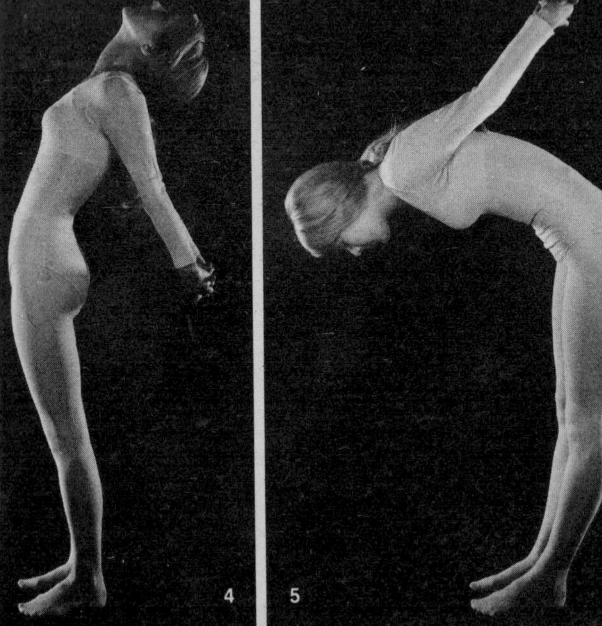

1 Stand in a relaxed posture
Spine straight
Arms at sides
Feet close together

Gracefully bring hands up to touch chest
Palms face outward

2 Slowly straighten arms outward at chest level
Feel elbows stretching

3 **Slowly** bring arms behind you
Keep them high at shoulder level
Feel shoulders stretching
Lower arms slightly so that fingers can be interlaced
Do not bend trunk at this point

4 **Very slowly and gently** bend backward
Bend several inches only
Do not bend farther than illustrated
Keep arms high; look upward
Hold without motion for 10
(Count this 10 rhythmically in approximate seconds)

5 **Very slowly and gently** bend forward
Do not bend farther than illustrated
Bring arms over back and keep them high
Neck muscles are relaxed; forehead points toward knees
Knees do not bend
Feel spine stretching gently
Hold without motion for 20

Slowly straighten to upright position
Unclasp hands; relax

Proceed to next exercise

1st DAY

back stretch

FOR STRENGTH AND FLEXIBILITY OF YOUR BACK AND SPINE

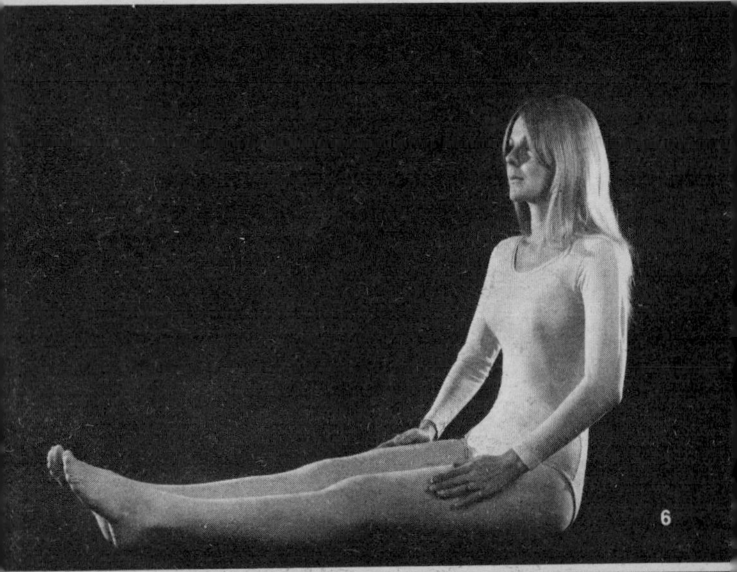

6

7

6 Sit as illustrated
Legs are together; feet touch
Hands rest on thighs
Spine straight

7 Think of the graceful movements of a ballerina
Raise arms slowly to shoulder level
Gracefully bring them overhead
Bend backward several inches (to firm abdomen)

8 Slowly, gracefully bend forward
Keep arms outstretched

9 Hold knees securely
Do not go farther than knees
Knees do not bend
Neck is relaxed; head bends forward

8

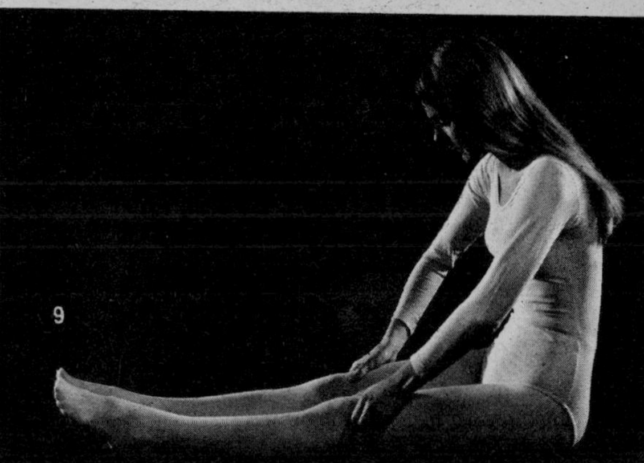
9

10 Hold knees firmly and draw trunk down
as far as possible
Forehead is aimed toward knees
Elbows bend outward (very important)
Knees remain straight
Feel spine stretching
But do not strain
Hold the posture motionless
Remain in your extreme position for 20

Slowly straighten to upright position of Fig. 6
Slide hands back up to knees

Proceed to next exercise

cobra

FOR REMOVING ALL TENSION FROM YOUR BACK AND SPINE

11

11 Lie on your mat as illustrated
Allow all muscles to relax completely

12 Rest forehead on floor
Gracefully place hands beneath shoulders
Fingers are together, pointing inward
(correct hand position is very important)

13 In **very slow motion** tilt head backward
Push hands against floor and begin to raise trunk
Spine must be curved

14 Raise trunk to position illustrated
Do not go farther than this position
Spine remains continually curved
Head remains tilted backward
Relax legs (note that they have a tendency to become tense)
Hold without motion for 15

Keep spine curved and **slowly** lower trunk
Slowly tilt head forward
Return first to position of Fig. 12
Then to position of Fig. 11
All muscles relax completely
(Note the feeling of deep relaxation)

Proceed to "Practice Plan"

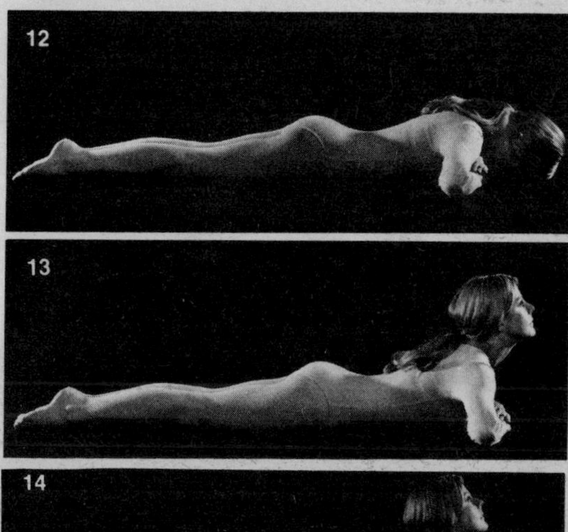

1st DAY

practice plan 1st day

Now that you have a feeling of the movements proceed as follows:

1. Return to Exercise 1, the Chest Expansion, and perform 3 times exactly as instructed *without pausing between repetitions.* Then relax for approximately one minute.

2. Next perform the Back Stretch 3 times without pausing between repetitions. Relax for approximately one minute.

3. Perform the Cobra 3 times without pausing between repetitions. Relax for approximately one minute.

4. Now perform each of the three exercises once, making the movements of one flow into those of the next as if performing a slow motion dance. Do this continuous dance-like routine of the three exercises twice.

Follow this Practice Plan to the letter. Do not do any additional Yoga exercising today.

thoughts for the day

STRETCHING FOR HEALTH AND BEAUTY

Today's exercises will provide a good indication as to how stiff, tight and tense you may have grown in many 'key' points of your body. The stiffer you find yourself, the greater your need for the gentle stretching movements of Yoga. A stiff, inflexible body cannot be a truly healthy and beautiful one. Remember that you must never strain, jerk or fight to achieve a more extreme position. Just go as far as you can, regardless of where it may be, and have the patience to hold as indicated. The "hold" will gradually impart the elasticity that is needed to accomplish the most extreme positions. This is true regardless of your age or physical condition. Once achieved, you will find that you can retain this wonderful flexibility for your entire life!

The Yogi (one who practices Yoga is a "Yogi") attaches great value in terms of both health and beauty to a strong, elastic spine and an ancient Yogic adage proclaims, "You are as young as your spine is flexible". You have only to look at the people around you to determine the truth of this statement. Young people whose spines have grown rigid will appear to be much older than their actual years. Conversely, people who have retained the elasticity of their spines and limbs appear youthful and "alive" in middle age and beyond. Therefore, a number of our exercises will be practiced for the express purpose of promoting the health, strength and flexibility of the entire spine, from the cervical vertebrae in the neck to the lowest of the lumbar vertebrae. If you follow our Yoga plan you will discover, to your delight, that the youthful "spring" is returning to your spine and joints within two to three weeks.

The Chest Expansion, Back Stretch and Cobra exercises learned today are not only powerful loosening techniques but they help to release energy that can be trapped in the spine and joints. You must never become discouraged or decide that any of these positions is too difficult. The response of even the most stubborn areas of the body to the ingenious Yoga movements is truly astonishing.

2nd DAY

triangle

1 Stand with legs approximately two feet apart
Gracefully raise arms to shoulder level
Palms face downward

2 Bend slowly to the left keeping arms outstretched
Take a firm hold on the left knee
Do not go lower than the knee
Knees remain straight
Bring right arm over as far as possible
Do not bend elbow

Feel right side tightening
Relax neck muscles
Hold without movement for 15

3 Slowly straighten to upright position

4 Perform identical movements to right side
Remember to move gracefully
Knees remain straight
Left arm is straight
Hold for 15

Slowly straighten to upright position
Slowly lower arms to sides
Slowly bring legs together; relax

Proceed to next exercise

2nd DAY

ADDITIONAL MOVEMENTS FOR THE

chest expansion

We will now continue with the movements of this exercise learned on the 1st day
Read the entire text below before actually performing the exericse.

Return to Exercise 1 Page 9 , 1st day

Perform the movements of Figs. 1-3 as instructed, Pp. 9-10

5 Compare with position of Fig. 4, Page 10
Fig. 5 depicts a slightly more extreme backward position
6 Do not bend farther than illustrated
Hold without motion for 10 counts

Slowly straighten to upright position
Unclasp hands; relax

Now that you understand these more advanced positions perform the entire exercise as instructed

Proceed to next exercise

TO FIRM YOUR THIGHS

knee and thigh stretch

7

8

7 In a seated position clasp feet firmly
Pull heels in as far as possible

Sit erect

Pull up against feet and slowly lower knees
Feel thighs tightening

8 Pull hard against feet
Continue to lower knees as far as possible
Sit erect
Hold your extreme position without motion for 20

Relax hold on feet and allow knees to be raised

Once again pull against feet and repeat movements

Release hold
Extend legs straight outward

Proceed to next exercise

2nd DAY

ADDITIONAL MOVEMENTS FOR THE

back stretch

9

10

We will now continue the movements of this exercise learned on the 1st Day.

Return to Exercise 2, Page 12 and perform as instructed, once

Now we wish to make the stretching more intensive

9 Perform the movements of Figs. 6-8 only, Pp. 12-13 but now bend foward several inches farther.

Attempt to hold the calves (If you cannot as yet hold calves, revert to knees)

10 Hold calves firmly and draw trunk down as far as possible
Forehead is aimed toward knees
Elbows bend outward
Knees must remain straight
Do not strain
Today hold your extreme position (as far down as you can come) without motion for 20 counts

Slowly straighten to upright position

Proceed to next exercise

TO TRIM YOUR WAISTLINE

simple twist

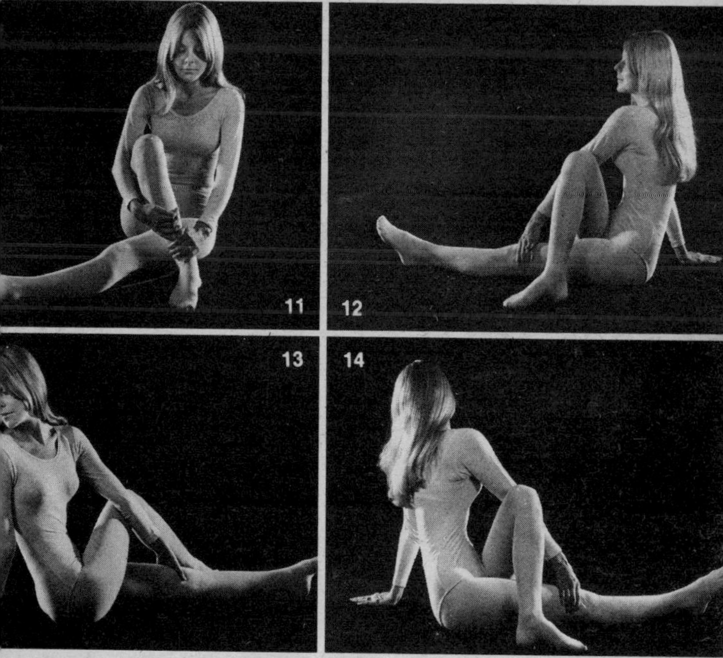

11 In a seated posture cross right leg over left
Place right foot as illustrated

12 Place right hand firmly on floor behind you
Bring left hand **over** to hold left knee firmly

13 Slowly twist as far as possible to **right**
Note position of head and chin
Hold without motion for 10

Keep hold on right knee; turn forward to position of Fig. 12 and relax
Now repeat twist to extreme right
Hold for 10
Turn forward; release hold; extend legs outward

2nd DAY

14 Perform identical movements to **left** side
Hold for 10
Turn forward and relax
Repeat twist to left
Hold for 10
Turn forward; release hold; extend legs outward

Proceed to next exercise

ADDITIONAL MOVEMENTS FOR THE

cobra

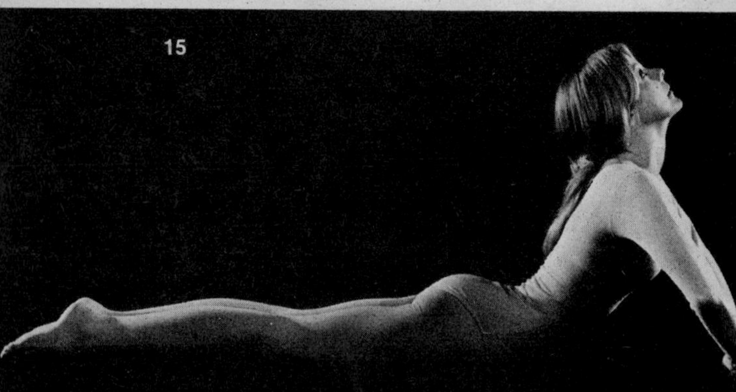

We will now continue with the movements of this exercise learned on the 1st Day
Read the instructions below before actually performing the exercise

Return to Exercise 3, Page 14

Perform the movements of Figs. 11-13 on Pp. 14-15

15 Compare with position of Fig. 14, Page 15
Fig. 15 depicts a slightly higher position of trunk
Do not raise farther than illustrated
Hold without motion for 15

Lower trunk exactly as instructed in Fig. 14

Now perform the entire exercise

Proceed to "Practice Plan"

practice plan 2nd day

1. Return to the Triangle and perform as instructed 3 times to each side *without pausing between repetitions.* Then relax for one minute.

2. Perform the more advanced Chest Expansion twice without pausing between repetitions. Relax.

3. Perform the Knee and Thigh Stretch 3 times without pausing between repetitions. Relax.

4. Perform the more advanced Back Stretch twice without pausing between repetitions. Relax.

5. Perform the Simple Twist twice on each side without pausing between repetitions. Relax.

6. Perform the more advanced Cobra once.

Now perform each of these 6 exercises once, without pausing between them, making the movements of each one flow into those of the next as if performing a slow-motion dance. Perform this continuous dance-like routine of the 6 exercises *once.*

Do not do any additional Yoga exercising today.

thoughts for the day

WHAT IS YOGA?

Many centuries ago, in that area of the world now known as "India," men of great intellectual and spiritual stature perceived in a very direct way that human beings are "disjointed." That is, the body, emotions, mind and spirit pull in their own directions as each, in turn, demands the fulfillment of its own needs and desires. This causes a continual separation and prevents the individual from functioning as an **integrated whole** wherein his full potential is realized. To make possible an integration of the body, mind and spirit, to unify the diverse aspects of the organism and end the "split", these wise men **(gurus)** of ancient times evolved and perfected, over the centuries, a system of self-development known as **Yoga,** a Sanskrit word meaning "union" or "joining together."

There are several major types of Yoga each employing different techniques but all designed to achieve the same **unifying** objective. The two major Yogas that concern us in this book are **Raja** (meditation) Yoga and **Hatha** (physical) Yoga, with the emphasis on the latter. The objectives of Hatha Yoga are twofold: (1) to cultivate the natural beauty of the body and attain a high state of health; (2) to awaken a great power that lies dormant in the organism and utilize it for developing one's own unique, individual potential; that is, to achieve **self-realization.**

From the above you can understand that Yoga is not simply another system of exercising. The word "exercise" is used in this book as a convenience. More precisely, Hatha Yoga is composed of a series of postures or poses **(asanas** in Sanskrit). As you perform the asanas you must be aware that they have been carefully designed to promote health and beauty as well as stimulate energies that will be of extreme importance in the days to come. Hence the necessity for poise, balance and concentration at all times during practice.

3rd DAY

circular motion

TO TRIM
YOUR
WAISTLINE

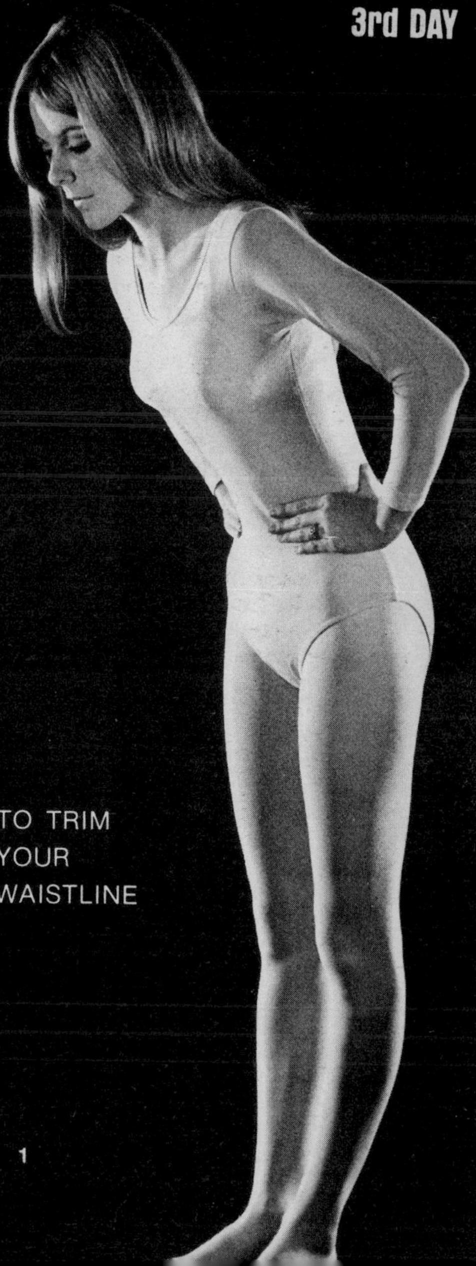

1

3rd DAY

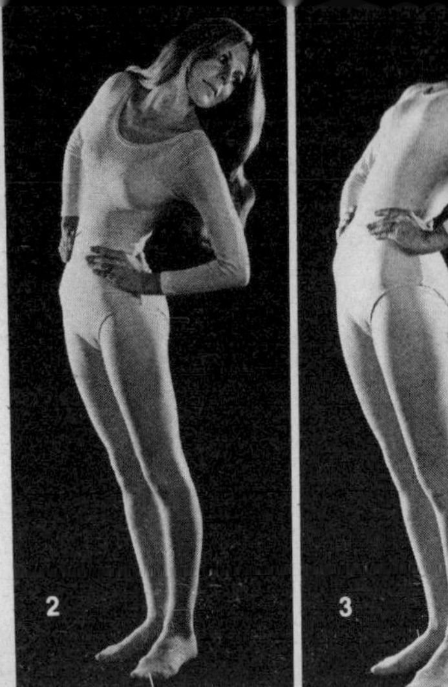

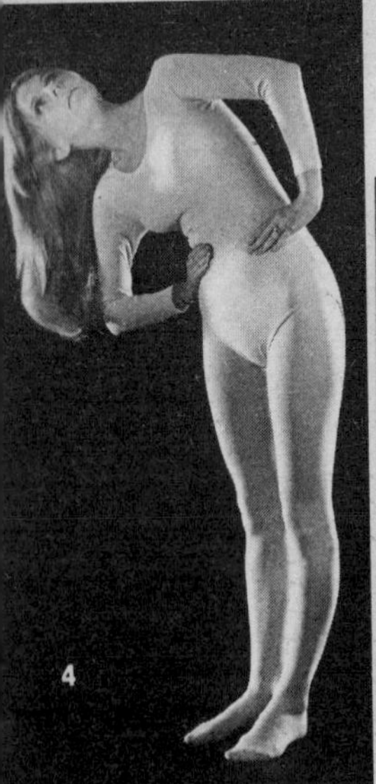

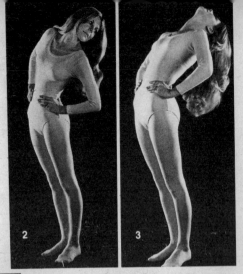

1 Stand with heels touching
Place hands on hips
Slowly bend forward a **short distance only,** as illustrated

2 Roll and twist trunk a moderate distance to left
Move slowly
Trunk does not only **bend** to left; it **rolls and twists** with exaggerated movement

Hold without motion for 5

3 Roll and twist trunk a moderate distance backward
Again, trunk must **roll and twist** with intensive movement in waist

Hold without motion for 5

4 Roll and twist trunk moderate distance to right
Hold for 5

Roll and twist trunk forward to original position
Hold for 5

5 Repeat movements but widen circle made with trunk
Bend forward several additional inches to intermediate position

Roll and twist trunk (slowly) increased distance to left
Rolling and twisting movements now become more intensive
Hold for 5

6 Continue wider circle by rolling and twisting to backward position
Hold for 5

Roll and twist increased distance to right
Hold for 5

Roll and twist to forward position
Hold for 5

7

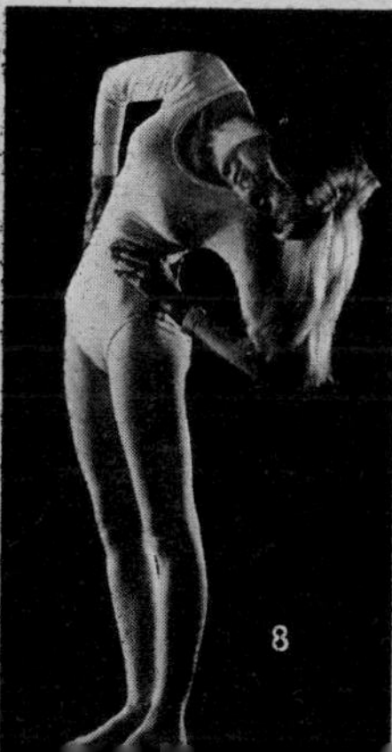
8

3rd DAY

7 Repeat movements and make widest circle possible
Bend forward to extreme position

8 Roll and twist trunk as far as possible to left
Hold for 5

Roll and twist with very exaggerated movements to extreme backward position
Hold for 5

Roll and twist to extreme right
Hold for 5

Roll and twist to forward position
Hold for 5

Straighten slowly to upright position
Lower arms; relax

Proceed to next exercise

ADDITIONAL MOVEMENTS FOR THE

triangle

9

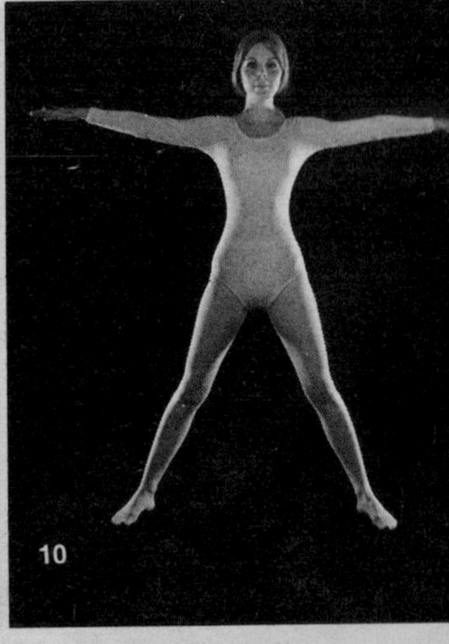

10

We will now continue with the movements of this exercise that we learned on the 2nd Day

9 Return to Exercise 4 and perform as instructed, once (Pago 19)

10 Now we wish to make the stretching more intensive
Therefore, widen the stance; feet are placed farther apart as illustrated
Compare with Fig. 1, Page 18

11 Bend slowly to the left as before
This time take a firm hold on the **calf** (Note increased pressure on insides of thighs)
Do not go lower than the calf
Knees remain straight
Bring right arm over as far as possible
Do not bend elbow
Feel increased tightening of right side
Relax neck muscles
Hold without movement for 15

Slowly straighten to upright position of Fig. 10

12 Perform identical movements to right side
Remember to move gracefully
Knees remain straight
Left arm is straight
Hold for 15

Slowly straighten to upright position
Slowly lower arms to sides
Gracefully bring legs together
Relax

Proceed to next exercise

3rd DAY

FROM THIS POINT ON,
TITLES PRINTED IN GRAY
INDICATE REVIEWED EXERCISES.

knee and thigh stretch

13 Return to Exercise 5, Page 21 and perform twice

Proceed to next exercise

back stretch

14 Return to Exercise 2, Page 12 and perform the knee movements, once

15 Return to Exercise 2, Page 22 and perform the calf movements, once

Proceed to next exercise

simple twist

16 Return to Exercise 6, Page 23 and perform twice on each side

Proceed to next exercise

TO TRIM YOUR WAISTLINE AND FIRM YOUR LEGS

leg over

3rd DAY

18

19

17 Lie on your back
Allow all muscles to relax
Bend right knee and raise as illustrated

18 Straighten right leg
Bring it as far toward your head as possible

19 Slowly bring leg over and down
Attempt to touch floor
Both shoulders remain on floor
Bring leg as far as possible toward head
Knee must not bend
Hold without motion for 10 -

Bring right leg back into position of Fig. 18
Lower to floor

Without pause perform identical movements with left leg
Hold for 10

Proceed to "Practice Plan"

practice plan 3rd day

(Do not pause between repetitions of the exercises below)

1. Return to Circular Motion and perform the entire routine of the three positions, 3 times. Relax.

2. Perform the Triangle in the following routine: first execute the movements to the knee only. Perform this twice to each side, alternating the sides (left-right, left-right). Then, without pause, perform the additional movements learned today twice to each side, alternating the sides. Relax.

3. Perform the Knee and Thigh Stretch 3 times. Relax.

4. Perform the Back Stretch twice with the knees; then, without pause, twice to the calves. Relax.

5. Perform the Simple Twist twice on each side. (Do not alternate sides.) Relax.

6. Perform the Leg Over 3 times, alternating sides. Relax.

Now perform each of these 6 exercises once, as directed above, without pausing between them, executing the same dance-like routine that was done on the 1st and 2nd Day.

Do not do any additional Yoga exercising today.

3rd DAY

thoughts for the day

BEAUTY THROUGH POISE AND BALANCE

"The body is the temple of the spirit, conceived in the image of its maker." This is the very first of the eternal truths that I attempt to impress upon students so that each one becomes aware of the infinite power and beauty of her own, individual body. As this fact begins to penetrate the consciousness there is a natural attempt on the part of the student to cultivate those characteristics of beauty which lie within her. The Yoga techniques are unsurpassed for this purpose, as we shall see.

We have already stressed the necessity for attempting to perform the Yoga movements with poise and balance, since these are essential qualities of beauty. There is something magnetic and radiant about the woman who moves, gestures, walks, sits and stands with natural grace and poise. She reflects an eternal aspect of true femininity. However, these movements cannot be successfully contrived, that is, you cannot copy or impose them upon yourself; they must flow rhythmically and naturally from the center of your being.

Poise, balance, grace and a beautiful carriage emerge naturally from the Yoga practice. Stiffness of the joints and limbs, a condition that inhibits poise and good posture are eliminated through the stretching exercises. The slow motion, "ballet-type" routines that we will perform later impart a strong sense of rhythm and balance. These qualities are carried over into all of your daily activities and, although subtle, are felt by everyone who comes in contact with them. People who have not seen you for some time will inquire, "What have you been doing? You look different but I don't know exactly what it is." The "difference" reflects the poise and confidence gained through Yoga.

Therefore, we make a conscious attempt to execute all of our exercises gracefully and rhythmically and, in turn, the very performance of these movements imparts the poise and balance we are seeking to manifest.

review chest expansion

Each 4th Day it will be very valuable for us to carefully review as much as possible of the material we have previously learned.

This review will help you to check your progress as well as aid you in "setting" your body in the various postures.

Whenever you have the slightest doubt concerning how any exercise is to be done make certain to refer to the pages indicated.

1

2

3

4

4th DAY

1-2 Perform this position learned on Page 9 twice without pausing between repetitions. Then relax for a moment

3-4 Perform this more advanced position learned on Page 20 twice without pausing between repetitions Then relax for several moments

Remember to:
Hold arms high at all times
Keep knees straight
Relax neck muscles in the forward bend so that head hangs limp

Proceed to next exercise

triangle

5

6

In this exercise we will not only review, but add an advanced position

5 Perform this position learned on Page 21 twice on each side, alternating the sides—left-right; left-right Relax for a moment

6 Perform this position learned on Pp. 30-31 twice on each side, alternating the sides. Relax for a moment

7 Now we wish to make the stretching still more intensive
Therefore, widen the stance once again
Feet are placed as far apart as possible
Arms are raised as before

8 Bend slowly to the left as before
This time take a firm hold on the **ankle**
(Note intense pull on insides of thighs)
If you cannot as yet hold ankle, revert to calf
Slowly bring right arm over as far as possible
Note now the triangles formed by the limbs
Hold without movement for 15

Slowly straighten to upright position

Perform identical movements to right side
Hold for 15

Slowly straighten to upright position
Slowly lower arms to sides
Gracefully bring legs together
Relax

Proceed to next exercise

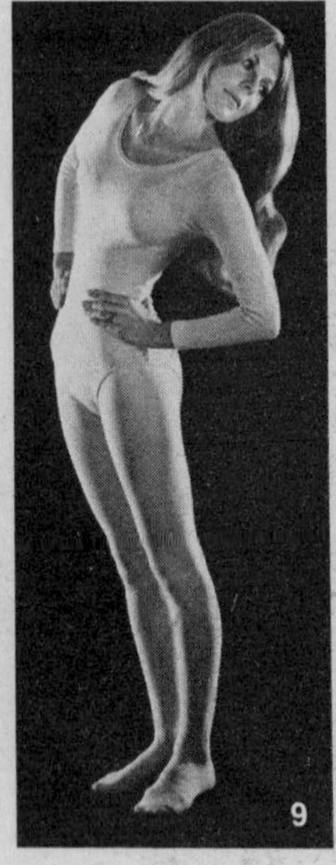

circular motion

9 10 11

Perform this exercise twice from **each** of the three positions learned on Page 27
Do not pause between any of the repetitions
Relax upon completion

Remember to:

Keep in mind the image of three circles being made as the trunk rolls and twists
These circles become increasingly larger and are to be considered as small, intermediate and extreme

Roll and twist the trunk with very exaggerated movements in the waist, even in the positions of the small circle

knee and thigh stretch

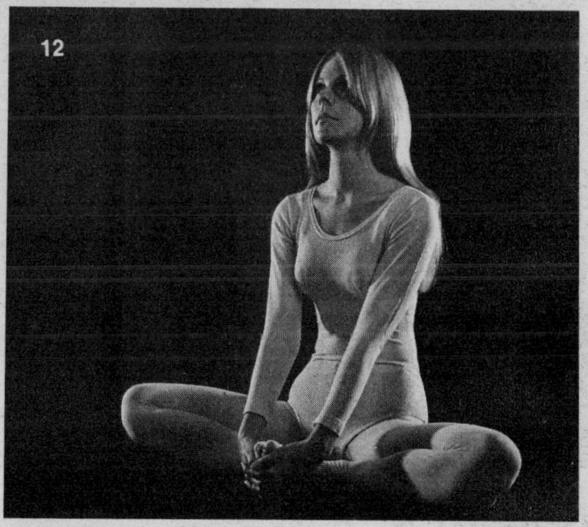

12 Perform 3 times without pausing between repetitions as learned on Page 21. Relax

Remember to:

Keep the spine straight
Pull hard against feet so that knees may be lowered

Proceed to next exercise

simple twist

13 Perform twice to right side, then twice to left side as learned on Page 23. Do not pause between repetitions. Relax upon completion

4th DAY

13

Remember to:

Turn head as far toward your back as possible to assist in complete twisting of spine

Proceed to next exercise

back stretch

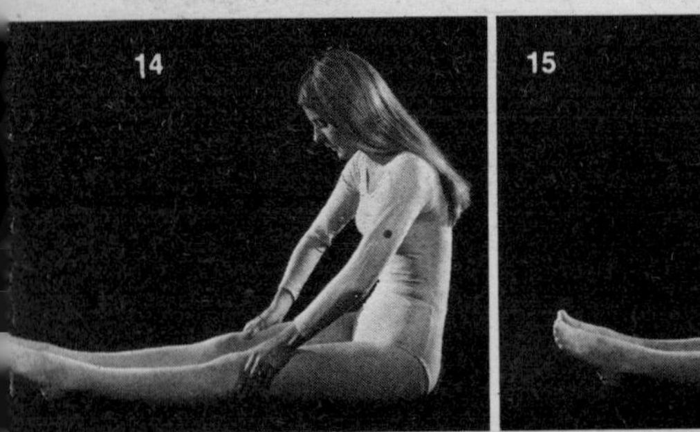
14

15

16

14-15 Perform this position learned on Page 12 twice without pausing between repetitions
Then relax for a moment

16 Perform this more advanced position learned on Page 22 twice without pausing between repetitions
Relax

Remember to:

Aim forehead toward knee (neck muscles relax)
Bend elbows outward
Remain motionless in extreme positions (do not pull, tug or fight to get down an extra inch)

Proceed to next exercise

leg over

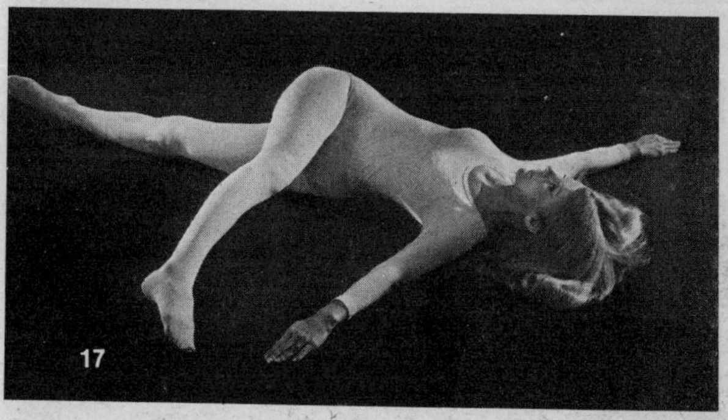

17 Perform three times to each side, alternating legs as learned on Pp. 33-34. Do not pause between repetitions. Relax

Remember to:

Keep leg as high toward the head as possible in the extreme position

Proceed to next exercise

4th DAY

cobra

18 Perform once, raising the trunk only to this position as learned on Pp. 14-15.

19 Without pause, repeat the movements raising the trunk to this hgher position as learned on Page 24. Relax

Remember to:

Place hands as instructed
Keep spine arched throughout exercise
Hold head back
Relax legs

18

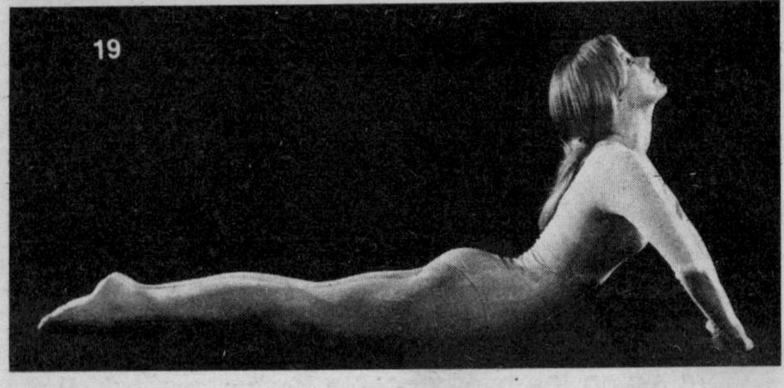

19

practice plan 4th day

To complete this review we will perform each of these 8 exercises once without pausing between them, executing the same dance-like routine we have attempted previously. The routine consists of the following:

Chest Expansion (2nd position only)—Triangle (ankle only)—Circular Motion (extreme circle only) —Knee and Thigh Stretch—Simple Twist (once on each side)—Back Stretch (calf position only)—Leg Over (once on each side)—Cobra (higher position only)

Do not do any additional Yoga exercising today.

thoughts for the day

TOTAL INVOLVEMENT IN YOUR PRACTICE

Inherent in most systems of calisthenics is the need to execute many quick repetitions of the exercises. huff puff, perspire and experience general discomfort and fatigue. Often it is only at the point of complete exhaustion that many women feel they have benefited from their "workout." But meaningful exercise, which I define in terms of **methodical body manipulation,** need contain none of the above. Indeed, the Yoga session is designed to be a highly pleasurable experience in which, as you now know, the exact opposites are true. That is, the movements are performed in relaxing, slow motion with very few repetitions, no strain should ever be felt and the practice sessions leave you feeling elevated and revitalized, not drained.

Contrasting the two concepts further, we find that in most systems of calisthenics it is not particularly important what the mind is thinking or where it wanders as long as the body is executing the required movements. As a matter of fact, in many calisthenics classes music is played as a type of distraction; the mind is encouraged to disengage itself from the boredom and discomfort that the body is experiencing. But again, the exact opposite is true of Yoga and it is this point that we now wish to impress strongly on the student. **Throughout the Yoga practice session we attempt to fix the consciousness fully on all movements of the exercises and not allow it to wander. We become totally involved in what we are doing.** You must **feel** what is happening in your organism, especially during the holding periods; learn to **feel** the stretching, **become** the stretch and do not run away from it; **feel** the stimulation; **feel** the release of energy within you; **feel** the relaxation. If you perceive that your attention is wandering, bring it back, gently but firmly to what you are doing. Before beginning each day's exercises remind yourself of this procedure.

The practice of deep concentration on the movements, excluding all interfering thoughts, results in a pronounced increase in the effectiveness of the exercises. Later, upon completion of the day's exercises, you will be instructed to sit very quietly for a brief period and become aware, to the greatest degree possible, of what is transpiring within you.

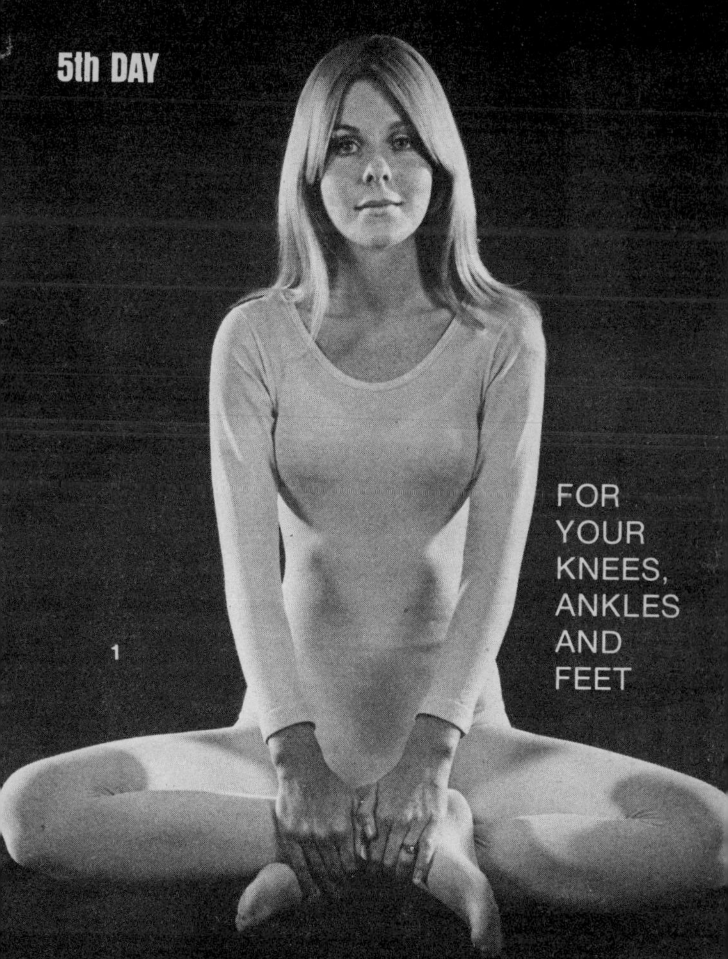

half-lotus

5th DAY

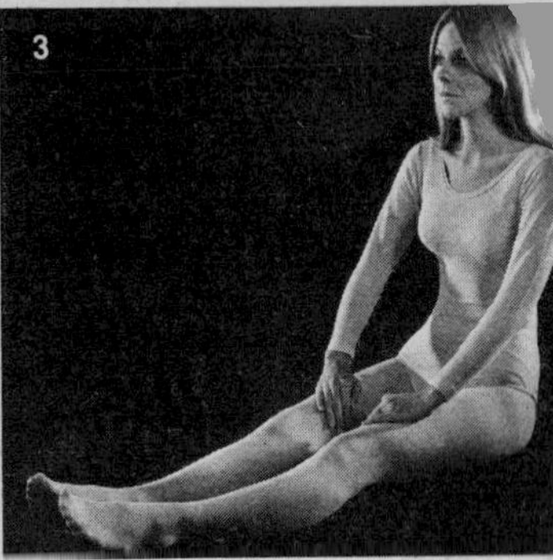

The meaning and importance of the Lotus postures are outlined at the conclusion of the 27th Day.

1 This is the simple cross-legged posture
It will be used by students who find the more advanced Lotus positions too difficult

Cross ankles and hold them firmly

2 Pull ankles in as far as possible
Sit erect but not rigid
Rest wrists on knees
Lower eyelids

3 Preparation for the Half Lotus
Extend both legs straight outward

4 Hold left foot firmly
Place left foot and heel as illustrated
Heel is in as far as possible
Foot rests against (not under) right thigh

5 Bring right foot in
Hold right foot with both hands
Place foot on left thigh or in fold of left leg (whichever is more comfortable)
If this position is not as yet possible, revert to the simple cross-legged posture

4
5
6
7
8

5th DAY

Sit erect but not rigid (very important)
Hands rest on knees; fingers are in position illustrated in Fig. 7
Lower eyelids

6 Attempt the same posture with the legs reversed

You may assume the position of either Fig. 5 or 6 (whichever is more comfortable) for all subsequent exercises where a "cross-legged" posture is indicated

7 A closeup of the hand and finger position

8 If Half-Lotus is difficult for you this position will assist in accomplishment

Foot rests on thigh
Forearm rests on raised knee
No movement is necessary
Sit in this posture one to two minutes whenever practicing the Lotus
Weight of forearm will gradually lower knee

Practice on both sides

complete breath

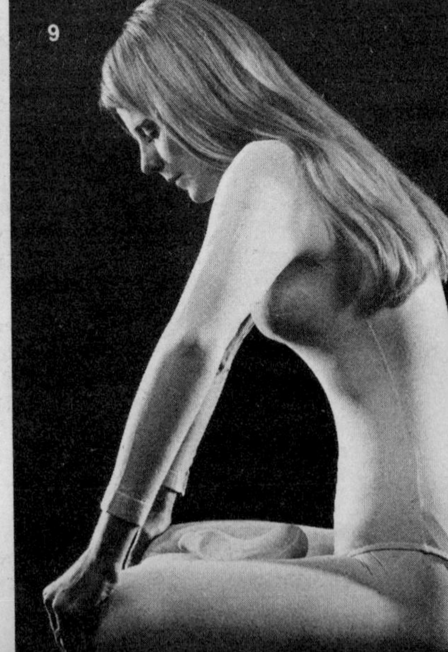
9

FOR ALL THE BENEFITS OF CORRECT DEEP BREATHING

10

11

9 Sit in a cross-legged posture (whichever one you have found most comfortable)
Our objective here is to empty all air from the lungs
Begin to slowly exhale **through the nose**
Simultaneously contract abdomen as far as possible to assist in complete exhalation

10 Begin a very slow, quiet inhalation (through nose)
Simultaneously attempt to slowly distend (push out) in abdominal area using abdominal muscles. This movement permits air being inhaled to enter lower area of lungs

(If abdominal movements seem difficult, breathe normally and concentrate temporarily on contracting and distending the abdomen to get your abdominal muscles working. Moving the abdominal wall only an inch or two will be sufficient for today. When you have gained some mastery over the abdominal muscles, resume the exercise)

11 Continue the slow, quiet inhalation
Simultaneously contract the abdomen slightly and attempt to expand the chest as far as possible

5th DAY

12 Continue the slow, quiet inhalation
Simultaneously raise the shoulders slowly as high as possible (This permits air to enter high area of lungs)

Hold breath with shoulders raised for a count of 5

Now slowly and quietly exhale deeply, relaxing shoulders and chest as you exhale and contracting as in Fig. 9
When exhalation is completed, repeat

Summary:
1. exhale deeply, contract abdomen
2. inhale slowly, distend abdomen
3. continue inhalation, expand chest
4. continue inhalation, raise shoulders
5. retain breath for count of 5
6. exhale deeply, relax shoulders and chest, contract abdomen. Repeat

The importance of this breathing exercise cannot be overstated. It has an effect on your entire Yoga study. Be patient and practice carefully. Inhale very slowly so that you have sufficient time to perform the necessary body movements. Practice to make the body movements flow into one another very smoothly.

Perform 10 times pausing between repetitions whenever necessary. If legs become tired in cross-legged posture extend them straight outward and massage knees. Then reverse position of legs and continue the exercise.

With just a few days of practice this invaluable breathing technique will become second nature to you.

complete breath standing

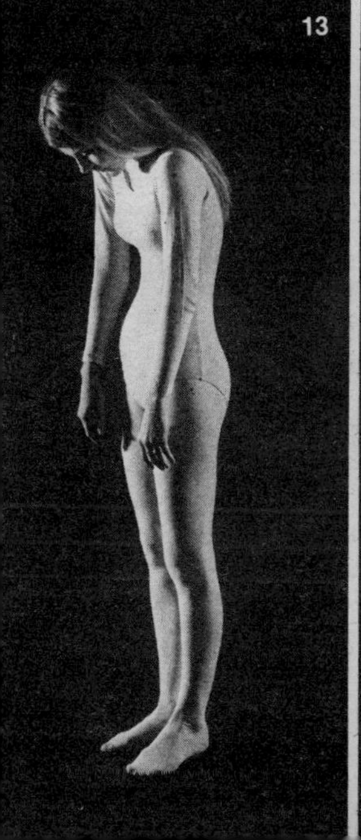

13

14

5th DAY

The movements of this exercise are performed in conjunction with the Complete Breath, just learned

13 Move off your mat and stand directly on the floor
Feet together as illustrated
Exhale and contract abdomen as previously learned
Simultaneously relax muscles so that trunk becomes limp

14 Begin deep inhalation (abdomen expands)
Simultaneously raise arms; palms face upward

15 Continue deep inhalation; chest expands
Bring hands to touch overhead
Simultaneously raise high on toes

Hold extreme position as steady as possible for 5

16 Begin deep exhalation
Very slowly lower to limp position of Fig. 13
Palms face downward

Perform 5 times without pausing between repetitions

Sit down on your mat; relax
Assume a cross-legged posture
Perform the Complete Breath twice

Relax

Do not do any additional Yoga exercising today

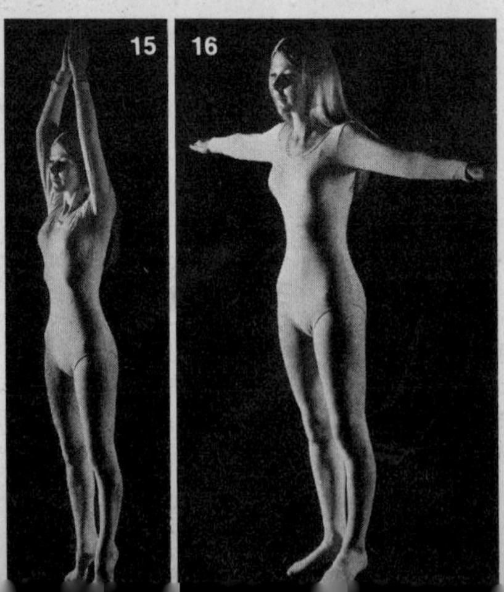

thoughts for the day

LIFE AND BREATH

"Life is in the breath; therefore he who only half breathes, half lives." This Yogic proverb attempts to impress upon us that the way in which we breathe directly affects our physical and mental well-being and determines to a great extent the length and quality of our lives!

The body can go for many weeks without food and for days without water or sleep but life will expire in a matter of minutes without air. Thus, the primary source of our sustenance is derived from an element in the air we breathe. In Yoga, this subtle element is known as **prana** or **life-force.** Prana is not the air itself but the subtle life-giving element extracted from the air. The more life-force you have in your body, the more "alive" you are; the less life-force, the less life. It's as simple as that. Life-force is present in all forms of nourishment but, obviously, it is most accessible and most constant in the air.

Most people have the habit of shallow breathing, using only the upper part of the lungs. Even when a so-called "deep breath" is attempted the lungs are only partially filled. Therefore, the primary objective of the Complete Breath, learned today, is to utilize the lungs in their entirety and extract the most life-force possible. Increased prana will improve the quality of your blood, complexion and general health. A secondary objective of the Complete Breath is to help make breathing slow and rhythmic whenever possible. The Yogi contends that people who are breathing in a rapid and erratic fashion develop nervous bodies and minds and shorten their lives. You will experience a very immediate, positive effect on your emotions and mind from Yogic breathing. When the breath is slow and rhythmic, anxieties and tensions lessen or dissolve completely and control of the mind for purposes of concentration is greatly increased. That is why we indicate frequent practice of the Complete Breath in this book and why we now advise you to take a few Complete Breaths whenever possible during the day. If you do not lift the shoulders you will not draw attention to yourself and consequently you can breathe fully and deeply anywhere and at anytime when you need to revitalize your body and clear your mind. Remember, **life is in the breath.**

6th DAY

complete breath standing

1 Perform three times as learned on 5th Day
Do not pause between repetitions. Relax

Remember to:

Breathe slowly and deeply so that all of the raising movements may be performed smoothly during the inhalation and exhalation

Proceed to next exercise

triangle

2 Perform this position learned on Page 18 twice on each side, alternating the sides
Relax for a moment

3 Perform this position learned on Pp. 30-31 twice on each side, alternating the sides
Relax for a moment

4 Perform this position learned on Pp. 38-39 twice on each side, alternating the sides

Hold each of the side bends in the above three positions for a count of 10, not 15 as previously instructed

Do not pause between any of the repetitions

Remember to:

Bring the arm far over the head and hold elbow straight

Proceed to next exercise

knee and thigh stretch

5 Perform three times without pausing between repetitions as learned on Page 21. Relax

Remember to: Keep spine straight

Proceed to next exercise

6th DAY

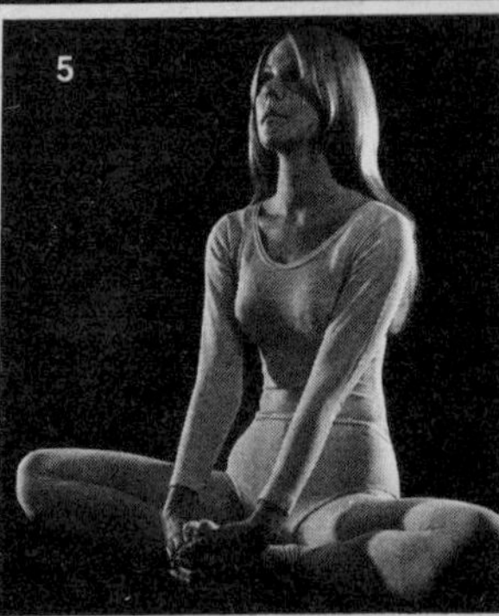

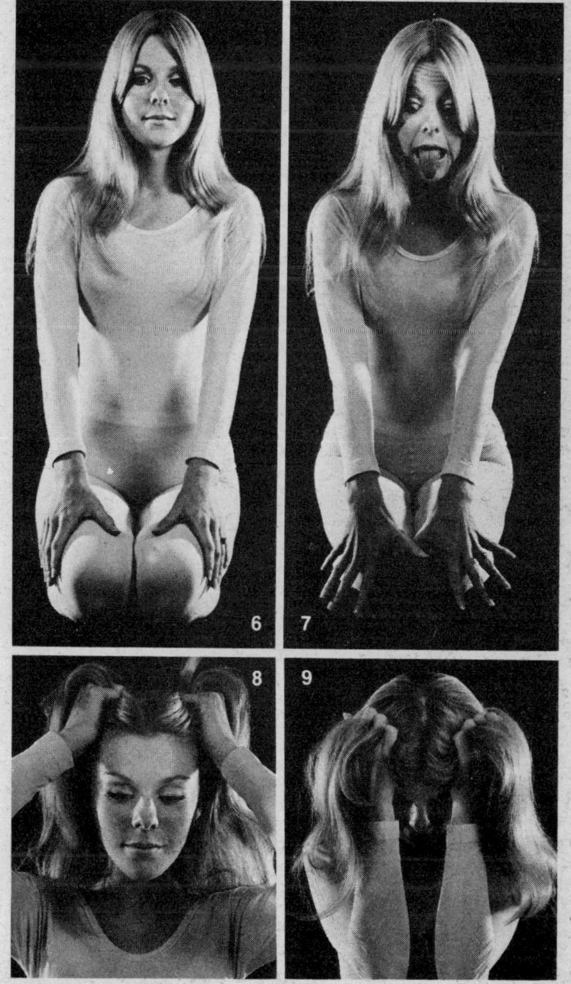
6
7
8
9

6th DAY

lion

TO FIRM THE MUSCLES OF
YOUR FACE AND NECK

6 Sit on heels
Hands rest on knees

7 Slowly move trunk forward
Simultaneously widen eyes and extend tongue
Fingers are spread far apart
You must feel a strong pull in all muscles of the face and neck; if not, you must intensify effort
Do not be reluctant to assume all the ferocity of a lion
Hold the extremely tensed position for 15

Very slowly withdraw tongue
Relax eyes and fingers
Settle back into position of Fig. 6; relax

Perform three times

Proceed to next exercise

scalp exercise

FOR THE HEALTHY
APPEARANCE OF YOUR HAIR

8 Sit in cross-legged posture
Grasp hair firmly at roots

9 Make scalp move as much as possible, first forward, then backward by pulling vigorously

Perform rhythmically and not too quickly 25 times without pause. Relax

At conclusion of movements scalp should tingle and feel "alive"

Proceed to next exercise

backward bend

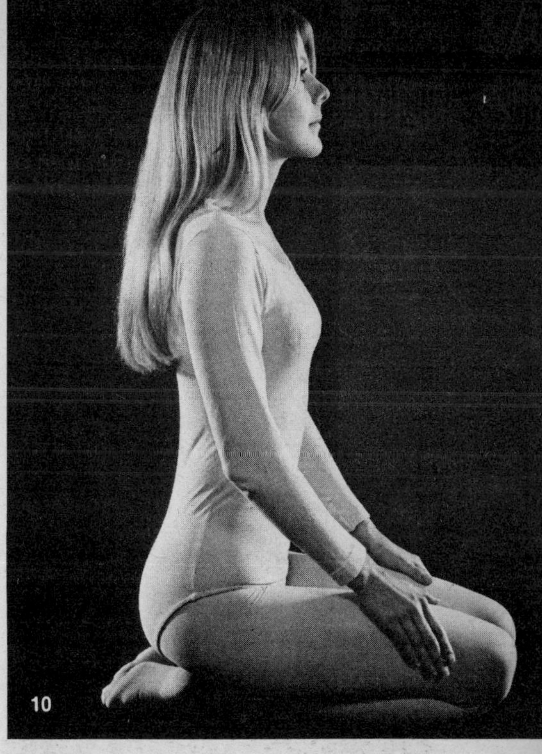

FOR FLEXIBILITY OF YOUR FEET, ANKLES AND TOES

10 Place knees together and slowly sit back on heels (as in the Lion)

11 Place fingertips on floor at your sides
Move arms **slowly** backward until you can rest hands on floor in position illustrated.
Note carefully that arms are parallel and fingers are together pointing behind you

12 Lower head backward slowly
Simultaneously arch spine inward; move trunk upward
Buttocks remain on heels

6th DAY

Knees remain together on floor
Hold without movement for 20

(If this position is not yet possible due to overweight or weakness of feet, revert to position of Fig. 10 and simply sit on heels for a count of 20 or only for as long as is comfortable. Ability to assume position of Fig. 12 should come with several days of practice)

13 If Fig. 12 presents no difficulty move hands as far backward as possible. Make sure hand position is correct
Keep knees together
Lower head and arch spine as before
Stretch is now more intensive
Hold without movement for 20

Raise head
Move hands **slowly** forward (never lunge in this exercise)
Return to position of Fig. 10

Without changing position, proceed to next exercise

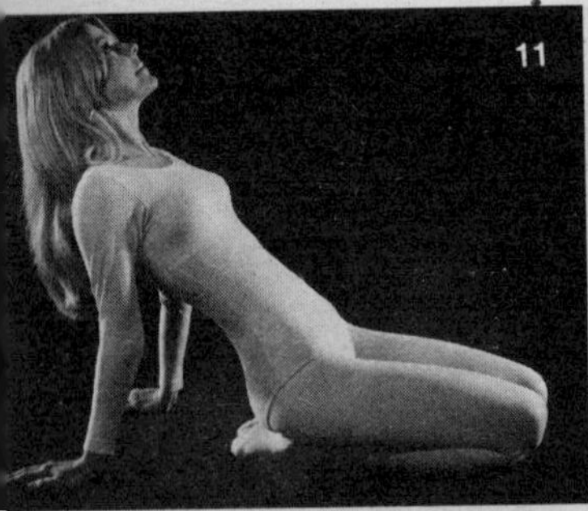
11

12

13

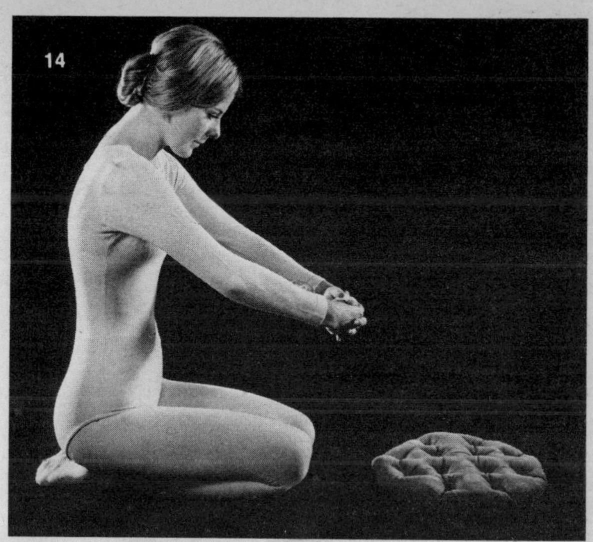

modified head stand

FOR BEAUTY OF YOUR COMPLEXION AND HAIR AND FOR CLARITY AND ALERTNESS OF THE MIND

This posture is performed with the aid of a small pillow

14 Seated on heels, interlace fingers

15 Place hands firmly on pillow

16 Place top of head on pillow
Cardle back of head in clasped hands
Rest toes on floor

17 Push toes against floor and raise body as illustrated

6th DAY

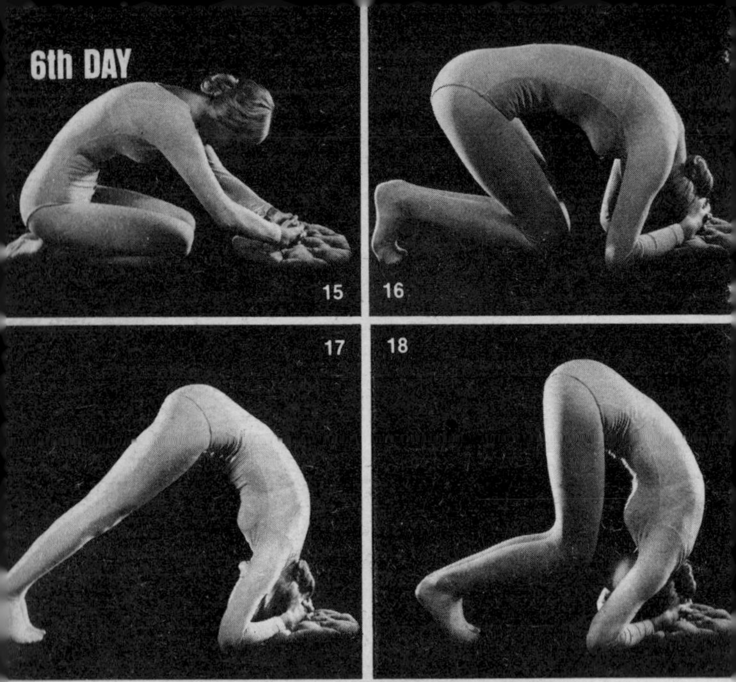

15 16

17 18

19

18 **Very slowly** inch forward with toes and bring bent knees as close to chest as possible
Do not go farther than this position at present
Do not attempt to raise legs
Hold without movement for a count of 20; do not hold longer

19 Lower knees to floor and **remain with head down** for additional count of 20

Raise head
Assume a cross-legged posture and relax

Perform two Complete Breaths (page 50)

No further practice is required today

thoughts for the day

THE SOLUTION TO TENSION

"Tension" is, for most people, quite a vague condition and there are almost as many feelings and descriptions regarding it as there are those who have experienced any type of discomfort or uneasiness. But let me offer the following definition which, if valid, can clarify the problem and provide a permanent solution: **Tension is a tightness or a squeezing that occurs in the organism mentally, emotionally and physically.** If you observe yourself carefully when you next experience a "tense" condition you will become aware that there is a "tightness" occurring at the point of discomfort. We "squeeze" ourselves mentally and induce a headache; when we get "up tight" emotionally we feel uneasy; we can "contract" ourselves physically and the result is a multitude of aches and pains. And indeed, it is exactly these things, in varying degrees, that are transpiring unconsciously within many people during a significant part of the day. Try this experiment: whenever you can remember to do so, "freeze" yourself in any of your working positions as you would stop a motion picture. Then take stock of the way in which you are performing physically. Run quickly over your body with your mind, beginning with your feet and working upward. Note all of the muscles being held tensed needlessly, muscles that are making no direct contribution to what you are doing at the moment. You may be astonished at the great amount of energy being wasted in this manner. If you agree that squeezing, tightening and contracting are indeed realities and responsibile for tension, then the relief of the condition would result from **decontracting** or, in other words, **letting go and relaxing.**

The procedure for "letting go" is as follows: as you observe the tensed muscles it is necessary to issue a calm (not angry or stern) order to these muscles to "relax." You actually tell them to do so. By repeating this self-observation process frequently and issuing the "relax" order you will be able to change the pattern and habits of the tensed muscles so that they decontract when not being used. This physical decontraction, which we emphasize with our Yoga exercises, not only frees a great amount of tied up energy but leads to emotional and mental relaxation. Psychotherapists are becoming more and more aware of the profound influence that the body exerts on the mind and emotions and, in the years to come, we can look for them to utilize many of the techniques for physical decontraction. Every one of the Yoga exercises will aid in this process.

ADDITIONAL MOVEMENTS FOR THE

chest expansion

7th DAY

1

1 Perform this position learned on Page 9 once

2 Perform this position learned on Page 20 twice without pausing between repetitions. Relax for several moments

3 We will now perform the extreme positions of this exercise
Bend slowly backward at the waist as far as possible **without strain.** If this position seems too extreme for you, revert to the more modified position
Eyes remain open
Knees do not bend
Hold without motion for a count of 5 only

7th DAY

2 3

4 Bend slowly forward as far as possible
In the extreme position for the forehead is close to the knees. Simply come as far forward as you can today and hold without motion for 20
Bring arms over back as far as possible; hold them high

Very slowly straighten to upright position
Unclasp hands; relax

Proceed to next exercise

circular motion

5-6-7 Perform this exercise twice from each of the three positions learned on Page 27

Do not pause between any of the repetitions. Relax upon completion

Remember to:

Envision the three circles as the trunk rolls and twists
Roll and twist the trunk with very exaggerated movements in the waist

Proceed to next exercise

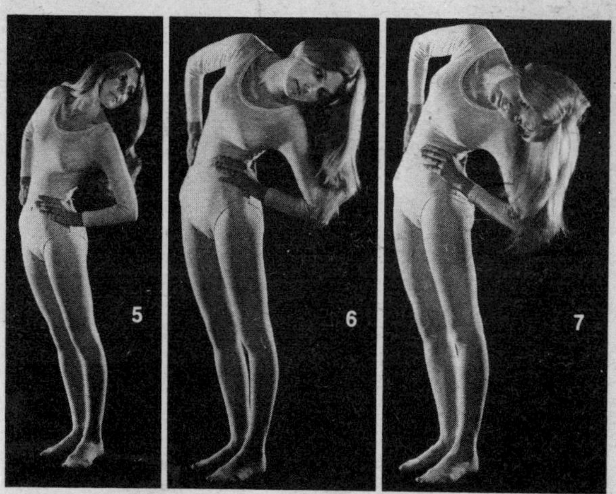

simple twist

8 Perform twice to right side, then twice to left side as learned on Page 23. Do not pause between repetitions. Relax upon completion

7th DAY

Remember to:

Trun head as far toward your back as possible to assist in complete twisting of spine

Sit erect during twist; don't slump

Proceed to next exercise

complete breath

9 Perform five times, seated in cross-legged posture, as learned on Page 50. Review the instructions on Pp. 51-52 before beginning

Proceed to next exercise

ADDITIONAL MOVEMENTS FOR THE

back stretch

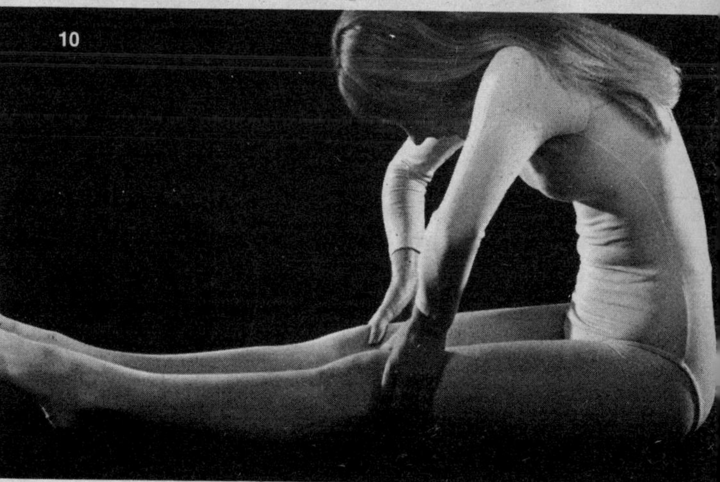
10

10 Perform this position learned on Page 12 once

11 Perform this position learned on Page 22 twice without pausing between repetitions
Relax upon completion

12 We will now continue with the movements of this exercise
Reach up and backward as far as possible

•

13 Attempt to hold the ankles
(If you cannot as yet hold ankles revert to a more modified position)

7th DAY

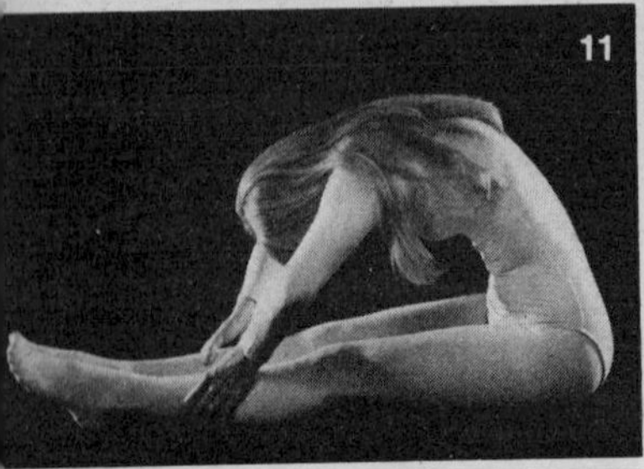

11

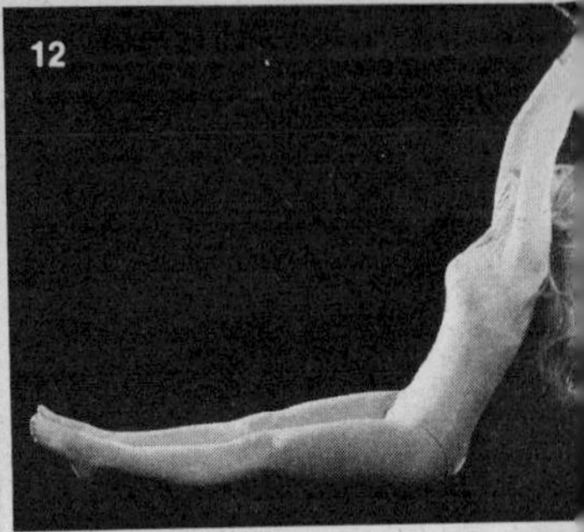

12

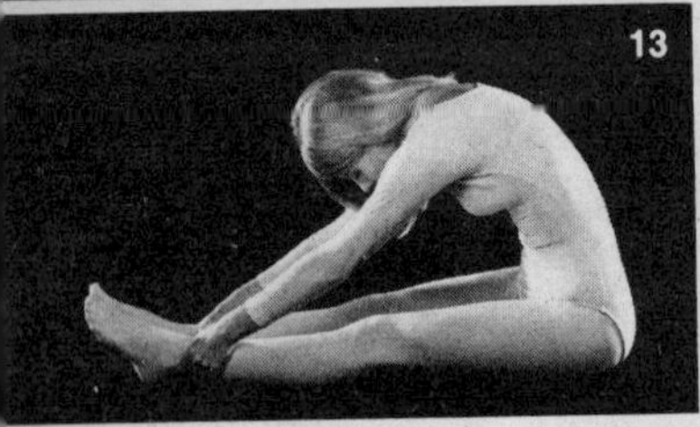

13

14

14 Hold ankles firmly and draw trunk down as far as possible
Forehead is aimed toward knees
Elbows bend outward
Knees remain straight
Do not strain
Hold your extreme position (as far down as you can come today) without motion for 20

Slowly straighten to upright position

Proceed to next exercise

ADDITIONAL MOVEMENTS FOR THE

cobra

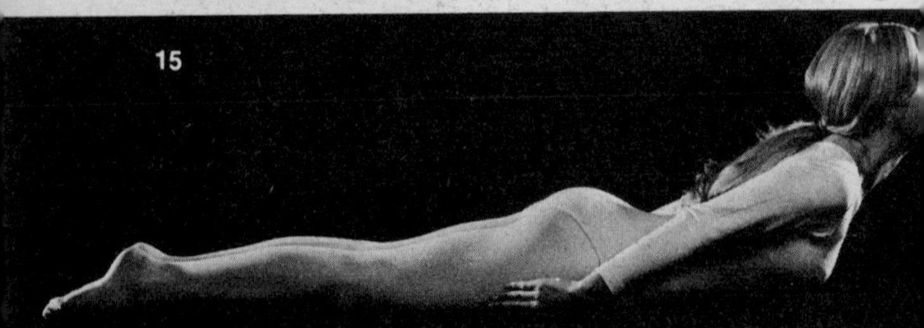

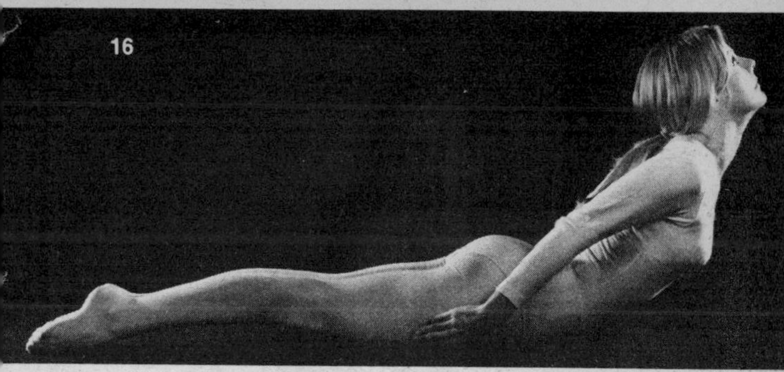

We have learned several preliminary movements of the Cobra on Pp. 11-12 and 24. The new movements below will complete the routine

15 Forehead rests on floor as previously learned
Arms are at sides
Head and trunk are now raised **without aid of hands**

16 Trunk is raised as high as possible without aid of hands

17 Hands are brought in very gracefully from sides and placed in correct position beneath shoulders
Trunk then continues to be raised with assistance of hands (move very slowly)

18 The extreme posture
Head is as far back as possible
Elbows straight
Spine in extreme arch
Lower abdomen remains on floor
Legs relaxed
Hold without motion for 15

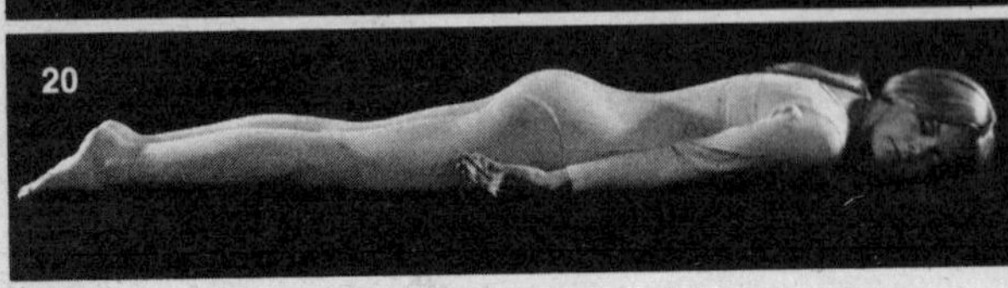

19 Very slowly begin to lower trunk
Return to position of Fig. 17
Gracefully return arms to sides
Make back muscles work to support trunk

20 Slowly return forehead to floor
Rest cheek on floor and go completely limp

Note feeling of deep relaxation

Repeat entire routine once

practice plan 7th day

To complete our 7th Day of practice we will perform each of today's exercises once, in the continuous motion, dance-like routine we have practiced previously. The routine consists of the following:

Chest Expansion (the most extreme position you can execute)

Circular Motion (once, from the extreme forward position)

Back Stretch (the most extreme position you can execute)

Simple Twist (once to each side)

Cobra (once, to the extreme position learned today)

Do not do any additional Yoga exercising today.

thoughts for the day

WORK IS NOT EXERCISE

It is important for the Yoga student to distinguish between ordinary activity and exercise. The housewife is often the classic example of one who confuses the **amount** of activity with the **type** of activity. She fails to distinguish between just plain activity (housework) and the systematic manipulation of the body that is true exercise. The duties of the housewife, as is the case with most types of work, actually **promote** conditions of physical and emotional stress and it is therefore essential that she take the time to relieve this stress through proper body movements. If the activities of housework (cleaning, shopping, child care) constituted true exercise we would not see the housewife tense, irritable, overweight, flabby, depressed and complaining of many types of aches and pains.

Many office workers and professional women also

mistakenly believe that they have had plenty of "exercise" during the workday and that what they should do after their day's work has been completed is rest. Of course, this is true to a certain extent but rest will not work out those conditions of tension, sluggishness and stiffness in the back, shoulders and legs that have resulted from the day's activities. Health and beauty must be renewed on a daily basis; you cannot play golf or tennis on the weekend, have an occasional massage or steam bath and expect to maintain true suppleness and flexibility of spine, joints and limbs.

Yoga is the perfect answer, since only a brief, enjoyable period is necessary to overcome tension on a daily basis. Naturally, no worker has much of a desire to engage in the leaping about of calisthenics when she finishes work. But Yoga will not drain energy; its movements are pleasant and stimulating. Here is our suggestion to the housewife, office worker and professional woman: at the end of the workday spend five to ten minutes in performing the Chest Expansion, Back Stretch, Simple Twist and Complete Breath. **Stretching is the key to relieving tension and releasing energy.** A few minutes, so spent before dinner, will revitalize you for the remainder of the evening.

Many of our students take a minute or two during their coffee break or lunch hour to stretch their backs and limbs with a modified Chest Expansion. Always remember that a stiff and tense body must detract from the efficiency of the mind.

8th DAY

review

Today's review will include all of the exercises learned in the previous seven days. If any of the positions are, as yet, difficult for you, simply do as much as you can. All of the extreme positions will be accomplished in time.

From this point forward we will make it a rule not to pause between the repetitions of any exercise unless so instructed. For example, if you are directed to perform the Complete Breath Standing 5 times, the only pause will be at the point where you hold the extreme position for a count of 5. Immediately upon completing the movements on Pp. 53-54, you repeat the exercise. When all 5 repetitions are completed, you relax briefly as instructed.

Whenever you have the slightest doubt concerning any of the movements make certain to refer to the pages indicated.

complete breath standing

1-2 Perform 5 times as learned on Pp. 53-54. Then relax

Remember to:

Breathe slowly and deeply so that all of the raising

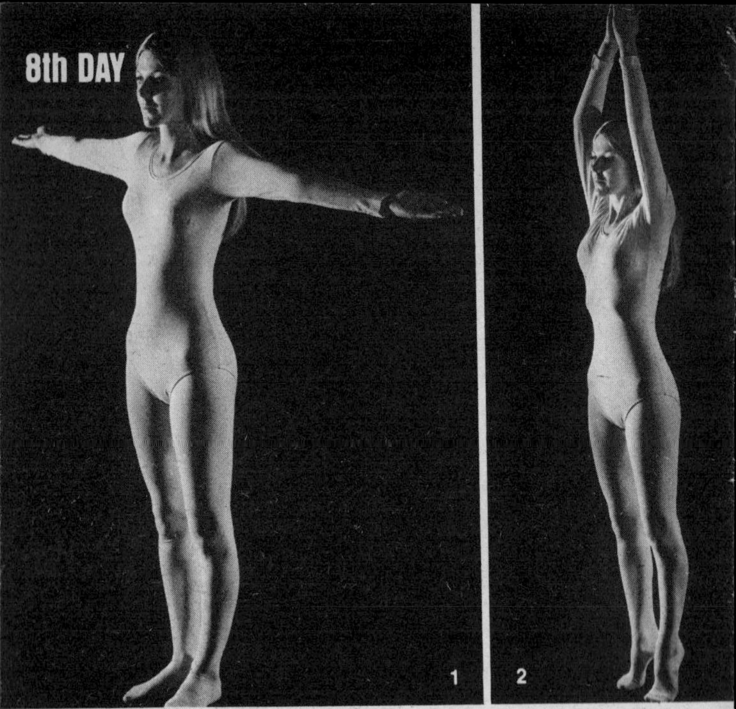

8th DAY

1

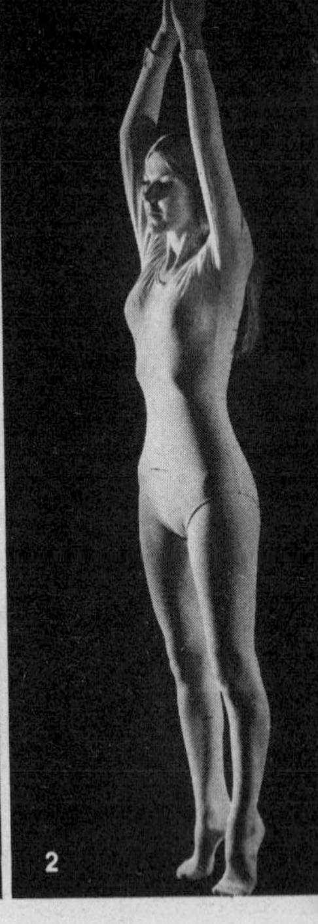

movements may be performed smoothly during the inhalation and exhalation

chest expansion

3 Perform this position learned on Page 9 once

4 Perform this position learned on Page 20 once
Relax

5 Perform this position (or your extreme position) as learned on Page 67 twice. Relax

Remember to:

Bend very slowly, both backward and forward
Hold arms high at all times
Keep knees straight
Count 5 in the backward and 20 in the forward positions

(Correct counting is essential in each of the exercises if we are to be successful in our "progressive" plan. Do not become careless in your counting)

Proceed to next exercise

3

4

5

8th DAY

triangle

6-7-8 Perform this exercise twice in each of the three positions (as learned on Pp. 18, 30-31, 38-39) Alternate the sides (left-right; left-right) in each position. Relax upon completion

Remember to:

Bring the arm far over the head and hold elbow straight in each of the side bends

Keep knees straight

Let neck muscles relax

Proceed to next exercise

6

7

8

circular motion

9-10-11 Perform this exercise twice from each of the three positions learned on Pp. 28-30
Relax upon completion

Remember to:

Roll and twist the trunk with very exaggerated movements in the waist

Proceed to next exercise

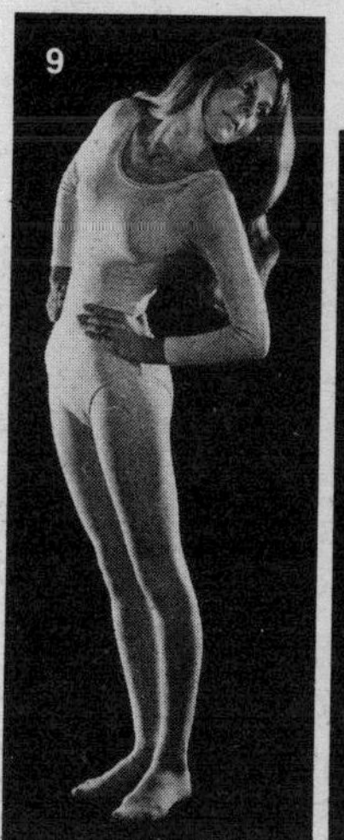

9

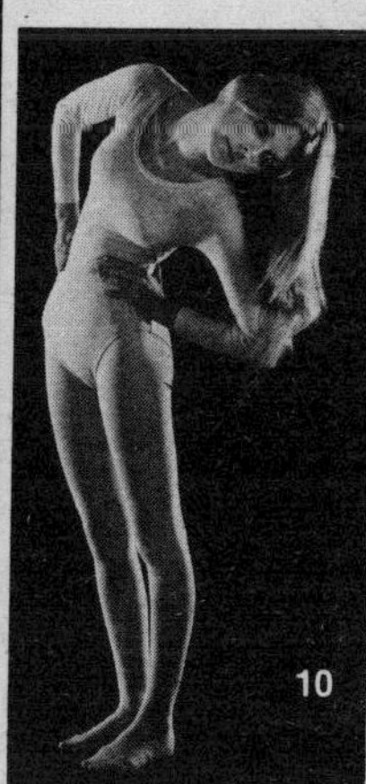

10

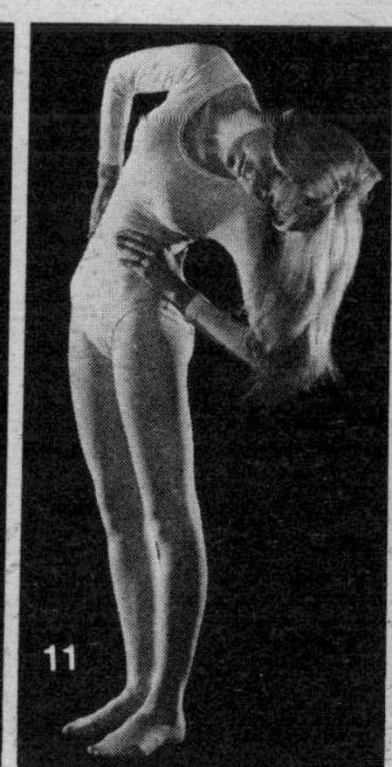

11

knee and thigh stretch

12 Perform three times as learned on Page 20

Remember to:

Keep spine straight

Proceed to next exercise

8th DAY

12

simple twist

13-14 Perform twice to right side, then twice to left side as learned on Page 23

Relax upon completion

Remember to:

Turn head as far toward your back as possible to assist in complete twisting of spine

Sit erect during twisting movements; don't slump

Breathe normally in extreme positions (This is true of the extreme positions of all exercises unless otherwise instructed)

Proceed to next exercise

13

14

lion

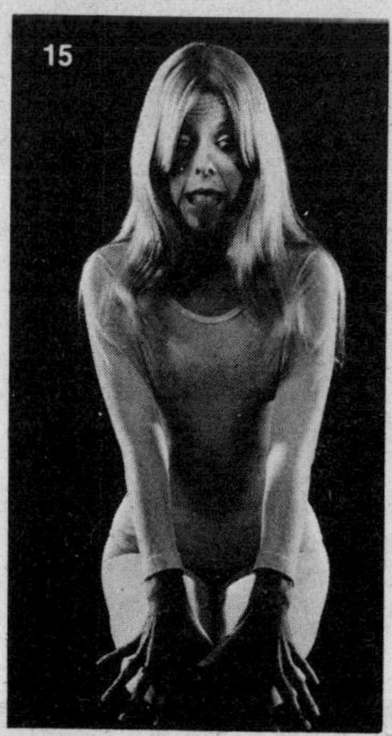
15

15 Perform three times as learned on Pp. 59-60
Relax upon completion

Remember to:

Extend tongue with sufficient intensity so that a strong pull is experienced in all muscles of face and neck

Hold eyes wide and fingers apart

Proceed to next exercise

scalp exercise

16 Perform 25 times as learned on Pp. 59-60

Remember to:

Grasp and pull hair forcefully
Don't be too gentle; movements should hurt a little

Proceed to next exercise

back stretch

17 Perform this position learned on Page 12 once

18 Perform this position learned on Page 22 twice

19 Perform this position learned on Page 71 twice
Relax upon completion

If you have been practicing faithfully you should experience good progress in all three positions today

Remember to:

Move slowly and count correctly
Aim forehead toward knees in all three positions
Bend elbows outward
Hold extreme positions motionless

Proceed to next exercise

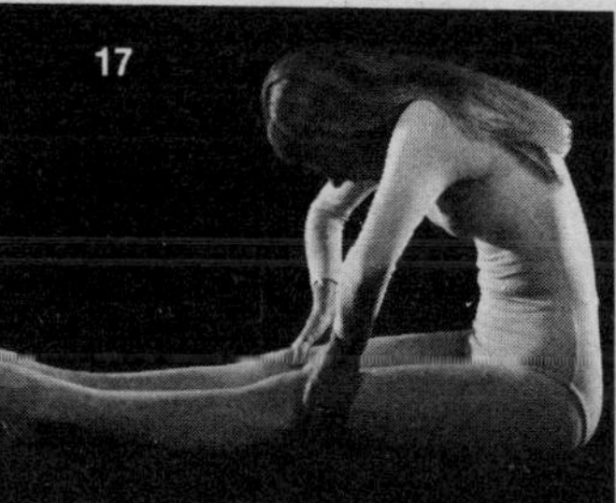

backward bend

20-21 Perform once in each of the positions learned on Page 61
Relax upon completion

Remember to:

8th DAY

Place arms and hands in correct position
Make as acute an arch with the spine as possible
Allow head to drop as far backward as possible
Keep knees together

Proceed to next exercise

20

21

modified head stand

22

22 Perform once as learned on Page 63
Relax upon completion

Remember to:

Hold for a count of 20 only
Use pillow if required
Bring knees close to chest
Remain with head down for additional count of 20 upon completion

Proceed to next exercise

cobra

23 Perform the entire Cobra routine, as learned on Page 72 twice.
Relax completely after each routine

Remember to:

24-25 Raise trunk as high as possible without aid of hands
Bring arms in from sides smoothly and gracefully
Keep head back and spine continually arched
Move as slowly as possible
Relax legs throughout exercise
Return arms to sides smoothly and gracefully
Experience deep relaxation upon completion

Proceed to next exercise

8th DAY

24

25

leg over

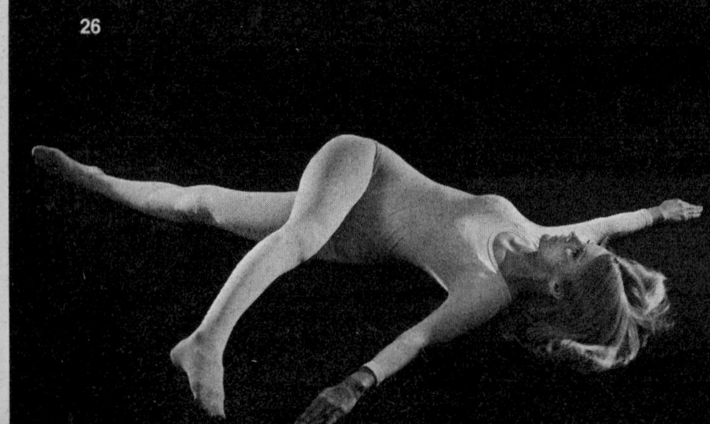

26

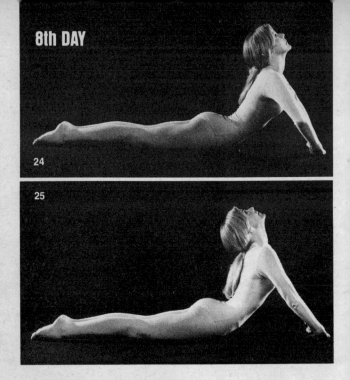

26 Perform three times to each side, alternating legs as learned on Page 33
Relax upon completion

Remember to:

Keep leg as high toward the head as possible in extreme position

Proceed to next exercise

complete breath

27 Perform three times, seated in a cross-legged posture, as learned on Page 50

28 Relax upon completion

29 Remember to:

Work for the smooth flow of the expansion movements during the long, slow, quiet inhalation

To complete today's review, return to Page 77 and perform your extreme position of each of the 14 exercises once, in the continuous motion, dance-like routine we

have practiced previously. Do not pause between the exercises.

Do not do any additional Yoga exercising today

thoughts for the day

HOW TO JUDGE YOUR PROGRESS

Today's "Review" should provide an opportunity to evaluate your progress. We are now practicing 15 important exercises, many of which require the use of muscles you may have not methodically exercised in years and some of which manipulate the body in ways that are totally new. You can begin to judge where you are weak (back, legs, balance, etc.) and devote a little extra attention to those areas as you perform the exercises. Remember that all of the Yoga movements are **natural;** the demands that are made on the body are never excessive and all of the positions can eventually be accomplished with patience, faithfully following our day-by-day **progressive plan.** This plan always takes into account the fact that the histories and conditions of no two bodies are alike and consequently there is to be no "competition" in the practice of Yoga. You will receive the full benefit of each of the movements according to your particular structure.

You have probably discovered (or soon will discover) that progress in the postures is irregular. That is, you will find that you can accomplish a more extreme position fairly comfortably one day, but that two or three days of practice may be needed before you can do this again. This is the Yoga learning process. There are days when you experience what appears to be a setback. We say "appears" because it is not truly a setback; the body is stiff on certain days and does not respond as well as on previous days. Actually, it is **setting** itself and preparing to make another stride forward. This is similar to the arrow, which is first pulled **back** before it leaves the bow. This pulling back movement provides greater impetus to fly forward. When you seem to be having difficulty, your body is usually drawing itself back like the arrow. If you simply "go easy" when you feel stiff and do not force your body or become discouraged, you will find that within a day or so your organism has completed its setting process and then will take a significant step ahead.

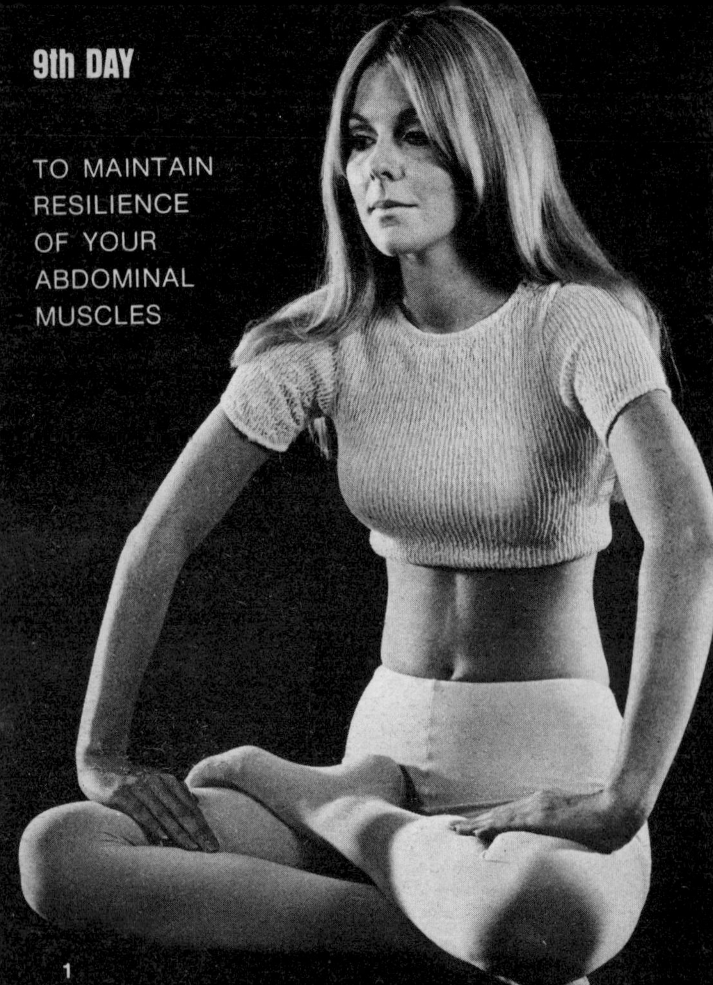
9th DAY
TO MAINTAIN
RESILIENCE
OF YOUR
ABDOMINAL
MUSCLES
1

abdominal lifts

This exercise, in its various positions, will be of such great value to you for your entire life, that we will spend the entire practice period of today in learning its movements.

Study the illustrations and read the text of Pages 92-97 carefully before actually attempting the movements.

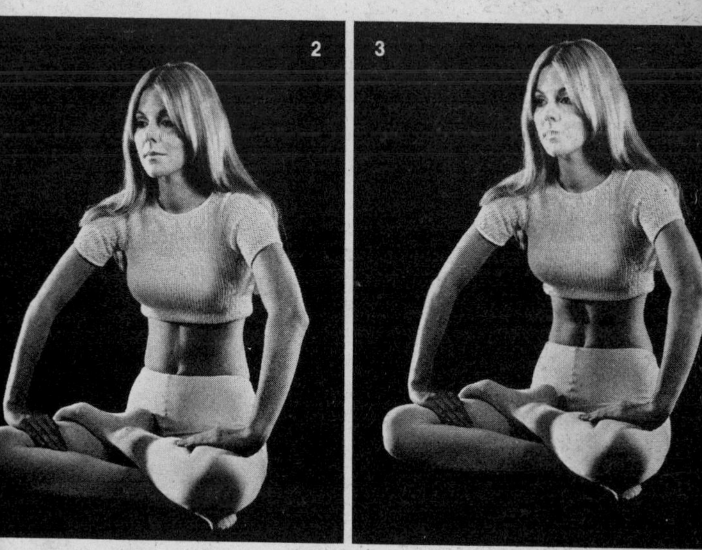

1 Sit in a cross-legged posture

2-3 Work the abdominal muscles to contract your abdomen as much as possible. The depth of the contraction can be increased by first pushing out with the muscles (as in the Complete Breath), then contracting, then pushing out again, etc. This will strengthen the abdominal muscles It is necessary to gain some control of these muscles before proceeding

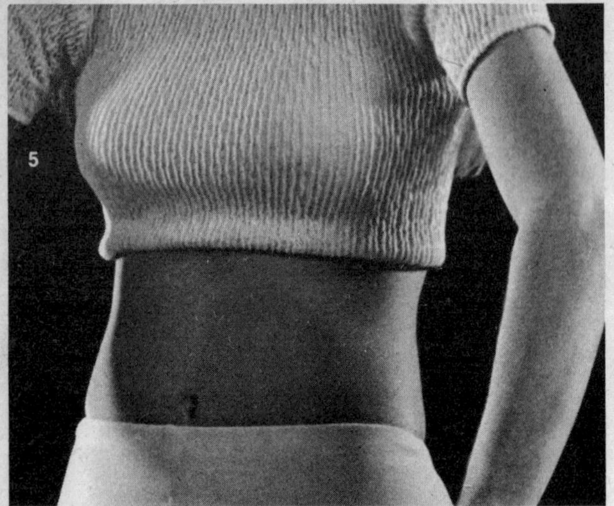

ABDOMINAL LIFT (16A)

4 This is the completed "lift"
Note the contrast between the "contraction" of Fig. 2 and the "lift" of this position
It is very important to understand that this lift can be accomplished successfully **only if all air is first exhaled from the lungs and no air is allowed to enter while the lift is being performed**

Therefore, it is the patient practice of this deep exhalation and then the lifting movements that is necessary

Now exhale deeply so that all air is emptied from your lungs
Keep the breath out and attempt to lift the abdomen as depicted

Hold whatever lift you have executed for a few moments; then inhale and relax

We can further describe this lifting movement as a "sucking in" of the abdomen—inward and upward
Imagine that you are attempting to breathe very deeply from the abdominal area
No air actually enters your lungs but the abdominal area goes through the motions of this deep breath during which it is sucked inward and upward

Now exhale deeply, empty the lungs and attempt the lift again

5 **Keep the breath out** and attempt to "snap" the abdomen out with a forceful push of the muscles
Inhale
Relax a few moments
Repeat

When you get a feeling of the movements, attempt to to 2 and then 3 of the lifting and snapping out movements to each exhalation
There is no pause between these movements
5 movements and more to each exhalation will become easy within a few days

Now practice the movements patiently for several minutes to gain some mastery of them

Regardless of your success at this point (even if you are able only to contract, not lift the abdomen) we will proceed to the next position

ABDOMINAL LIFT STANDING (16B)

6 Stand as illustrated
Heels together
Knees bend slightly
Hands rest firmly on upper thighs
All fingers (including thumb) point inward

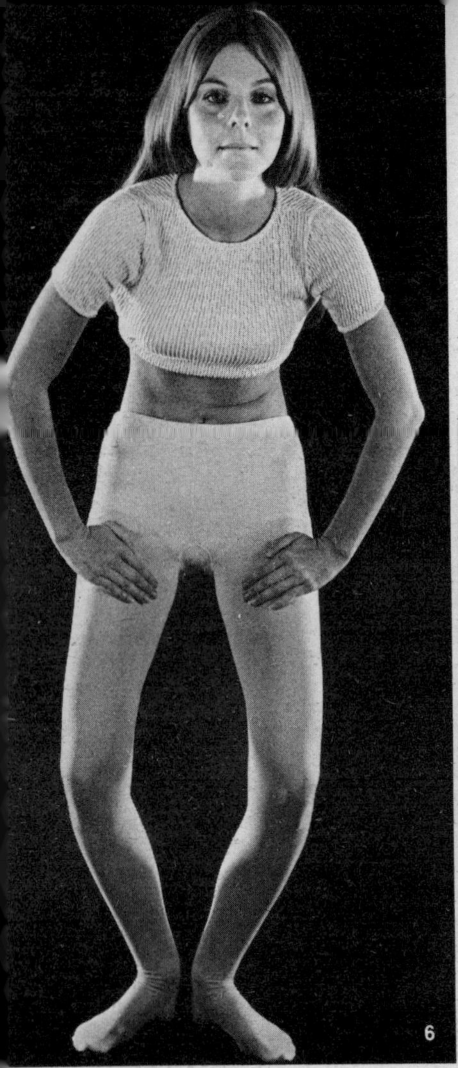

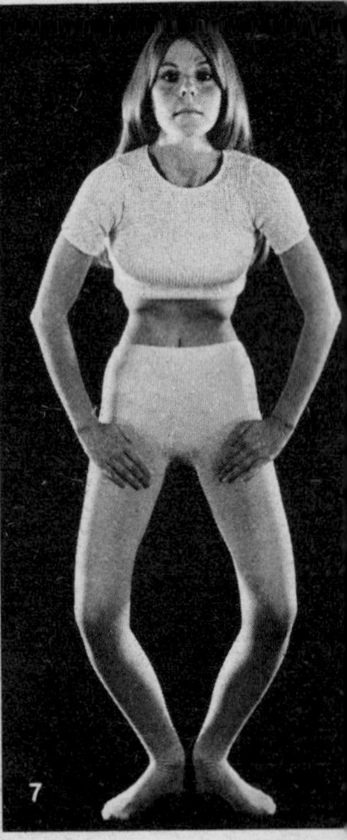

7 Exhale deeply
Perform the lifting movement (press down hard on thighs)
Snap the abdomen out
Inhale and straighten to the upright position; relax
Now resume the squatting position and perform as many lifts to the exhalation as possible

Inhale and straighten to the upright position, relax
Repeat; perform 5 times

Proceed to next exercise

ABDOMINAL LIFT—ALL FOURS (16C)

8

9

8 Place body in position illustrated
Knees touch
Arms parallel, fingers point straight ahead
Head is lowered
Abdomen is relaxed

9 Exhale deeply
Perform lifting and snapping out movement
Inhale and relax (stay in All Fours position)
Repeat; perform 5 times

Relax in cross-legged posture

Do not be discouraged if complete success has not been attained today. This is not an easy exercise. Even if you succeeded only in "contracting" the abdomen today you will begin to benefit greatly. The extreme value of this exercise makes it worthy of your patient practice on subsequent days. Your abdominal wall will not "drop" in later years if the abdominal muscles have the good tone that this exercise imparts. Also, there are many benefits for your visceral organs and glands as is explained on the next page.

If your time permits you may practice these movements again later today. However, do not practice any of the other Yoga exercises. After the intensive review of yesterday (8th Day) it is prudent to allow your body to rest and "set" itself today.

thoughts for the day

"EXERCISING" THE ORGANS AND GLANDS

With today's exercise, the Abdominal Lift, you will begin to truly appreciate the inestimable value of Yoga for promoting physical fitness. In almost all methods of exercise the emphasis is placed on the muscular system, while the endocrine, nervous and circulatory systems are sadly neglected. A major value of Hatha Yoga lies in the fact that it takes into consideration the methodical stimulation necessary for organs and glands of the various body systems. For example, the brain and pituitary gland are affected by the Head Stand, the heart and thyroid are involved in the Shoulder Stand, the Locust strengthens the reproductive organs and glands and the kidneys are stimulated through the Cobra and Bow. The Abdominal Lift provides a type of natural "massage" for the stomach, colon, intestines, liver, kidneys, gall bladder and pancreas—all with one movement! That is why this wonderful exercise deserves all the practice you can give to it.

Constipation is a serious and frequent problem for many people, particularly for those who must spend a great deal of time in a sitting position. Long periods of inactivity cause the peristaltic action to grow sluggish. There is no better solution to this problem than observing the Yogic dietary suggestions and regular practice of the Abdominal Lifts in both the Standing and All-Fours positions. Today, we have practiced a minimum number of lifts, since the exercise is new and somewhat difficult. In subsequent days we will increase the number until, within a few weeks, you will be doing up to twenty-five lifts with each exhalation.

The best time of the day to deal with sluggishness is upon arising. Drink four to six ounces of cool (not cold) water with a pinch of lemon. Allow a minute or two for the water to reach the stomach and then perform the lifts in both positions as learned today. This exercise greatly strengthens and firms the abdominal wall, preventing it from sagging. Good muscle tone in this area helps to maintain the organs and glands of the viscera in their correct positions. You may have observed the unsightly and unhealthy results of a "dropped" abdomen.

The All Fours position is particularly valuable for new mothers to help restore organs and glands to their proper positions.

Let us reiterate: this priceless technique is worthy of your most patient practice since it will certainly be utilized for your entire lifetime.

10th DAY

1

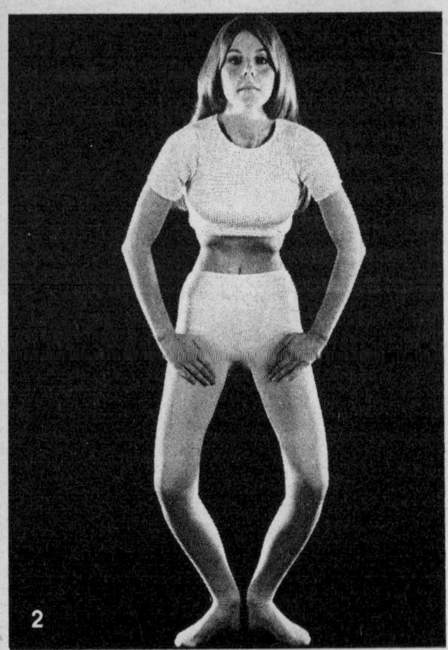

2

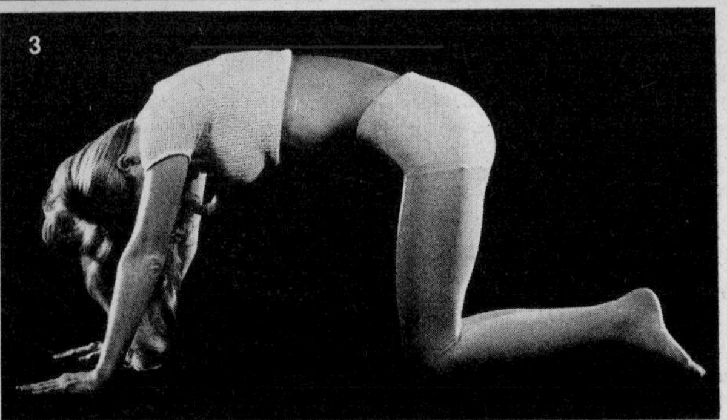

3

Having had one day of rest you should find your body responding well to today's exercises

complete breath standing

1 Perform 5 times as learned on Pp. 53-54
Then relax

Remember to:

Breathe slowly and deeply so that all of the raising movements may be performed smoothly during the inhalation and exhalation

Come up high on the toes and hold the extreme position as steady and motionless as possible
Proceed to 16 (below)

abdominal lifts

ABDOMINAL LIFT STANDING (16B)

2 This exercise was learned on Page 96
Practice as follows: assume the squatting position (make certain the position is correct); exhale and perform as many lifts as possible to the exhalation; straighten up and relax a moment; repeat. Do 5 groups in all. Today you should be able to do 3-4 lifts to each exhalation.
Relax upon completion

Remember to:

Exhale very deeply; the more completely the lungs are emptied, the easier it is to execute the lifts

Keep the air out during the lifts

Perform the lifts and snapping out movements as **rhythmically** as possible

Practice patiently. Do not be discouraged if complete success has not been achieved. Simply continue to work the abdominal muscles as intensively as possible

Proceed to next exercise

10th DAY

ABDOMINAL LIFT—ALL FOUR (16C)

3 This exercise was learned on Page 97
Practice as follows: assume the All Fours position and follow the exact directions given **for Fig. 2 above**
Relax upon completion

Proceed to next exercise

side bend

TO REDUCE FLABBINESS

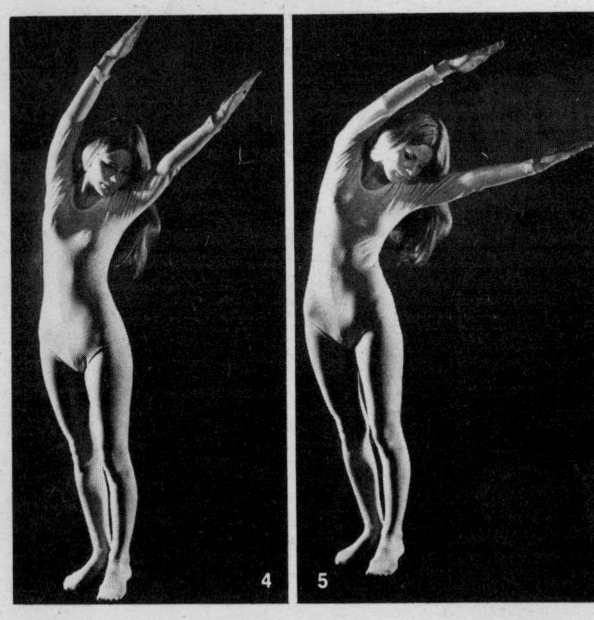
4 5

4 Stand with heels together
Gracefully raise arms overhead; palms turned inward
Very slowly bend several inches to the left
Arms must remain parallel
Knees do not bend
Hold without motion for 5

Slowly straighten to the upright position
Perform the identical movements to the right
Bend only several inches
Hold for 5
Straighten to the upright position
Lower arms to sides and relax; stand still; do not fidget

5 Raise arms to overhead position
Now bend slowly to an intermediate position
Arms remain parallel
(this is essential to firm and tighten sides)
Hold for 5

Straighten up
Perform identical movements on right side

Lower arms to sides and relax for several moments

6 Raise arms to overhead position
Now bend as far to the left as possible
Arms remain parallel
Feel firming and tightening in right side
Hold for 10

Straighten up (slowly)
Perform identical movements on right side

Lower arms to sides and relax

Proceed to next exercise

10th DAY

backward bend

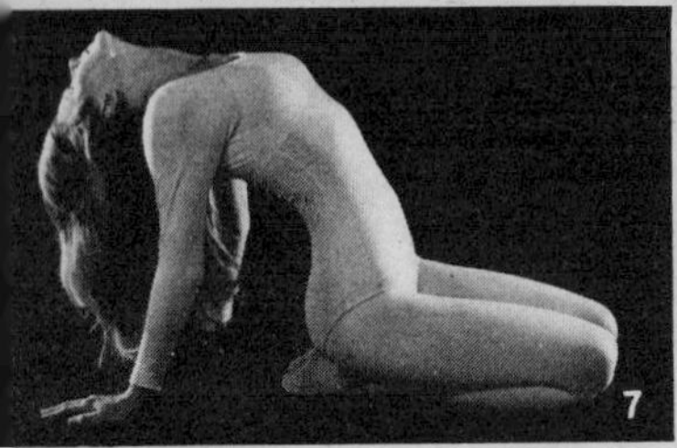

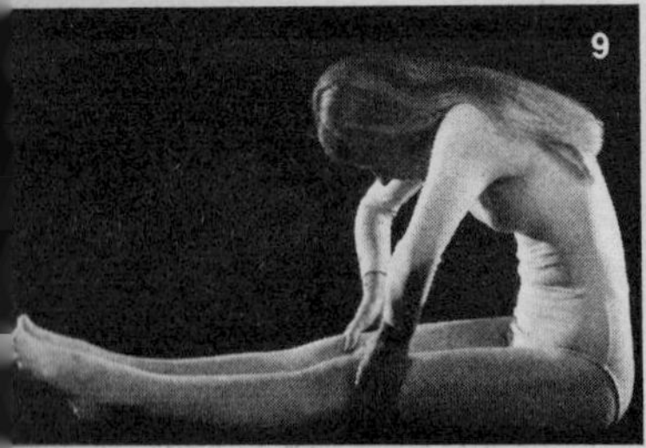

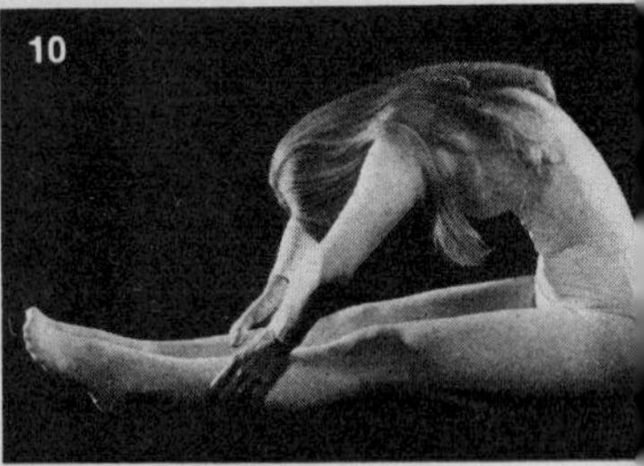

7-8 Perform once in each of the positions learned on Page 61. Hold the extreme positions for 20 Relax upon completion

Remember to:

Place arms and hands in correct position
Make as acute an arch with the spine as possible
Stay seated on the heels
Allow head to drop as far backward as possible
Keep knees together (very important)

Proceed to next exercise

back stretch

9-10-11 Perform twice in each of these positions learned on Pp. 12, 22 and 71. Hold each extreme position for 10. Relax upon completion

Remember to:

Bend elbows outward
Lower head as far as possible toward knees in all three extreme positions
Hold extreme positions absolutely motionless

Proceed to next exercise

locust

TO FIRM YOUR LEGS

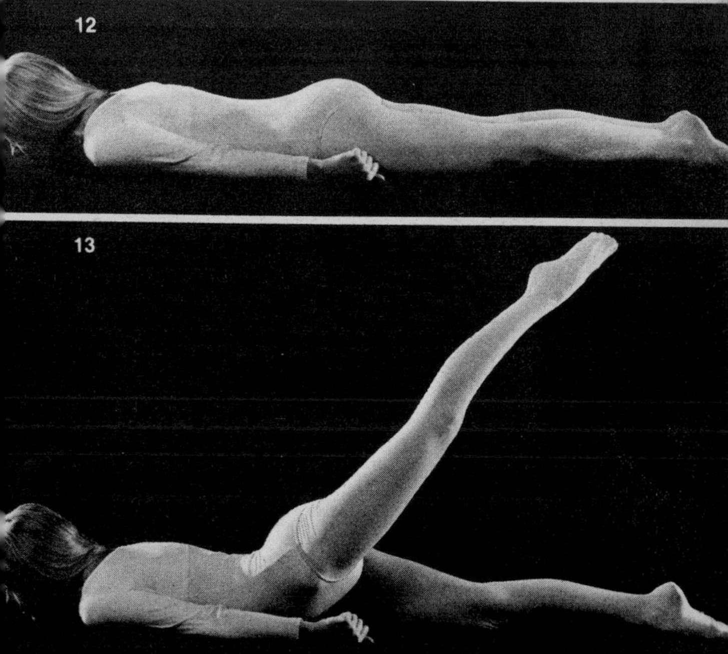

10th DAY

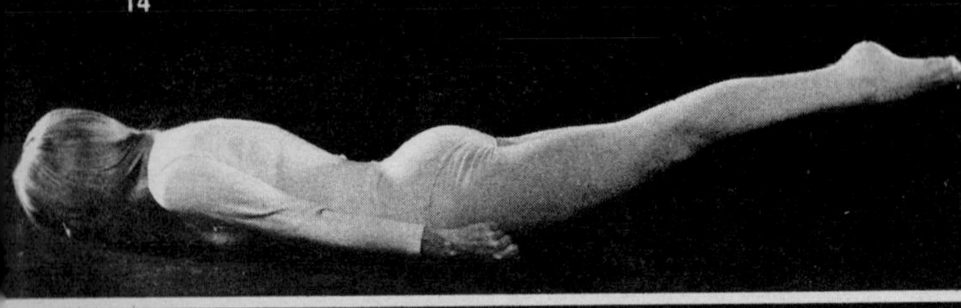
14

15

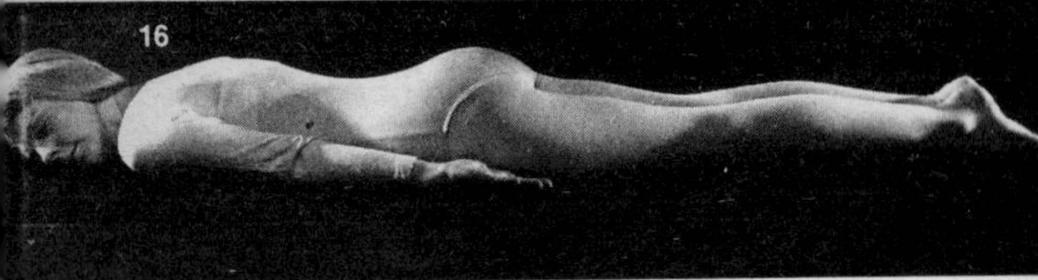
16

12 Rest ball (not point) of chin on floor
Place fists, thumbs down, firmly against floor at sides

13 Push against floor with fists
Raise left leg very slowly as high as possible
Hold for 5
Lower leg slowly

Very slowly raise right leg as high as possible
Hold for 5
Lower leg slowly

Repeat movements once with each leg

Relax for a few moments

14 Push against floor with fists
Raise both legs a few inches only
Do not raise higher than illustrated
Hold for 5

Lower legs slowly; relax

Repeat once

15 Inhale a shallow breath and retain
Push against floor with fists
Attempt to raise both legs slightly higher than the previous position
Hold for 5

Lower legs slowly and simultaneously exhale; relax

Repeat once

16 Relax in this position for approximately one minute

practice plan 10th day

To complete our 10th Day of practice we will perform each of today's exercises once, in the continuous motion, dance-like routine we have practiced previously. Remember to move with all of the grace, poise and balance of a ballet dancer while performing this routine. If you keep this image in mind you will be astonished at how quickly your body assumes these very attributes!

The routine consists of the following:

1. Complete Breath Standing (once)
2. Abdominal Lift Standing (one group only)
3. Abdominal Lift—All Fours (one group only)
4. Side Bend (once on each side to the extreme position.)
5. Backward Bend (once in the extreme position)
6. Back Stretch (once to your most extreme position)
7. Locust (once to your most extreme position)

Do not do any additional Yoga exercising today.

10th DAY • thoughts for the day

RELAXATION AS A WAY OF LIFE

Under "Tension" we discussed relaxation in terms of a physical and mental "letting go." Ideally, one should be able to maintain the "letting go" feeling at all times since it is in this state that our best work is done. Most tasks can be accomplished with ease and you are probably aware that the less anxiety that goes into a job, the more successfully that job is done. But unfortunately we have come to think of relaxation as something that is done only at specific times. That is, we set aside **periods** for relaxation. We believe that our ordinary work is hard, tedious and boring and when the workday is over and the necessary chores are completed we attempt to engage in some type of relaxation. However, most people are finding it more and more difficult to let go even when they are supposed to be relaxing and having a good time. This is because all of the anxious and irritating experiences that have piled up during the workday refuse to put on their collective hats and take a temporary leave. You cannot relax "on cue." Consequently it is not relaxation that is sought but rather **escape** and the result is that tons of drugs and oceans of alcoholic beverages are now consumed each year in the United States.

True relaxation must become a continual way of life. Relaxation, to the Yogi, does not mean lethargy, collapse or escape. It does not even necessarily mean inactivity. Exactly the contrary. Real relaxation implies becoming much more "alive" and aware than we usually are, even in the midst of our workday activities! Escape or distraction is desirable only when you are not experiencing the miracle of your true "self." Through the centuries it has been proven that there is nothing more effective for achieving a state of sustained relaxation, for "getting with yourself," than Yoga. At first, the delightful experience of letting go may be confined solely to the time you are actually practicing your Yoga exercises. But gradually this feeling begins to carry over more and more into your everyday activities. As this occurs you often find that work, chores and tasks that were formerly irritating lose the power to drain your life-force. When you are truly relaxed you can accomplish your work, whatever it is, expending a minimum of energy. You will experience the truth of this before our 28 days are concluded.

11th DAY

ADDITIONAL MOVEMENTS FOR THE

chest expansion

1

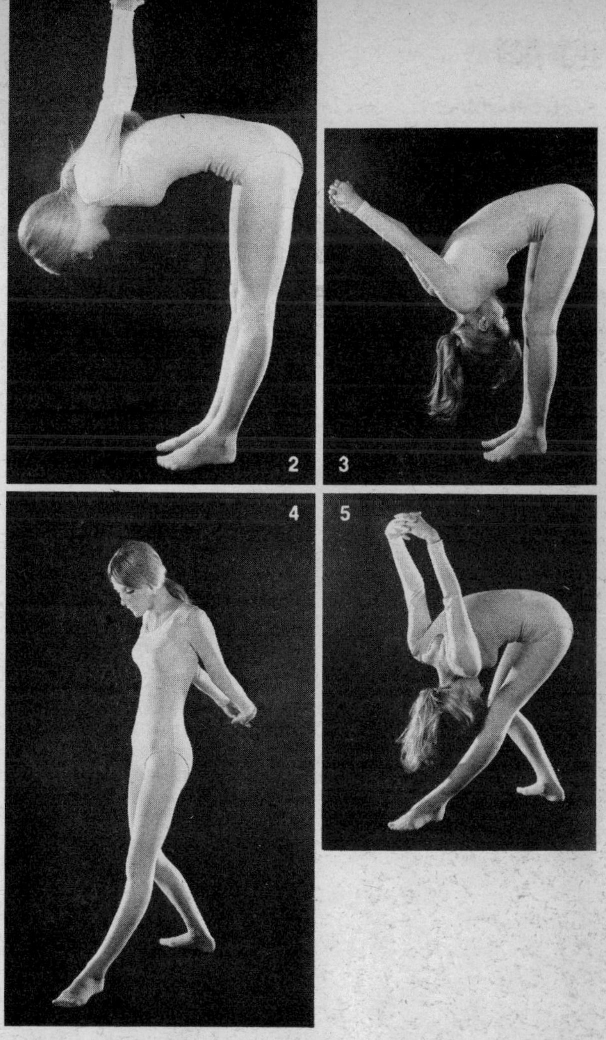

1
2 Perform once in each of the three positions as learned on Pages 9, 20 and 67. Count only 5 in the backward position and 20 in each forward position
3

4 When you have completed the third position, straighten up so that you can extend your left leg to the side. Note the position of the leg and foot

5 Bend forward once again
Twist trunk slightly to the side
Bring forehead as close to knee as possible
Arms come over back as before
Knee remains straight
Feel stretching of the "hamstring" muscles
Hold without motion for 10

Straighten to upright position
Bring left leg in
Extend right leg
Perform identical movements to right leg

Straighten to upright position
Perform entire routine of Chest Expansion in extreme position followed by leg movements, once

Relax upon completion

Proceed to next exercise

circular motion

6-7-8 Perform this exercise twice from each of the three positions learned on Page 27
Relax

Proceed to next exercise

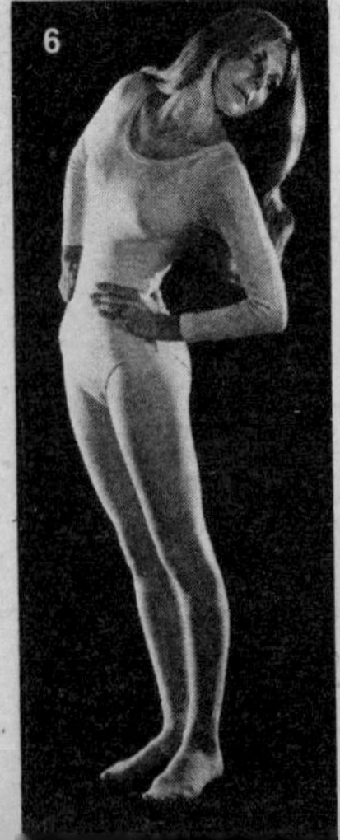
6

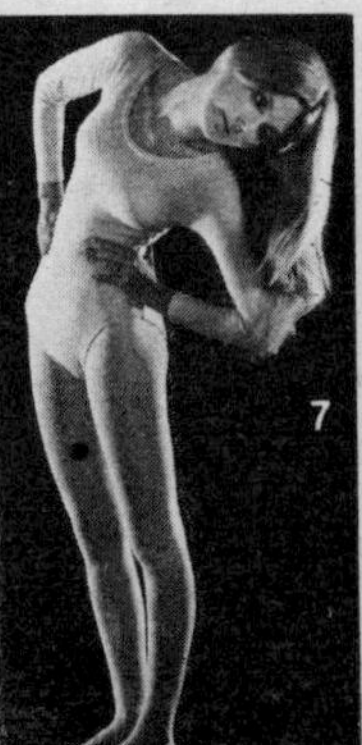
7

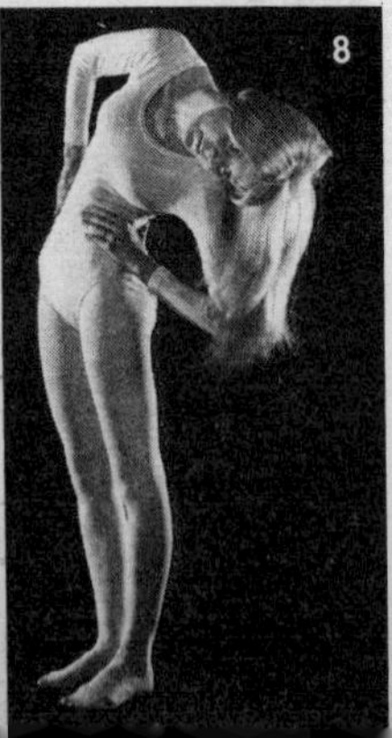
8

knee and thigh stretch

9 Perform three times as learned on Page 21

Proceed to next exercise

simple twist

10 Perform twice to right side, then twice to left side as learned on Page 23

Relax

Proceed to next exercise

lion

11 Perform three times as learned on Page 60

Relax upon completion

Remember to:

Extend tongue with sufficient intensity so that all muscles of the eyes, face and neck are brought into play

Hold eyes wide and fingers apart

Proceed to next exercise

11th DAY

11

ADDITIONAL MOVEMENTS FOR THE

cobra

12

13

12 Perform the Cobra as learned on Page 72 once
Relax completely (with cheek on floor)

The additional Cobra movements are performed following the extreme position of Fig. 12

13 Bend elbows slightly
Very slowly twist head and trunk to right
Attempt to see right heel (if this is not possible simply twist as far as you can)

Hold without movement for 10

Slowly turn forward and return to position of Fig. 12

14 Bend elbows slightly
(Do not bend farther than illustrated)
Twist to left
Attempt to see left heel (or as far as possible)
Hold for 10

Slowly return to position of Fig. 12

Proceed to lower trunk as previously described

Now perform the entire Cobra routine, including the twisting movements, once

Relax completely

Proceed to next exercise

11th DAY

head twist

TO REMOVE ALL TENSION FROM YOUR NECK

15

16

17

15 Lying on abdomen, place elbows on floor
Arms are parallel
Place head between hands
Close eyes
Slowly push head downward with hands until chin touches chest
Hold without motion for 10

16 Raise head
Place chin in right palm and left hand firmly on back of head
Note position of fingers
Elbows remain on floor
Very slowly twist head to right
Hold for 10

17 Turn head frontward
Now place chin in left palm and right hand on back of head
Very slowly twist to left
Hold for 10

Turn head frontward

Proceed to next exercise

•

•

leg over

18 Perform three times to each side, alternating legs (right leg goes to left side; left leg goes to right side, etc.) as learned on Page 33
Relax upon completion

Remember to:

Keep leg as high toward the head as possible in extreme position

Proceed to next exercise

11th DAY

complete breath

19 Perform five times, seated in a cross-legged posture, as learned on Page 50. You should be making progress with the Halt-Lotus. That is, the knees should gradually be lowering themselves toward the floor. If this is not the case, remember to practice the position of Fig. 8, Page 49

You can sit in this posture while performing the Complete Breath

Remember to:

Work for the smooth flow of the expansion movements (abdomen, chest, raising of shoulders) during the long, slow, quiet inhalation

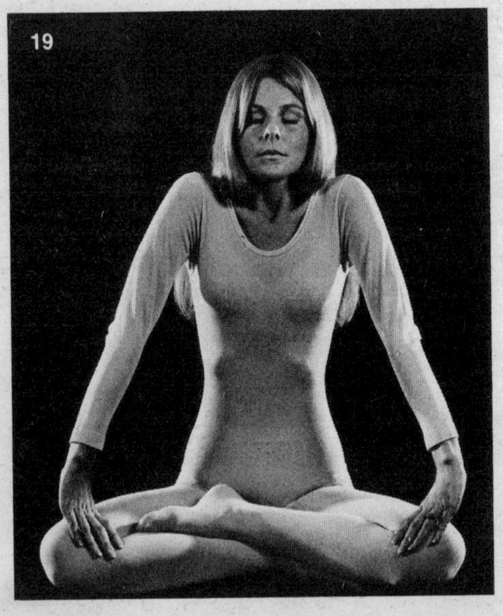
19

practice plan 11th day

To complete our 11th Day of practice we will perform each of today's exercises once, in our continuous motion routine.

The routine consists of the following:

1. Chest Expansion (your extreme position only, followed by the leg movements learned today)
2. Circular Motion (from the extreme forward position)
3. Knee and Thigh Stretch
4. Simple Twist (once to each side)
5. Lion
6. Cobra (your extreme position, followed by the twisting movements to each side as learned today)
7. Head Twist (once to each position as learned today)
8. Leg Over (once to each side)
9. Complete Breath (once, very slowly and very deeply)

Upon completion, sit very quietly in a cross-legged posture for several minutes and become aware of the "awakening" of your organism.

thoughts for the day

"AWAKENING"

Previously, we have stated that one of the two major objectives of Hatha Yoga is "to awaken a great power that lies dormant in the organism and utilize it for developing one's own unique, individual potential; that is, to achieve "self-realization." It is the very postures we have been doing that provide the necessary stimuli and it is approximately at this point in our work that you can begin to actually experience the "awakening" of the dormant forces. This awakening process is a subtle one; the elevation and increased energy are very different from the response to artificial stimuli such as coffee, drugs or alcohol. **At first, you must make a conscious attempt to become aware of the manner in which this awakened life-force is manifesting; you have to turn your attention inward and look for it.** Once recognized, it continues to grow and develop in a way that can effect very great, positive changes in your life. Hence the instructions that concluded this 11th Day of practice: "Upon completion (of the continuous motion routine) sit very quietly in a cross-legged posture for several minutes and become aware of the 'awakening' of your organism."

The advantages of deep concentration on all movements of the exercises were discussed under "Total Involvement In Your Practice." I hope you have remembered to do this. Now, we are suggesting that upon conclusion of the day's exercises, you sit quietly and focus your full attention on **how you feel.** What effect have these profound physical movements had upon your organism? What is your body saying to you? How revealing is that moment when you are able to transcend your ordinary mind and reach deep into your center; when you begin to achieve "self-realization!" This practice of awareness is an exercise in feeling, not thinking. We are temporarily suspending our thoughts so that we may focus fully on what is transpiring within the body. If you perceive that your attention is wandering, bring it back gently and firmly to what you are **feeling.** Within several weeks you will look forward to your Yoga exercises and the few minutes of "silent awareness" that follow as one of the most meaningful periods of the day.

review

12th DAY

Our review for today calls for an intensive workout. Practice exactly as instructed, concentrating very carefully on all of your movements. If any of the positions are, as yet, difficult for you, simply execute **your** extreme position. Remember: never strain. All of the extreme positions will be accomplished in time.

Do not pause between the repetitions of any exercise unless so instructed.

complete breath standing

1 Perform three times as learned on Page 53
Hold the extreme raise for 5

chest expansion

2-3 Perform once in each of the three positions as learned on Pp. 9, 20 and 67. Increase the count in the backward positions to 10. Forward positions remain at 20. Perform the leg movements of Fig. 3 following the extreme positions only. Relax upon completion

side bend

4-5-6 Perform once in each of the three positions as learned on Pp. 102-103. Alternate the sides for each

12th DAY

1

2

3

4

5

position. Hold each bend for 10. Relax upon completion

Remember to:

Bend very slowly to each of the three positions
Keep arms parallel in each of the three positions (very important)

triangle

7 Perform once in each of the three positions as learned on Pp. 18, 30 and 38. Alternate the sides for each position. Hold each bend for 10.
Relax upon completion

12th DAY

circular motion

8 Perform this exercise twice from each of the three positions learned on Page 29
Hold each of the rolling movements for a count of 3
Relax

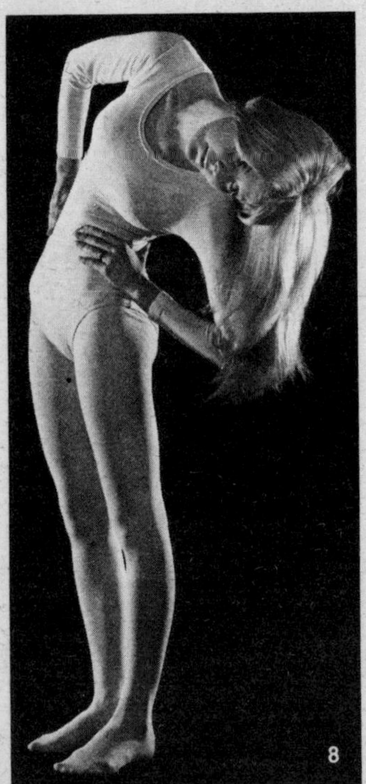

abdominal lifts

ABDOMINAL LIFTS (16 B & C)

9 This exercise was learned on Pp. 95-96
Perform as many rhythmic lifts as possible to each

exhalation. Do 5 groups in all. Today you should be able to do approximately 5 lifts (or contractions) to each exhalation. Relax briefly after each group; relax for one minute after the 5th group

Remember to:

Keep the air out of the lungs during the lifts
Perform the lifts **rhythmically**
"Snap" the abdomen out using the muscles (do not allow it to simply "fall" back)
Practice patiently. Do not be discouraged if success with the lifting movement has not yet been achieved; if 5 lifts are too many for you, simply execute as many as you can comfortably and **rhythmically**

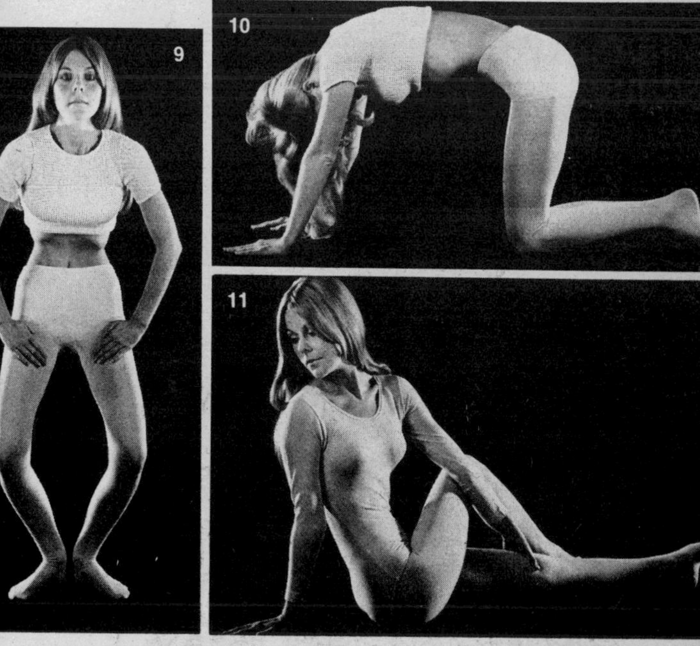

10 This exercise was learned on Pp. 97-98
Assume the All Fours position and practice exactly according to the directions given under Fig. 9. Relax for one minute after the 5th group

12th DAY

simple twist

11 Perform twice to right side, then twice to left side as learned on Page 23. Hold each extreme position for 10. Relax upon completion

knee and thigh stretch

12 Perform three times as learned on Page 21. Hold each extreme position for 10. Relax briefly

backward bend

13 Perform once in each of the two positions learned on Pp. 61-62. Hold the extreme positions for 20. Relax upon completion

back stretch

14 Perform once in each of the three positions learned on Pp. 12, 22 and 71. Hold each extreme position for 20. Relax upon completion

cobra

15-16 Perform the complete Cobra routine as learned on Pp. 72-73 and 114-115 twice. Hold the extreme position of Fig. 15 for 20 and the twisting of Fig. 16 for 10 on each side. Relax deeply after **each** repetition

12th DAY

head twist

17-18 Perform once in each of the three positions learned on Page 116. Hold each extreme position for 20

Remember to:

Use hands to move head gently but **firmly** to each of the extreme positions

17

18

locust

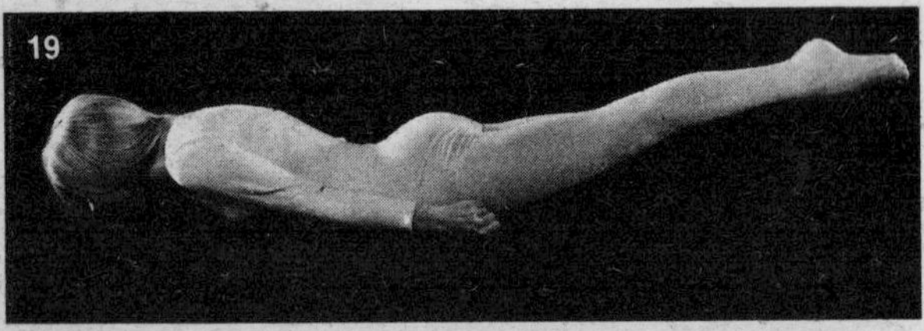
19

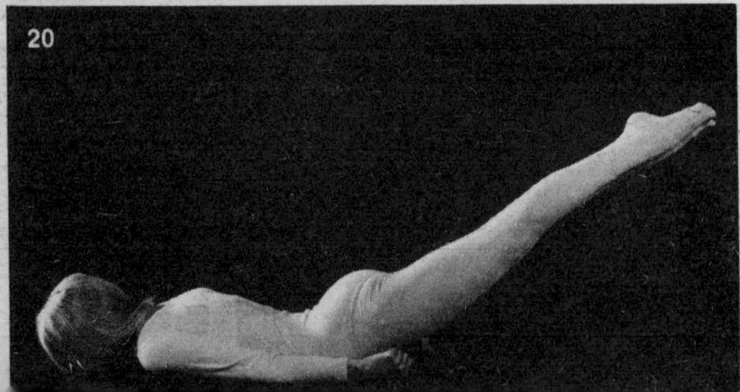
20

19-20 This exercise was learned Pp. 105-106. First, raise each leg once to prepare the muscles. (See Fig. 13, P. 105) Then perform twice in the position of Fig. 19 and twice in the position of Fig. 20. Hold each raise for 5. Relax briefly after **each** repetition. Do not be concerned with the distance you are able to raise legs. Repeated **attempts** are the important thing to strengthen the neglected leg and abdominal muscles

Remember to:

Rest ball (not point) of chin on floor
Push hard against floor with fists

modified head stand

21 Perform once as learned on Page 63. Hold extreme position for 30. Relax with head down upon completion

21

12th DAY

complete breath

22 Perform five times, seated in a cross-legged posture as learned on Page 50. Sit quietly for several minutes and become aware of what is occurring in your organism as explained in yesterday's lesson

thoughts for the day

YOGA NUTRITION (1)

The chief sources of life-force **(prana)** are: air, water, sleep, food and sunlight. Breathing, drinking and sleeping are almost automatic processes about which there is not too much choice. You must continually breathe (and we have discussed this in detail), you drink when you are thirsty and generally sleep when tired. But you are free to choose from a multitude of food products. Therefore, it is essential that the Yoga student understand certain vital principles regarding this choice. **You must make certain that you are getting the most possible life-force from the foods that you eat.** Otherwise, since foods can sap your vitality as well as nourish you, your eating habits may well be doing you more harm than good! By eating too often and consuming too many heavy, rich, indigestible and devitalized foods you will allow your stomach to drain vital energies from other parts of your body, especially from your physical defense agents and your mental and spiritual bodies. The Yogi believes that the less you eat, the better you will feel, providing your food is of a **high quality**. If you are forcing your body to digest several of the typical "American" meals each day, you may well find that your strength, vitality and endurance are decreased and that your mind functions less efficiently. Your organism is a precision instrument designed to function at its peak on small amounts of high-quality food. Such light, high quality food, eaten sparingly has the ability to nourish you and leave important vital energies free to help activate those little-used forces with which we are concerned in this study.

Here is the guiding principle to govern your selection and preparation of foods: **All foods should be consumed in a form that is as close to their natural state as digestion permits.** In their natural state, most foods contain life-force. When foods are boiled, fried, roasted, refined, canned, frozen, preserved, fumigated, aged, pasturized, "enriched" and otherwise subjected to the innumerable modern processes, the life-force is seriously reduced or killed. You can fill your stomach and appear to satisfy your "hunger" with boiled vegetables, frozen fruits, aged cheeses, white bread, refined sugar candies, etc. but the real nourishment (life-force) of these products is highly questionable. Thus the Yogi is concerned not with the amount of food he eats but with the amount of life-force in that food.

Consider carefully the above statements and we will continue this discussion shortly.

13th DAY

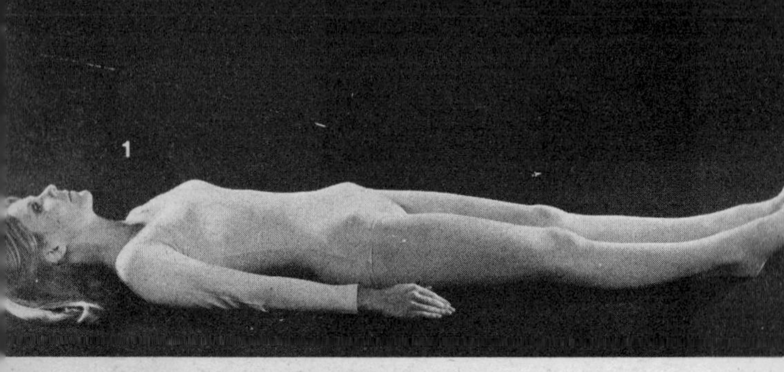

Shoulder Stand

FOR WEIGHT CONTROL
THROUGH THYROID STIMULATION

1 Lie in the completely relaxed position illustrated

2 Brace palms against floor
Tense abdominal and leg muscles
Slowly raise legs

3 Swing legs back with sufficient momentum for hips to leave floor
Brace hands against hips

4 Very slowly straighten up to whatever extreme position you find comfortable

5 The completed posture
Chin is pressed against chest
Legs are straight but relaxed
Eyes can be closed
Position is held for one minute (not longer today)
If this completed posture is difficult, revert to any less extreme position

6 Come out of the posture exactly as instructed (very important to maintain smoothness and balance)
Bend knees and lower them toward head
Place hands on floor

7 Roll forward with knees bent
Arch neck upward **to keep back of head on floor**

8 When hips touch floor straighten legs upward
Slowly lower legs to floor
Relax completely for approximately one minute

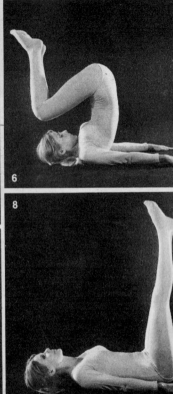

13th DAY

5

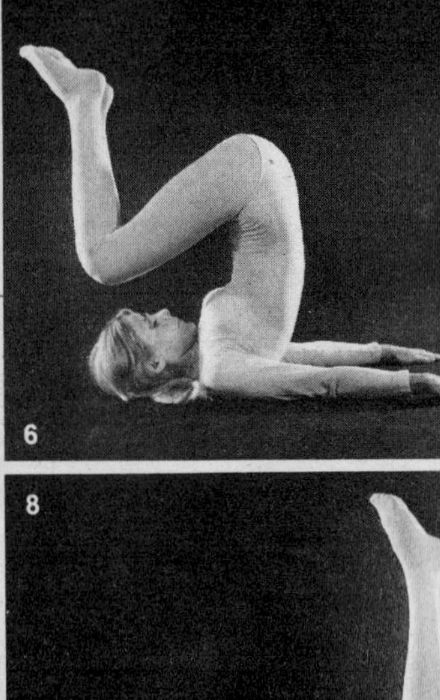

6

8

7

If you are unable, at this time, to raise the hips as in Fig. 3 simply hold the legs in the position of Fig. 2 Allowing the blood to flow out of the legs for one minute is healthful for the veins and arteries. Remember that many Yoga students have experienced remarkable weight normalization with the aid of the Shoulder Stand. The count in the extreme position will be increased on subsequent days.

Proceed to next exercise

plough

TO STRENGTHEN AND MANIPULATE YOUR SPINE

9 Lying on back brace palms against floor and raise legs

10 Push against floor and swing legs back (as slowly as possible)

11 Continue to move trunk upward and slowly lower legs to floor
Keep knees straight

12 The completed posture
Toes rest on floor
Chin is pressed against chest
Attempt to breathe normally
Hold for 10

If this completed posture is too difficult, revert to any less extreme position where the legs are lowered (as in Fig. 11)

13 Come out of the posture with the identical movements performed for the Shoulder Stand
Bend knees and bring them forward to head

14 Roll forward, arching neck to keep head on floor
When hips touch floor, straighten legs upward
Lower legs slowly to floor
Relax for approximately one minute

Repeat once

Proceed to next exercise

11

12

13

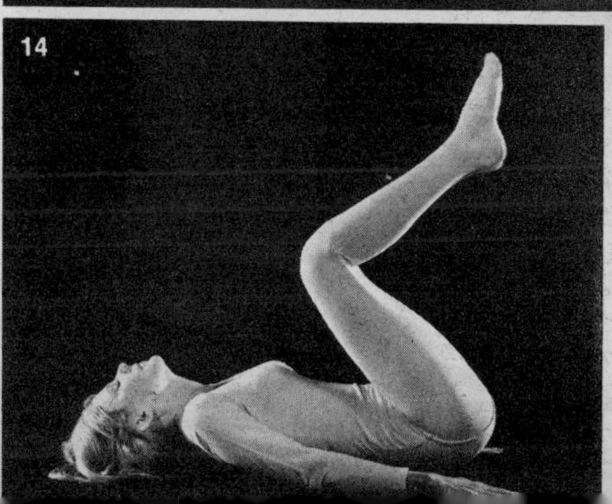
14

13th DAY

ADDITIONAL MOVEMENTS FOR THE

back stretch

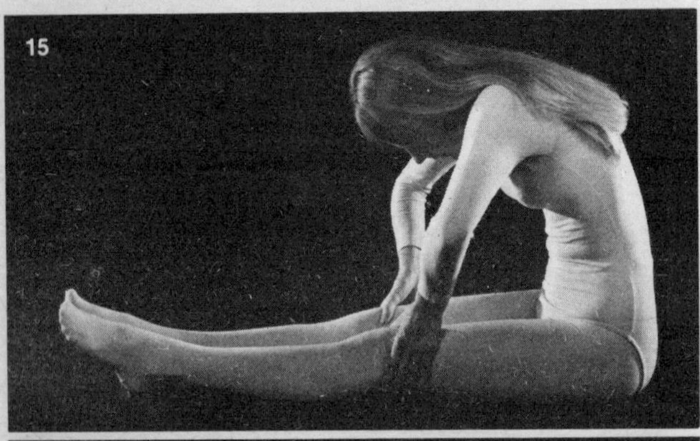

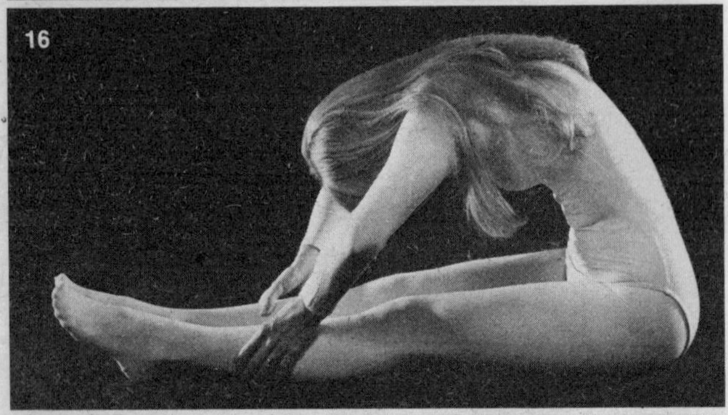

15-16-17 Perform once in each of the three positions learned on Pp. 12, 22 and 71
Hold each extreme position for 20
Relax briefly upon completion

18 Raise arms overhead and perform the backward movement as usual
Reach forward and attempt now to hold the feet

19 Bend forward as far as possible
Elbows need not bend outward as previously
Knees remain straight
Hold your extreme position (as far down as you can come today) without motion for a count of 20
If this position is too difficult revert to a less extreme posture

Slowly straighten to upright position

Repeat this extreme position once

Proceed to "Practice Plan"

18

19

20

21

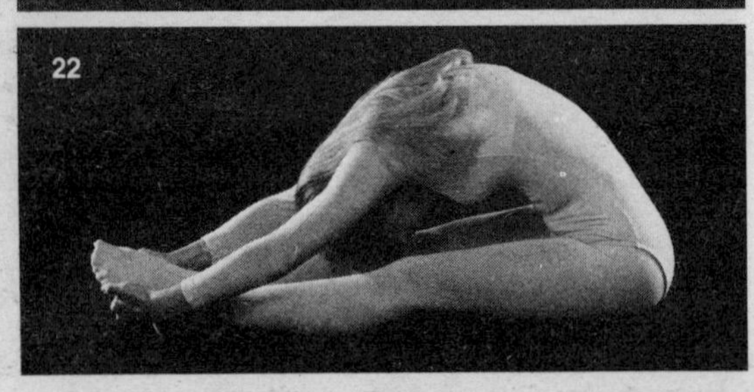
22

practice plan 13th day

1. Perform your extreme position of the Shoulder Stand once as learned today. (Fig. 20)

Hold for one minute

Instead of coming out of the posture, begin to lower legs behind you and place palms on floor.

2. Execute your extreme position of the Plough as learned today. Hold for 20. (Fig. 21)

Come out of the posture as directed.

Rest briefly, then raise your trunk to upright position.

3. Execute your extreme position of the Back Stretch. (Fig. 22)

Sit in a cross-legged posture and perform the Complete Breath five times.

Then sit quietly for several minutes and become aware of what is occurring in your organism as explained previously.

thoughts for the day

THE INVERTED POSTURES

If you hold your arm overhead for several minutes the blood will drain from your fingers, hand and forearm into the upper arm and shoulder. Gradually, your arm will become numb. To a lesser degree this is what can occur when your body is held continually in an upright or a sloping position. Gravity is always at work upon your body exerting its pull on many vital organs and glands and causing the blood to flow in a predominantly downward direction. Since most of our daily activities require that we sit and stand in upright positions you can appreciate the efficacy of inverting the body for a brief interval each day.

Inversion is accomplished in our Yoga study through such postures as the Head Stand, Shoulder Stand, Plough, Chest Expansion and others. These exercises have had a marked effect on the blood circulation of many of my students. For example, the thyroid gland, located in the throat area, secretes into the bloodstream a vital substance that regulates weight, promotes the health of the sexual glands and is responsible for the smooth tempo of many important body functions. People who suffer from over-active or under-active thyroids are deficient in the timing of their activities as well as in their metabolic processes. The Shoulder Stand helps to promote the correct functioning of the thyroid by bringing an increased supply of blood into the throat area. Hence the great value of this posture. The Head Stand has been responsible for improvement in hearing and vision as well as for added beauty of the hair and complexion. One of the finest, natural ways to restore and maintain alertness is to allow an increased supply of blood to flow into the brain. Thousands of professional people throughout the world are aware of this and many practice the Head Stand for up to 15 minutes each day! It is also important to note that the Yogi regards the Head Stand **(Sirshasana)** as the major posture to increase the capacity and power of the brain. I always advise students who have had a history of illness with regard to circulation, heart, brain or other organs and glands to obtain their physician's approval before attempting any of the inverted postures.

To summarize: The heart is always pumping **against** gravity to circulate the blood into the vital organs and glands situated **above** it. With the body in the inverted positions those organs and glands are now **below** the heart. The effect of this simple maneuver on the entire organism is truly remarkable.

1 2

chest expansion

1-2 Perform once in each of the three positions as learned on Pp. 9, 20 and 67 Count 10 in each backward position and 20 in each of the forward positions

Perform the leg movements of Fig. 2 (as learned on Page 110) following the extreme position only Hold the leg positions for 10. Relax upon completion

side bend

3 Perform once in each of the three positions as learned on Pp. 102-103. Alternate the sides (first left, then right) for each position. Hold each bend for 10
Relax upon completion

14th DAY

Remember to:

Bend very slowly to each of the three positions
Keep arms parallel in each of the three positions

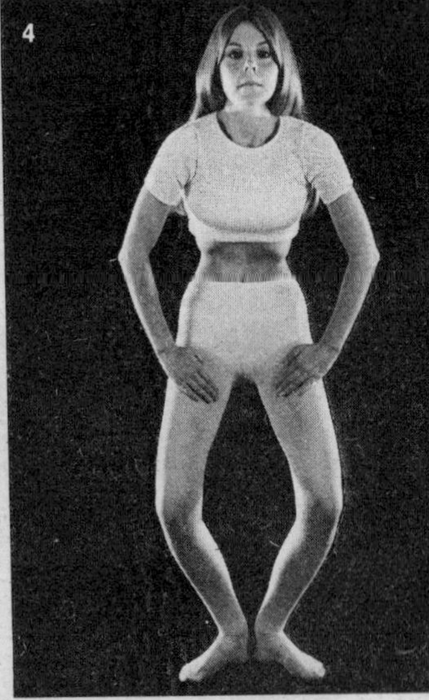

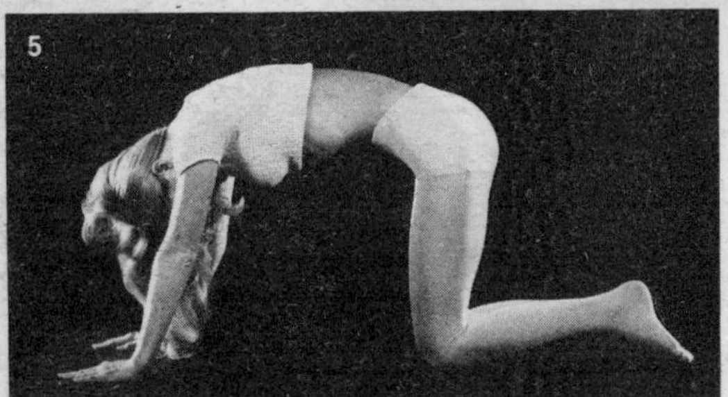

abdominal lifts

ABDOMINAL LIFTS (16 B & C)

4-5 This exercise was learned on Pages 96 and 97
Perform 5 rhythmic lifts to each exhalation. (Do less

if necessary but not more than 5)
Relax briefly after each group

Perform 5 groups in the standing and 5 groups in the All Fours position

ADDITIONAL MOVEMENTS FOR THE

backward bend

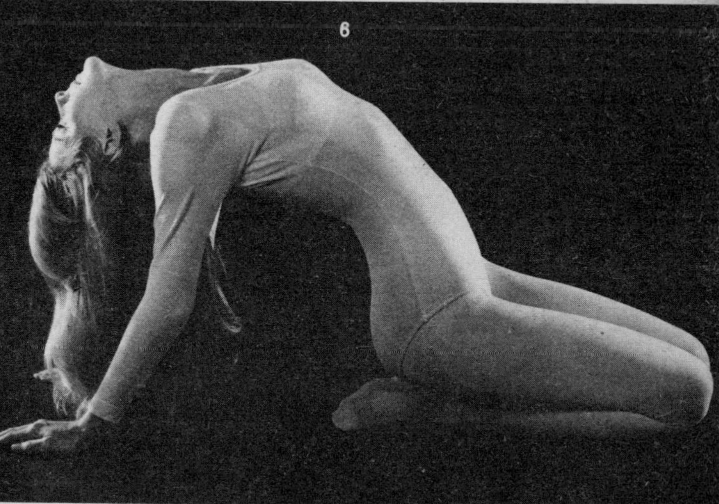
6

6 Perform once in each of the two positions learned on Page 61
Hold the extreme positions for 20

7 Change position of feet so that toes are as illustrated
Sit on heels

8 Lean backward so that additional pressure is placed on toes

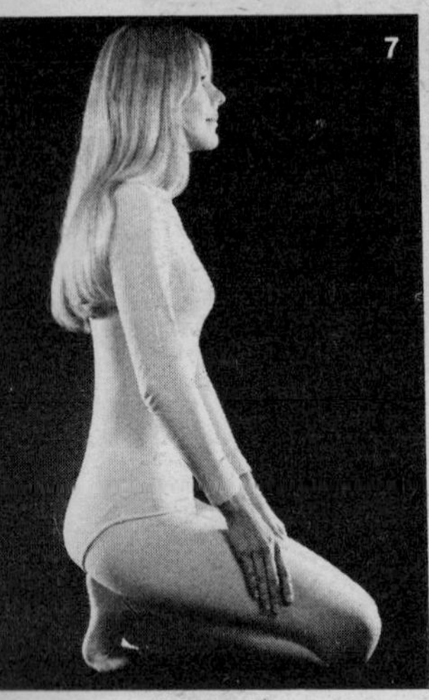

Touch fingertips to floor
Do not go farther than depicted
Hold for 10
Straighten up and proceed to next exercise

If this position causes discomfort, remain on toes for a few moments only.
With each attempt in subsequent days your toes will become better able to support weight of body

simple twist

9 Perform twice to right side, then twice to left side as learned on Page 23. Hold each extreme position for 10. Relax upon completion

back stretch

10 Perform once in each of the four positions learned on Pages 12, 22, 71 and 138. Hold each extreme position for 20. Relax upon completion

If any of the positions is too difficult, revert to a more simple posture

9

10

bow

TO FIRM FLABBY AREAS OF YOUR BACK

11 Rest chin on floor
Arms at sides

12 Bend knees and bring feet forward
Reach back and attempt to hold feet
Chin remains on floor

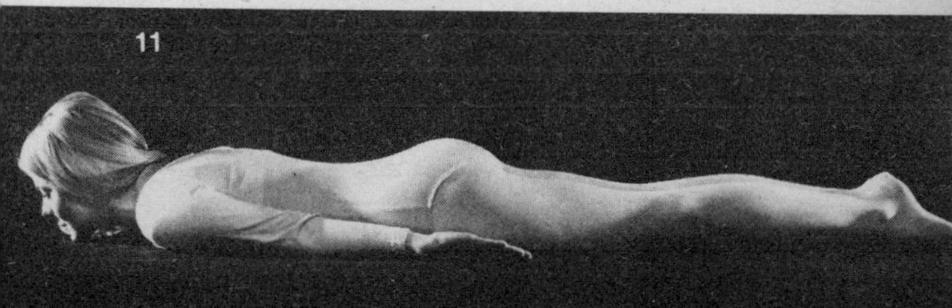

11

14th DAY

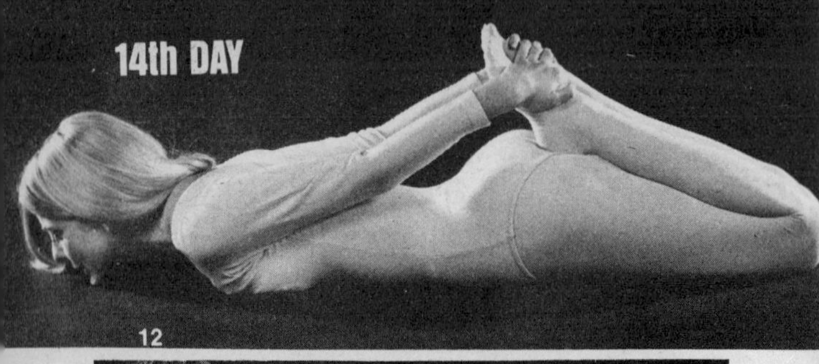

12

13

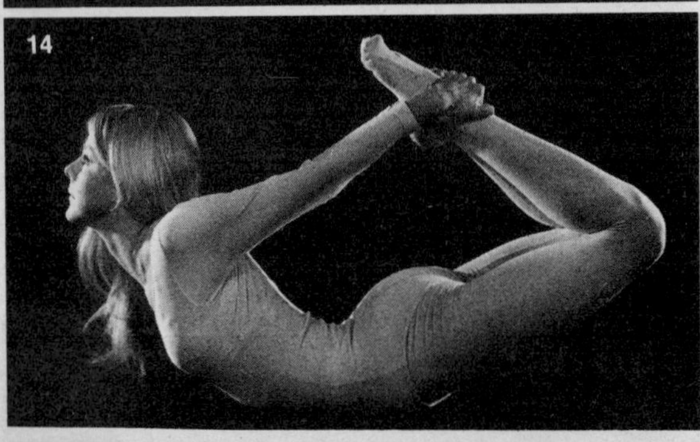

14

15

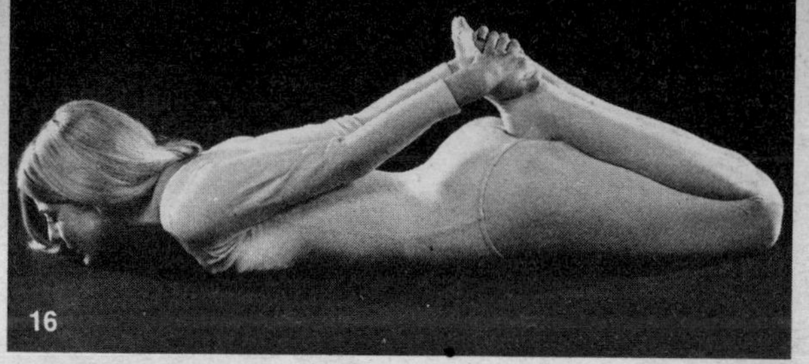

16

13 Hold feet firmly
Slowly raise trunk

14 Continue to raise trunk
Simultaneously raise knees
Head bends backward
Attempt to bring knees together
(feel how entire back becomes firm)
Move cautiously and do not strain
This is the completed Bow posture
Hold as still as possible for 10

15 Slowly lower knees to floor
Retain hold on feet

16 Slowly lower trunk and chin to floor
Retain hold on feet

17 Release feet and lower legs to floor
Rest cheek on floor and relax completely

Repeat once

If you cannot hold both feet (as in Fig. 12) hold one foot only for count of 20. Ability to hold both feet will come with practice on subsequent days.

If you cannot raise knees (as in Fig. 13) raise trunk only and hold for 10. Repeated attempts on subsequent days will develop muscles necessary to raise knees.

Move very slowly and extremely cautiously at all times in this exercise so that you never strain or go beyond a comfortable position.

Proceed to next exercise

17

14th DAY

head twist

18 Perform once in each of the three positions learned on Page 116. Hold each extreme position for 20

ADDITIONAL MOVEMENTS FOR THE

modified head stand

19 This is the extreme position, learned on Page 63, that we have been practicing.

20 This position follows directly that of Fig. 19
It must be executed very cautiously
Move knees as close to chest as possible
Place your complete weight on head and arms
Straighten back
Push lightly against floor with toes; attempt to bring body into position illustrated
Do not go farther than this position; do not attempt to straighten legs
Hold for 10
Slowly lower feet to floor and relax with head down as previously

If balance cannot be maintained in Fig. 20, continue to return feet to floor and try again
Make the surrounding area soft with a few pillows in the event you lose your balance and tumble over or to the side

If you feel you absolutely cannot execute the position of Fig. 20 revert to Fig. 19 and hold for 30 as previously

Proceed to next exercise

19

14th DAY

20

complete breath

21 Perform 5 times, seated in a cross-legged posture, as learned on Page 50. Continue to alternate your legs when attempting the Half-Lotus, i.e. right on top one day, left the next

Upon completion, sit quietly for several minutes and become aware of what is occurring in your organism as practiced previously

No further practice is necessary today

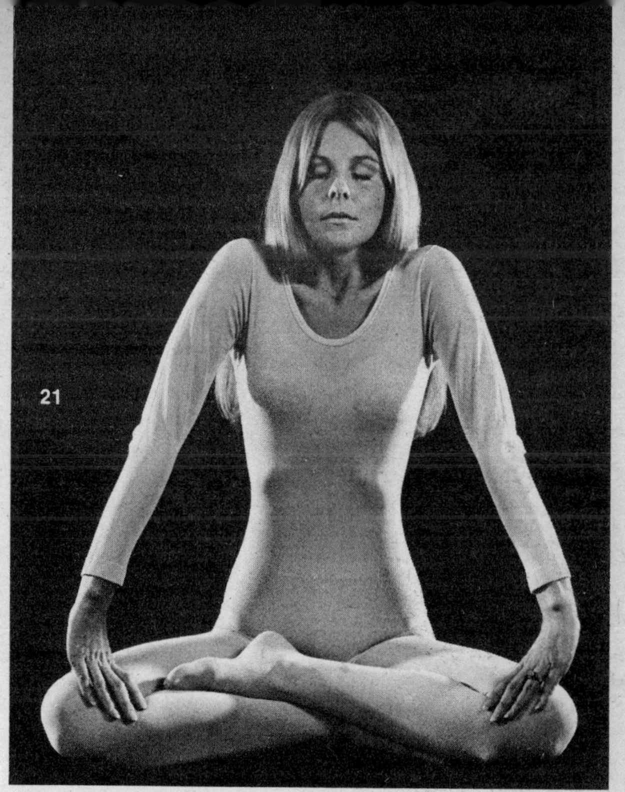

thoughts for the day

YOGA AND THE HOUSEWIFE

Housework and all that it entails may not be fun but it is important and must be accomplished with a sense of fulfillment and satisfaction. Work, according to the Bhagavad-Gita, is a great privilege and through it inner growth and development are achieved. If the housewife does not experience such satisfaction from her work, if housework is continual drudgery and without meaning, she becomes irritable, frustrated and depressed and these feelings are passed on to other members of the family. This morbid situation prevails in many homes and makes for very unhappy living.

A housewife usually works under a certain amount of continual pressure (which is increased if there are small children) and she must be able to handle this pressure day after day; she usually needs to function with more continuous, sustained energy than her husband at the office! To cope successfully with pressure, to find pleasure, meaning and some degree of fulfillment in her work, the housewife's physical and psychological conditions must be particularly healthy. Now we have already stated (in our 7th Day's notes) that housework is often mistaken for "exercise," whereas the truth of the matter is that these chores **promote** conditions of stress and tension. It is essential, therefore, that the housewife take the necessary time out from her work each day and do whatever is necessary to maintain a high level of physical and mental fitness. Yoga provides the perfect method. The exercises we are learning in this book will impart energy, offer relaxation when needed and provide a firm, streamlined body with good muscle tone. At any point in the day when her work is "getting her down" the housewife can devote a few minutes to her Yoga routines and find herself refreshed and energized. She need no longer experience the "let downs" that can occur at various times during the workday and, in addition, she will be able to revitalize herself for the evening's activities (something that is greatly appreciated by husbands).

Here are two important tips for the housewife, or for any person who must take care of her home: (1) Stretch often during your housework; (2) Make it a rule to always move with poise and balance regardless of how mundane you may think your activities are. If you begin to make a ballet (longer, smoother arm, leg and trunk movements) out of sweeping, cleaning, etc. you will be surprised at how quickly your body assumes added grace and beauty and at how quickly this is noticed by your family and friends.

15th DAY

rishi's posture

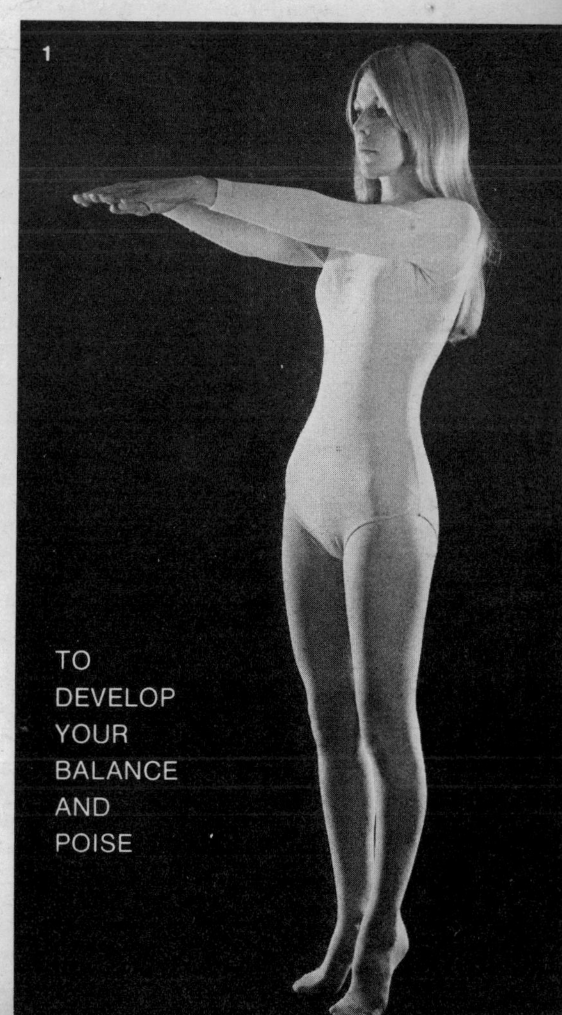
1
TO
DEVELOP
YOUR
BALANCE
AND
POISE

15th DAY

Today marks the beginning of the second half of our program. If we are to successfully complete our 28 day plan you must practice very seriously and carefully for the next 14 days. Do not allow anything to take precedence over your daily practice periods.

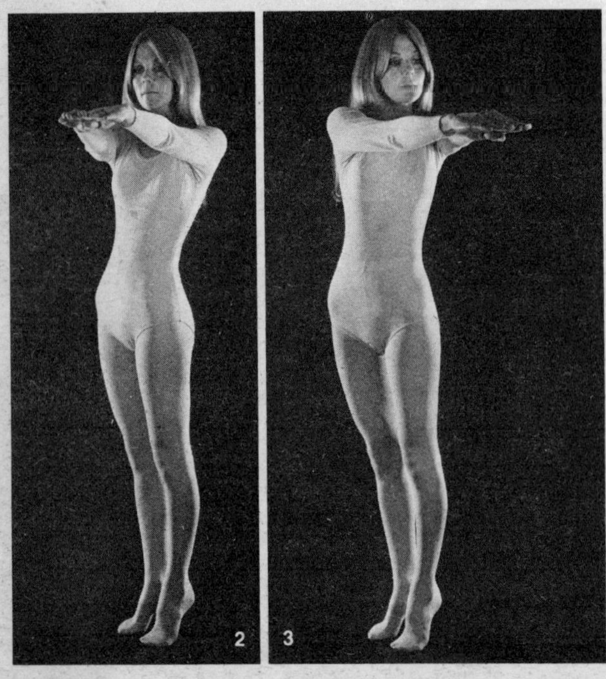

1 Stand with heels together
Raise arms slowly and gracefully from your sides
Simultaneously come up on toes as high as possible
If you lose balance, pause a moment and try again
Fix gaze on back of hands

2 As slowly as possible begin to twist to left
Hold gaze on back of hands

Remain high on toes
If you lose balance, simply come back up on toes and continue with movements

3 The 90 degree twisting posture
Hold gaze on back of hands
Keep spine straight

4 Come down on soles of feet
Bend forward slowly
Knees remain straight
Right hand moves slowly down **back of right leg** and stops at back of knee
Gaze follows back of left hand to position illustrated
Hold for 10

5 Slowly straighten to the upright position
Hands meet in front
Simultaneously raise high on toes

4

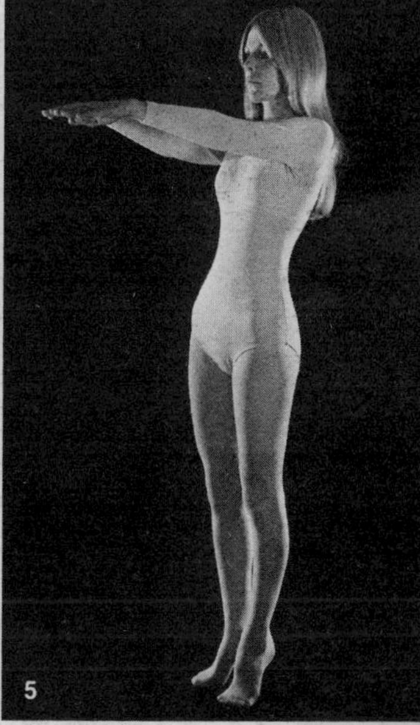
5

15th DAY

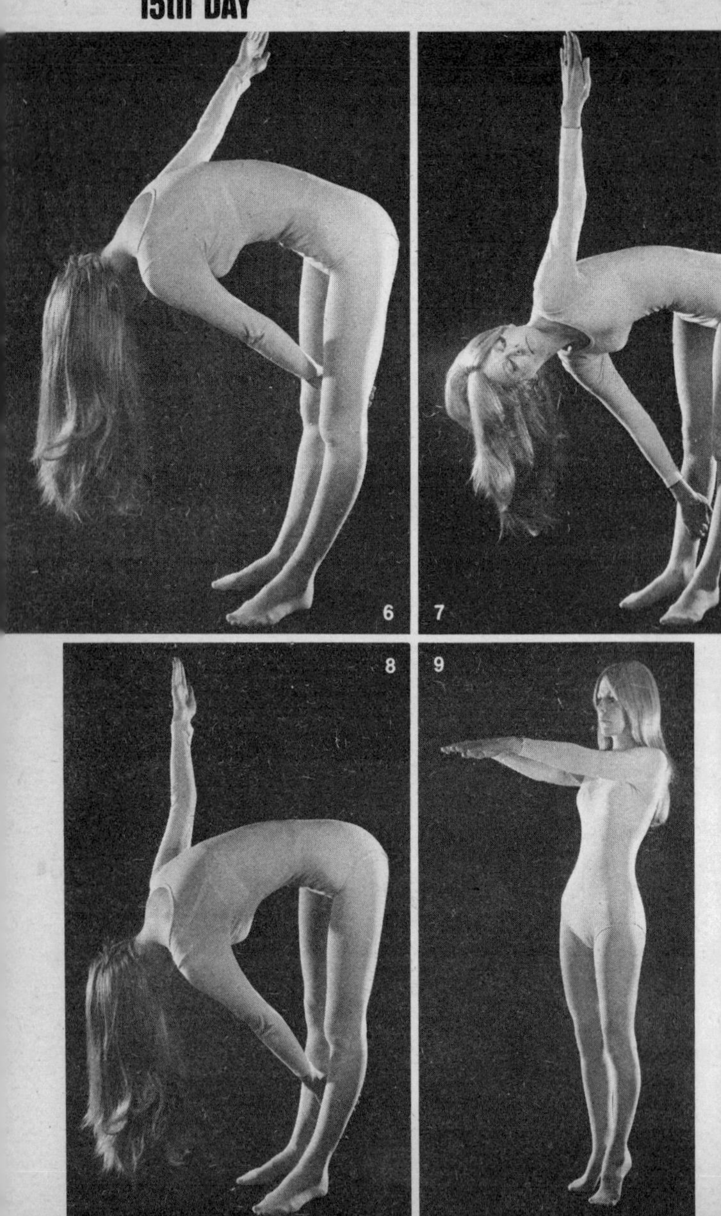

6 Fix gaze on hands and perform identical movements to right side
Left hand holds back of left knee
Eyes follow right hand to position illustrated
Soles of feet rest on floor
Hold for 10

7 Slowly straighten to upright position
Hands meet in front
Simultaneously raise high on toes once again
Perform identical twisting movements to left
This time right hand moves down to hold **right calf** (If this position is difficult, revert to knee)
Hold for 10

8 Slowly straighten to upright position
Raise high on toes
Perform identical movements to right
Remember to move very slowly
Left hand holds right calf for 10

9 Straighten to upright position
Raise high on toes
Hands meet in front
Very slowly lower arms to sides and soles to floor
Relax

Repeat entire routine once

Proceed to next exercise

circular motion

10 Perform this exercise twice from each of the three positions learned on Page 27. Hold each of the rolling movements for a count of 3. Relax

knee and thigh stretch

11 Perform three times as learned on Page 21
Hold each extreme position for 10. Relax briefly

15th DAY

lion

12 Perform three times as learned on Pp. 59-60

Hold each extreme position for 15. Relax briefly

scalp exercise

13 Perform 25 times as learned on Pp. 59-60
Relax briefly

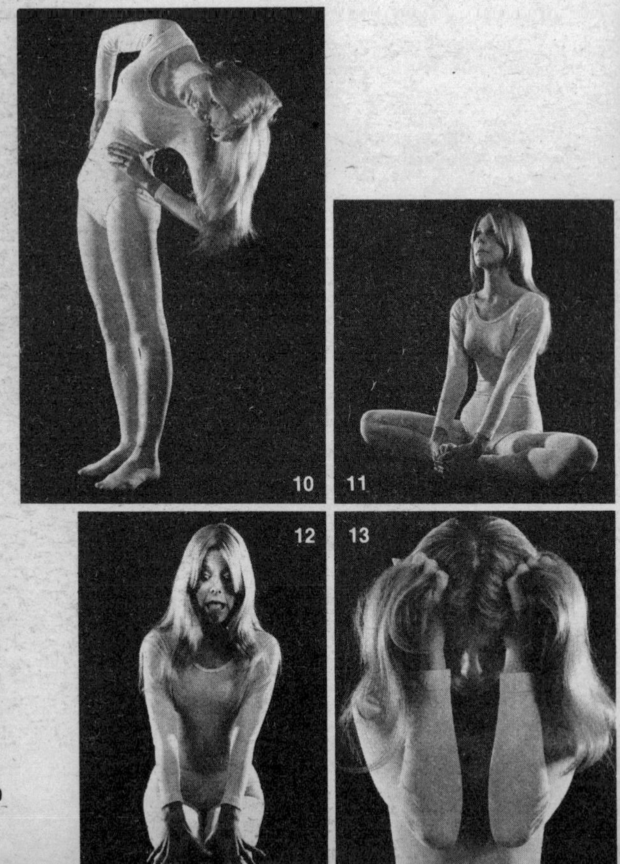

bust exercise

TO FIRM AND DEVELOP YOUR CHEST AND BUST

14

15

16

15th DAY

14 Sit in a cross-legged posture
Interlace fingers behind back

15 Very slowly raise arms as depicted
Keep spine straight

16 Continue to raise arms to extreme position
Hold your extreme position for 10

Lower arms to position of Fig. 14

Repeat twice

Proceed to next exercise

locust

This exercise was learned on Pp. 105-106
Raise each leg once to prepare muscles; hold for 10

17 Perform twice
Hold each raise for 5
Relax briefly after each raise

18 Perform twice
Hold each raise for 5
Relax briefly after first raise
Relax for approximately 20 seconds after final raise

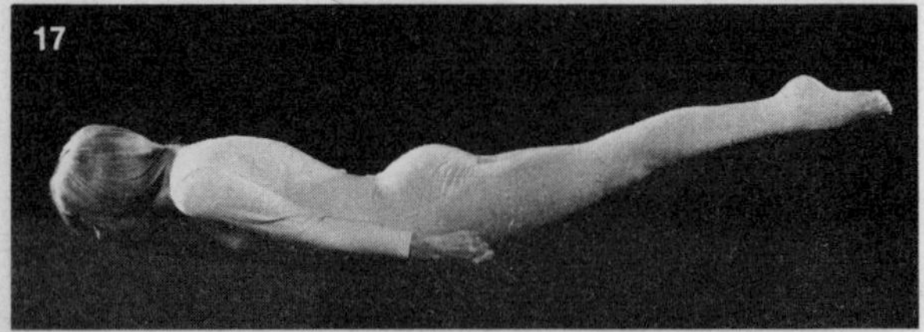
17

18

leg over

19 Perform three times to each side, alternating legs (right leg goes to left side; left leg goes to right side, etc.) as learned on Pp. 33-34. Hold each extreme position for 10. Relax upon completion

shoulder stand

20 Perform your extreme position of the Shoulder Stand as learned on Page 132. Increase the hold of the inverted posture to a count of 90 (1½ minutes) Do not hold longer

Come out of the posture exactly as instructed and relax for one minute

plough

21 Perform your extreme position of the Plough as learned on Page 135. Increase the hold to a count of 20. Do not hold longer

Come out of the posture exactly as instructed and relax

20

21

practice plan 15th day

To complete our 15th Day of practice we will perform each of today's exercises once, in our continuous motion routine. We do not pause between any of the exercises.

The routine consists of the following:

Rishi's Posture (your extreme position, once to each side)

Circular Motion (from the extreme forward position)

Knee and Thigh Stretch

Lion

Bust Exercise (your extreme position, once)

Locust (your extreme position, once)

Leg Over (once to each side)

Finally, perform the extreme position of the Shoulder Stand but do not hold; go directly from Fig. 20 into 21 and hold for 20. Then return to the prone position and relax completely for several minutes.

Beginning today, you may practice more than once a day if your time permits. The second practice period should consist of attempting to perfect the various postures in which you are weak.

thoughts for the day

YOGA NUTRITION (2)

Let us continue our discussion of the 12th Day.

If you have been following our daily plan faithfully you will find that you are now at a point where your sensitivity is heightened to all things that are occurring in your organism. You will become very aware that what you are eating has a pronounced effect on the way you feel and act. After some meals you will observe that you are alive and energized whereas others will leave you heavy, dull, lethargic in both body and mind. This is an important revelation; it will become very clear that the difference between the two states can be attributed to the foods you have consumed and you will begin to think about eating not simply to satisfy your taste buds or fill your stomach, but for life-force. One grows more and more sensitive to the fact that light, high-quality foods can give great reserves of life-force, help regenerate the body and impart many of the qualities of youth, while heavy, rich or devitalized foods can sap life-force and add to the symptoms of aging.

Overeating as well as incorrect eating may also be the cause of a great many physical disorders. Indeed, certain nutritionists believe that almost all illnesses can be attributed directly or indirectly to the toxins, acids and waste products continually formed by inferior foods that cannot be properly digested and eliminated. These nutritionists maintain that the body is capable of coping with most germs that enter it, providing that this body is in a pure, clean, healthy state with ability to call upon its defense agents as needed. But a physical organism that is low in resistance because its defense agents are occupied in other areas, trying to cope with toxins, congestions and deposits, is greatly weakened in its attempt to fight these germs. Therefore, the Yoga student must make certain that her diet does not inhibit either the life force already existent in the organism or the new life-force that will be gained through the Yoga exercises.

Before proceeding with this discussion I am going to ask you to perform an experiment: Put the book down and without further statements from me take an imaginary trip to your market. Go up and down the aisles and determine whether you know **instinctively** which foods are "alive," that is, those which contain life-force as opposed to those that are devitalized, without real nourishment. In my classes this experiment has proven most valuable since it has made students think about foods in a totally different light. Do that now and we will continue this discussion shortly.

review

complete breath standing

1-2 Perform three times as learned on Page 53. Hold the extreme raise for 5. At this point you should be able to hold the extreme position on tip toes without movement. Relax upon completion

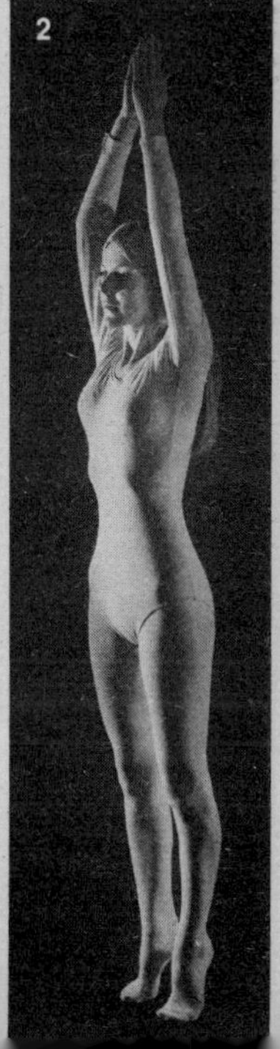

16th DAY

3

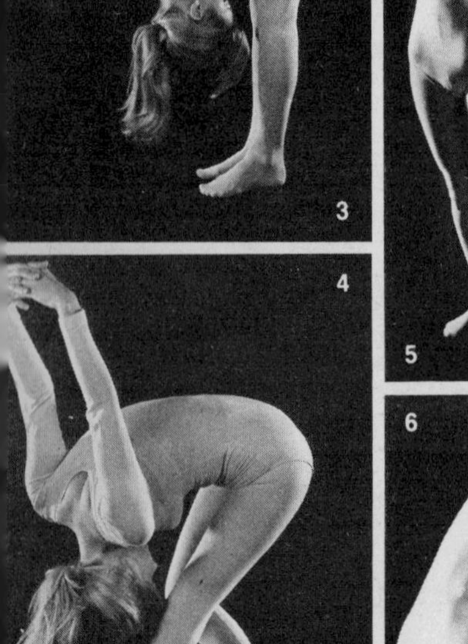
4

5

6

chest expansion

3-4 Perform once in each of the three positions as learned on Pages 9, 20 and 67. Count 10 in each backward position and 20 in each of the forward positions

Perform the leg movements (learned on Page 110) following the extreme position only. Hold the leg positions for 15. Relax upon completion

side bend

5-6 Perform once in each of the three positions as learned on Pp. 102-103. Alternate the sides (first left, then right) for each position. Hold each bend for 10. At this point you should be able to bend the full 90 degrees of the extreme position
Relax upon completion

triangle

7-8 Perform once in each of the three positions as learned on Pp. 18, 30-31 and 38-39. Alternate the sides (first left, then right) for each position. Hold each bend for 10. At this point you should be able to bring the arm over to the 90 degree position as depicted in Fig. 8. Relax upon completion

rishi's posture

9-10-11 Perform once in each of the two positions as learned yesterday on Page 166. Alternate the sides (first left, then right) for each position. Hold each bend for 10. Relax upon completion

Remember to:

Raise as high as possible on toes whenever so instructed
Twist very slowly
Keep gaze on back of hand when bending

9

10

11

circular motion

12-13 Perform twice from each of the three positions learned on Page 27. Hold each of the rolling movements for a count of 3. At this point you should be able to get a great deal of exaggerated movement into the waist in each of the three circles. Relax upon completion

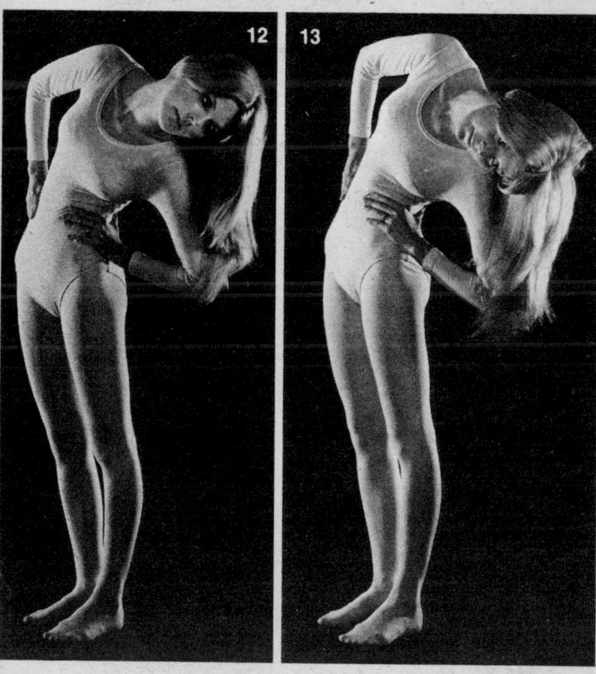

abdominal lifts

ABDOMINAL LIFTS (16 B & C)

14-15 This exercise was learned on Pages 101 and 102
Perform 5-7 rhythmic lifts to each exhalation
(Do less if necessary but not more than 7)
Relax briefly after each group

Perform 5 groups in the standing and 5 groups in the All Fours position

At this point you should be able to begin executing the "lift" and not simply a contraction. However, if this is not the case, be patient and continue to practice as deep a contraction as possible

Remember that the movements must be rhythmic

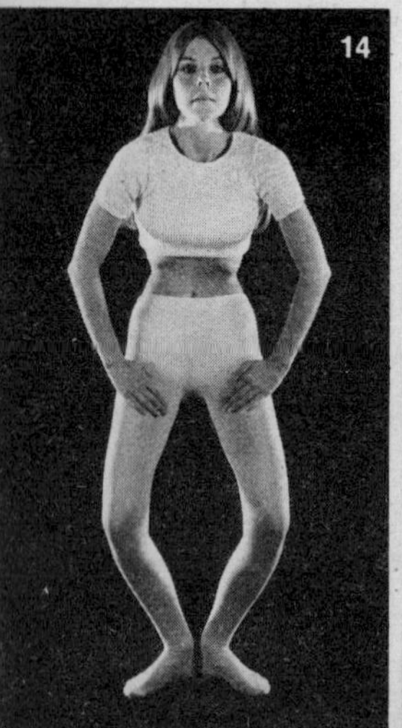

bust exercise

16–17 Perform 5 times as learned yesterday
Hold each raise for 5. Relax upon completion

Remember to:

Hold arms as straight as possible
Keep spine straight; don't slump

lion

18 Perform three times as learned on Pp. 59-60
Hold each extreme position for 15. Relax briefly

Remember to:

Make the tongue movements very intensive so that all the muscles of the face and neck are brought into play

16th DAY

backward bend

19-20 Perform once in each of the two positions learned on Page 61. Hold the extreme positions for 20

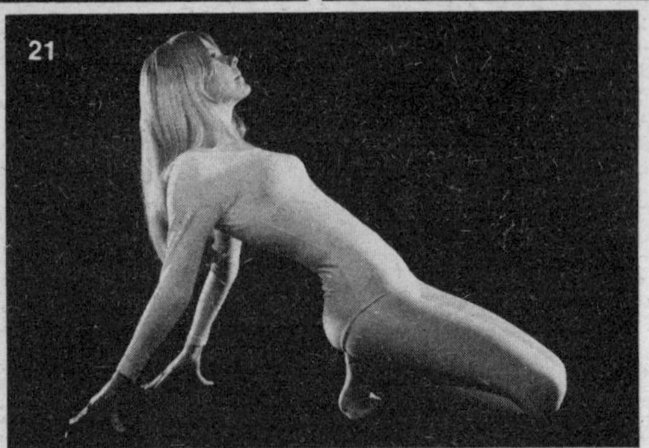

21 Change position of feet
Sit on heels and attempt to touch fingertips to floor as learned on Page 145
Attempt to sit more heavily on heels and place more pressure on toes than previously
Hold for 10
(If you experience discomfort, lessen pressure and hold for a few seconds only)
Relax

shoulder stand

22 Perform your extreme position of the Shoulder Stand once as learned on Page 132. Increase the hold of the inverted posture to a count of 105 (1¾ minutes). Do not hold longer. Today you should be able to straighten your trunk to a position that is close to Fig. 22

23 Come out of the posture exactly as instructed and relax for one minute

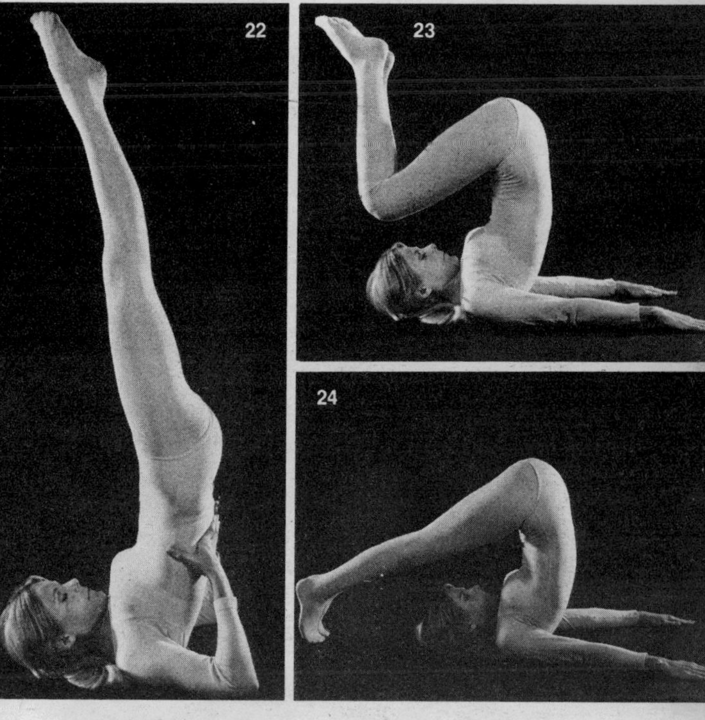

plough

24 Perform your extreme position of the Plough once

as learned on Page 135. Hold for 20. Do not hold longer. At this point you should be able to lower your legs behind you a few more inches than previously. Do not strain; simply hold whatever extreme position you can execute for 20

Come out of the posture exactly as instructed (work for smoothness) and relax

back stretch

25-26 Perform once in each of the four positions learned on Pp. 12, 22, 71 and 138-139. Hold each extreme position for 15. Relax upon completion

If you cannot, as yet, perform the fourth position, do the third position twice; if you cannot perform the third position, do the second position twice

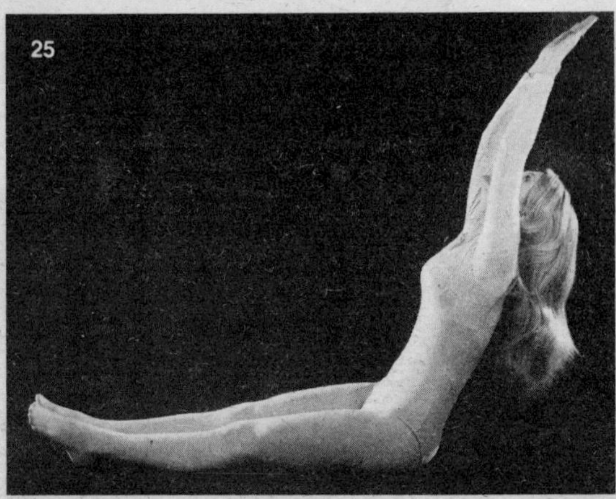

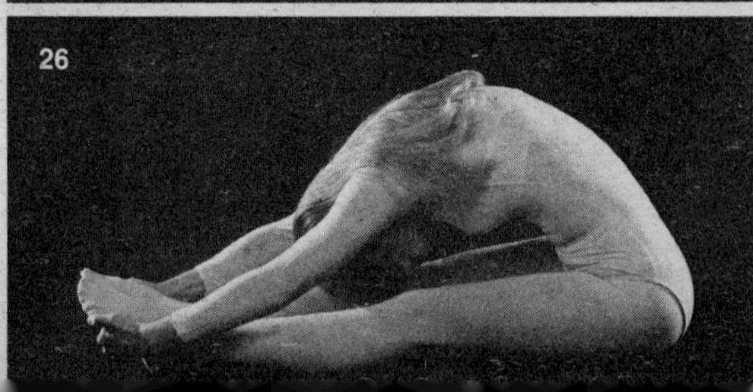

leg over

27 Perform three times to each side, alternating legs (right leg goes to left side; left leg goes to right side, etc.) as learned on Pp. 33-34. Hold each position for 10. Remember to keep the leg high toward the head. Relax upon completion

27

modified head stand

29

28

28-29 Attempt to perform the position of Fig. 29 as learned on Page 151. Hold for 15 only. If this is not yet possible revert to the position of Fig. 28. Hold for 45

Relax with head down as previously

practice plan 16th day

To complete today's Review we will perform a group of the exercises once in continuous motion but we will make this departure from our previous practice: there is to be no pause either between the exercises or *within each exercise. That is, there will be no holding of the extreme positions.* As soon as the extreme position of a posture is reached we will begin immediately (slowly of course) to come out of the posture and proceed to the next. Therefore, once you begin the routine you do not interrupt the continuous motion from beginning to end. You move very slowly with deep concentration on all movements and the postures must be made to flow, one into another, like a slow motion ballet. Sitting down, lying down, rolling over, etc. all become part of the routine and are executed in graceful slow motion.

Today's routine consists of the following:

Complete Breath Standing (do not hold extreme position)

Chest Expansion (your extreme positions only, do not hold backward, forward or leg positions)

Side Bend (to each side; do not hold)

Triangle (to each side; do not hold)

Rishi's Posture (to each side; do not hold)

Circular Motion (from the extreme forward position; do not hold) (sit down in continuous motion)

Bust Exercise (do not hold)

Backward Bend (the extreme position only; do not hold) (lie down in continuous motion)

Plough (your extreme position; do not hold) (sit up in continuous motion)

Back Stretch (your extreme position; do not hold)

complete breath

30 To conclude the routine, assume the cross-legged posture and perform three Complete Breaths. Then sit very quietly as we have practiced previously

thoughts for the day

ARTHRITIS

Arthritis, as a national tragedy, and the positive effect that the practice of Yoga has had upon it, should be included in our discussions. This painful inflammation of the joints, once confined primarily to the elderly, is now experienced widely not only among those of middle age but young people as well. Millions and millions of Americans suffer agonizing pains each day and, seeking relief, resort primarily to the various drugs that offer to alleviate the pain. As you probably know, arthritis victims seldom improve. The pain intensifies and the inflammation may slowly spread. The chances for a "cure" through currently employed methods appear to be extremely slim.

It is our opinion, based solely on extensive experience with many students, that the very patient and cautious self-manipulation of the joints, coupled with the elimination of all foods that might be the cause of "deposits" (and these include most dairy products and all other foods that have any significant fat content), could greatly decrease arthritis symptoms and even approach a natural cure. Notice that we stress **self-**manipulation, for while the various types of massage and heat therapy have proven helpful, they seem to offer only temporary relief. The term **self-manipulation** implies body movement and here we encounter the dilemma of the vicious circle: the arthritis victim does not wish to exercise because her body hurts when she does so, and her body hurts more and more because she refuses to exercise.

The Yogic movements, performed in slow motion, without strain, requiring that the student attain to a position in which only the slightest discomfort is experienced, are ideal. The various stretches and holds are able to reach deep into the joints and, apparently, loosen the deposits. The methodical repetition of the movements, practiced very slowly and cautiously seems, within the course of time, to produce excellent results.

If the arthritis victim, in undertaking Yoga, is able to move only one inch and hold a position for only five seconds, she is already beginning to exercise and manipulate. Each day she should attempt to move only an inch farther and hold one second longer. Only the most simple of the exercises can be attempted in the beginning. With perseverance, even during those periods of discomfort, improvement will be noted. It is also our opinion that regular Yoga students increase their chances of preventing arthritis.

A person with a severe case of arthritis who desires to practice Yoga should receive the approval of her physician.

At this point in our study it becomes extremely valuable to group the exercises according to the specific parts of the body that they manipulate. Through these groupings you will discover the wonderful possibilities of using the Yoga exercises for a complete plan of physical fitness as well as for dealing with problems that may exist in a particular area of your organism.

TODAY WE WILL EMPHASIZE
THE MAJOR TECHNIQUES
FOR THE BACK AND SPINE

chest expansion

1-2-3 Perform once in each of the three positions as learned on Pages 9, 20 and 67. Make a serious effort today to bring your forehead close to your knees (or touch them) in the extreme position
Your arms are brought far over your back

1

2

Count 10 in each backward position and 20 in each of the forward positions. Relax upon completion

We will not perform the leg movements today

back stretch

4-5 Perform once in each of the four positions learned on Pp. 12, 22, 71 and 138-139. Hold each extreme position for 15. Relax upon completion

If you cannot, as yet, perform the fourth position, execute the third position twice. Remember that the first and second positions are as important as the more advanced positions since they manipulate different areas of the spine. Do not neglect them

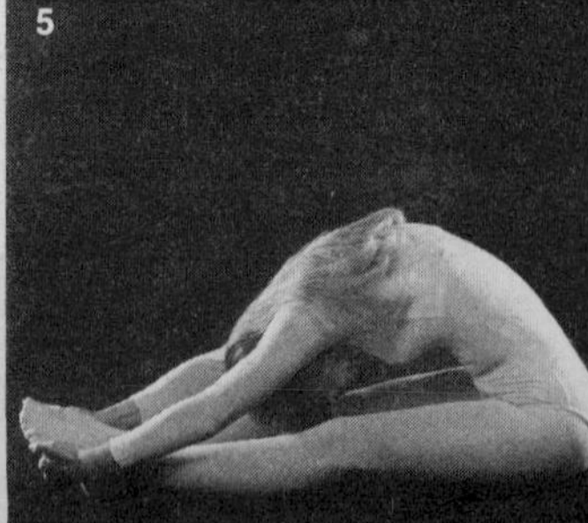

6

full twist

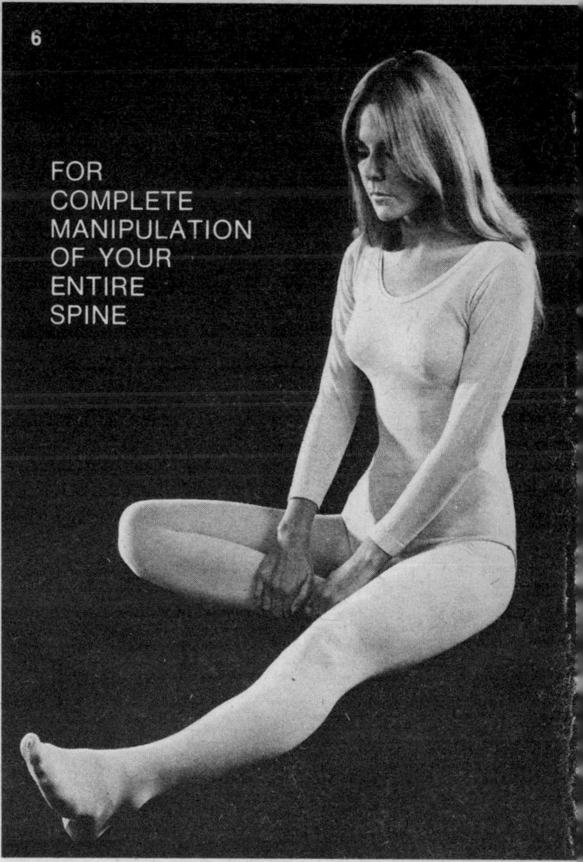

FOR COMPLETE MANIPULATION OF YOUR ENTIRE SPINE

This is the very finest exercise for an immediate loosening of the entire spinal column. At first, the "corkscrew" movements may appear complicated, but once learned you will be able to execute it within a matter of seconds and experience the most wonderful relief of spinal pressures and tensions. Therefore study the movements carefully and learn them well. This ingenious posture will become a lifelong friend.

6 Extend legs straight outward
Place right sole against left thigh (as in Half Lotus)

7 Take a firm hold on the left ankle

8 Swing left foot over right knee and rest sole on floor

9 Place left hand on floor behind you

10 Now bring right arm **over** left leg and take a firm hold on **right** knee (study illustration; this position locks lumbar area)

11 The completed posture (study illustration)
Slowly twist trunk and head as far to **left** as possible
Left hand moves around back and holds **right** side of waist
Hands holds knee firmly
Chin is close to shoulder
Spine is straight
Hold for 10

7

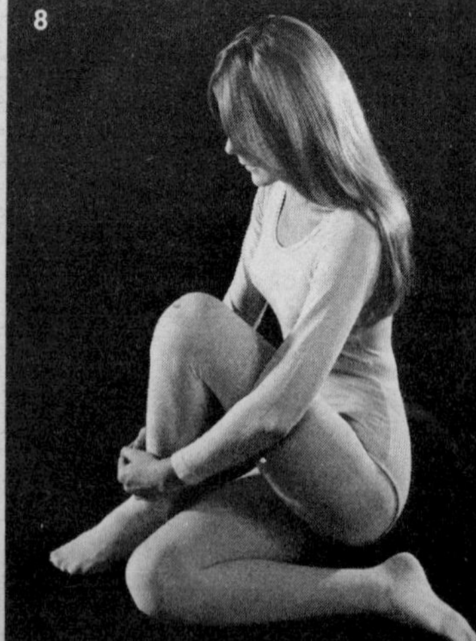
8

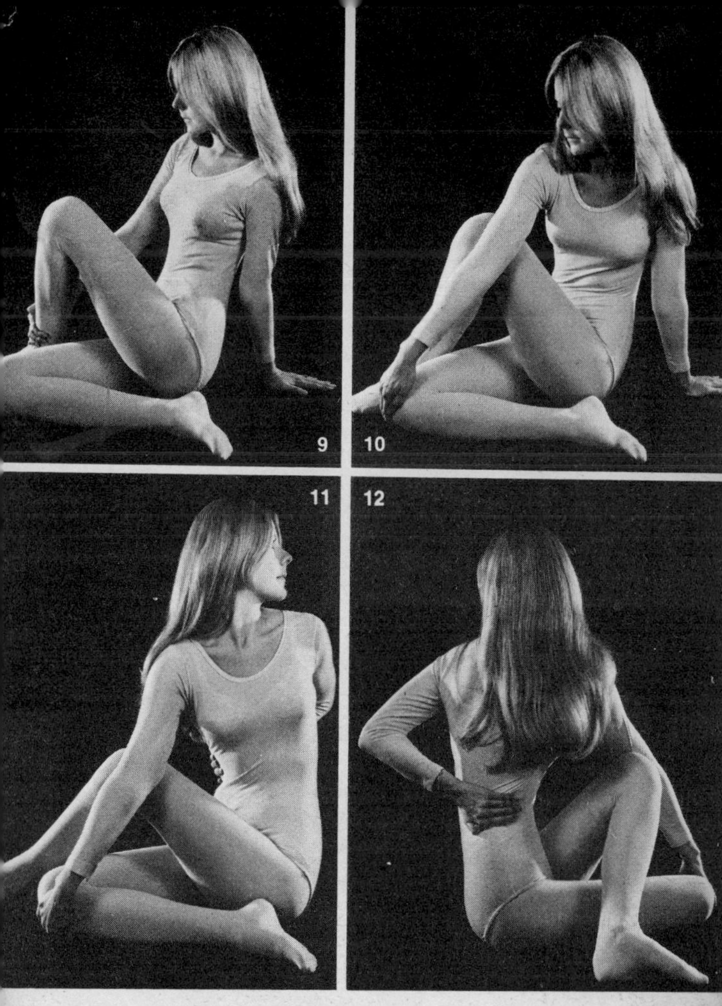

12 A back view of the position

When count of 10 is completed lower hand to floor, turn trunk and head forward and return to Fig. 10. Relax briefly but maintain hold on knee

Repeat twice; hold extreme position for 10

Come out of posture and extend legs outward as in Fig. 6

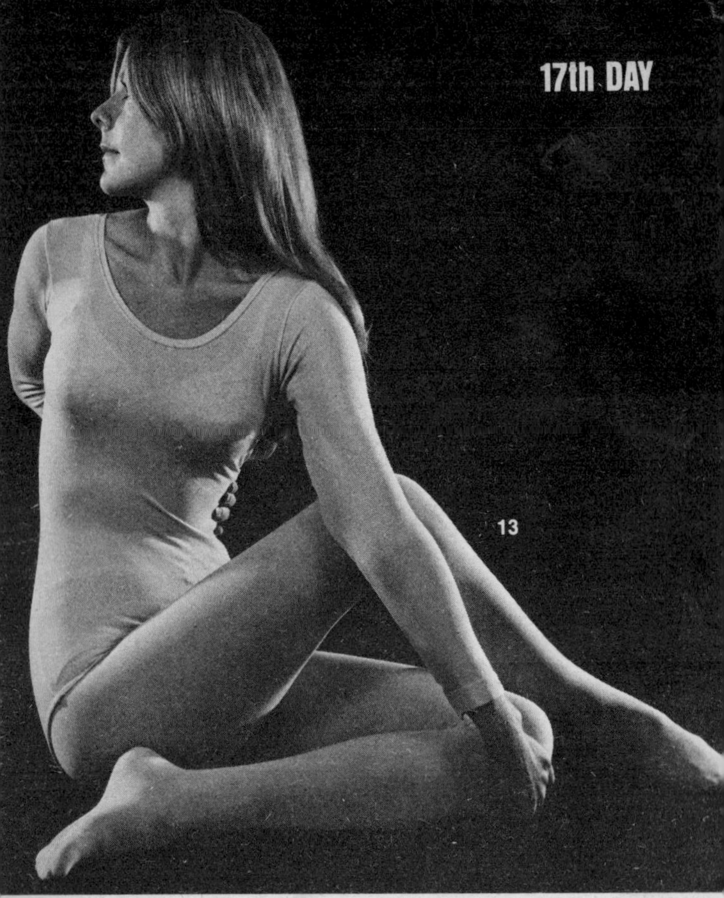

13 Perform identical movements on opposite side
Exchange the words "right" and "left" in above directions
Perform extreme twist three times; hold for 10 each

Come out of posture and extend legs outward. Relax

At first you may feel tight and cramped in the waist and legs; this is natural and will disappear with a few days of practice. Note that in Fig. 10 the lumbar area is locked and that the dorsal areas twist against this lock in Fig. 11. If you cannot hold the knee in Fig. 10, revert to practice of the Simple Twist (6) learned on Page 23.

cobra locust bow

14-15-16

Today we will combine these three intensive back and spine exercises into a routine. Note that all three are powerful **convex** positions; that is, they bend the spine **inward.** The Locust is both a leg and back exercise. When you are able to raise your legs into the extreme Locust position, it is the lumbar area that is exercised.

Perform the three exercises as follows:

Cobra: the complete routine, including the twisting movements, once as learned on Pages 72 and 114; hold the extreme raise for 30 today and the twisting movements for 10 each. Relax deeply

Locust: the legs separately (Page 83), then your extreme position once; hold for 7 today. Relax

Bow: your extreme position once (Page 147); hold for 10. Relax

Perform this entire routine of the three exercises **three times**

Upon completion relax deeply with cheek resting on floor and listen to your body

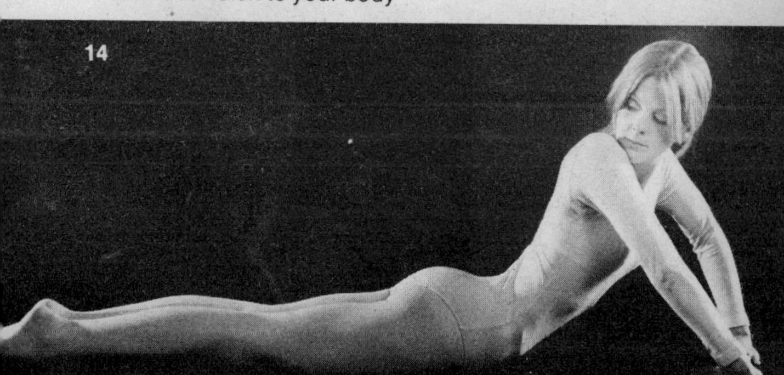

17th DAY

15

16

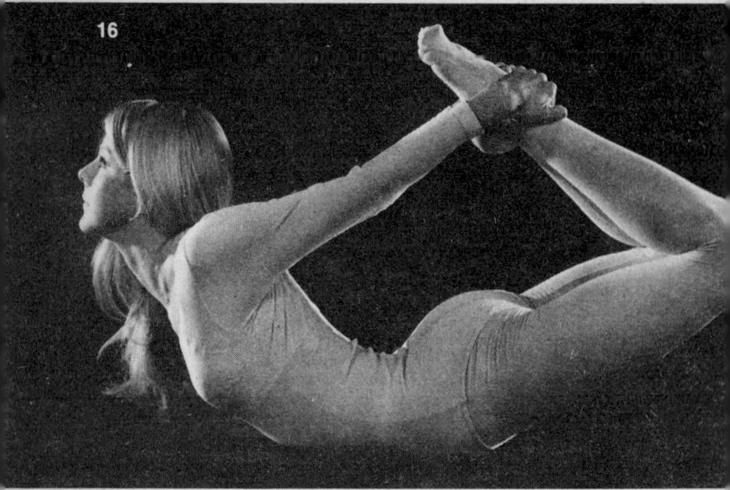

thoughts for the day

YOGA AS PHYSICAL THERAPY

Because of their great antiquity, it is difficult to determine whether certain of the Yoga postures were originally devised to aid in specific health problems or whether the pronounced therapeutic value inherent in the exercises is simply a by-product, a bonus. Most of the Hatha Yoga institutions in India make very specific health claims for the various techniques and a number of Hindu physicians have explained and substantiated these claims in medical journals. Recently, many physicians in Europe and America, seeing the postures performed, have offered their approval of Yoga, particularly because the mildness of the movements makes them so advantageous to those who wish to remain physically fit without straining.

Beginning today (17th Day) and extending through the 23rd Day, various Yoga exercises are grouped so that they may be applied to specific areas of the body. The primary objectives of this grouping are to strengthen, develop, firm and streamline. You may find that a number of your health and beauty problems are eventually solved in the course of practicing these groups. For example, a pain in the shoulder, a habitual cramp in the leg, excessively cold hands and feet or poor muscle tone may be overcome. If you have a problem in a particular area of your body, you may wish to emphasize the group of exercises that pertain to it by practicing only that group at a different time of the day. This is perfectly satisfactory, but do not neglect any of the regular routines.

It is well to remember that most physical problems have developed over a period of time, months or years, and when attempting to deal with them through **natural** means, such as Yoga, it is unrealistic to expect an immediate solution. If the laws of nature have been abused for prolonged periods, no sudden reversal of the resultant condition can be anticipated. It is possible that many minor conditions **will** respond quickly; more serious problems require sustained, patient practice. However, you can be assured that **in stimulating the life-force you are increasing your organism's healing power** and this is the esoteric explanation for the marked improvement in health that is so often experienced by Yoga students.

18th DAY

MAJOR EXERCISES
FOR THE SCALP,
FACE AND NECK

scalp exercise

1 Perform 25 times as learned on Pp. 59-60. Relax briefly

lion

2 Perform three times as learned on Pp. 59-60. Hold each extreme position for 15. Relax briefly

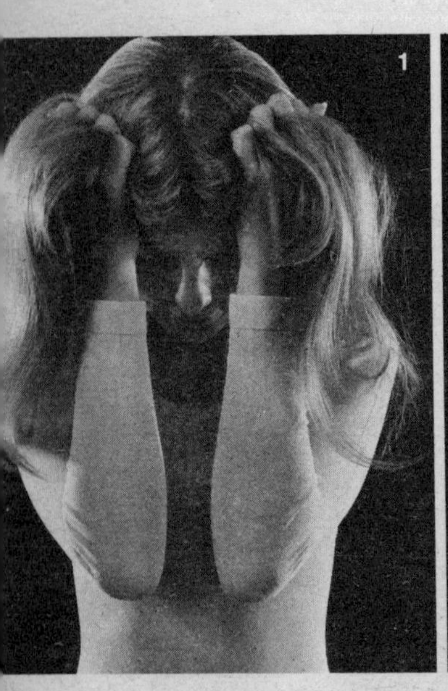

1

2

neck roll

3 Sit in a cross-legged posture
Bend head forward slowly and rest chin against chest
Sit erect
Close eyes
Hold for 10

4 Very slowly roll head to extreme left
Trunk does not move
Sit erect
Hold for 10

5 Very slowly roll head to extreme backward position
Feel chin and throat muscles tightening
Hold for 10

Very slowly roll head to extremc right
Trunk does not move
Hold for 10

Very slowly roll head forward to position of Fig. 3

Repeat entire routine once; relax briefly

Proceed to next exercise

3

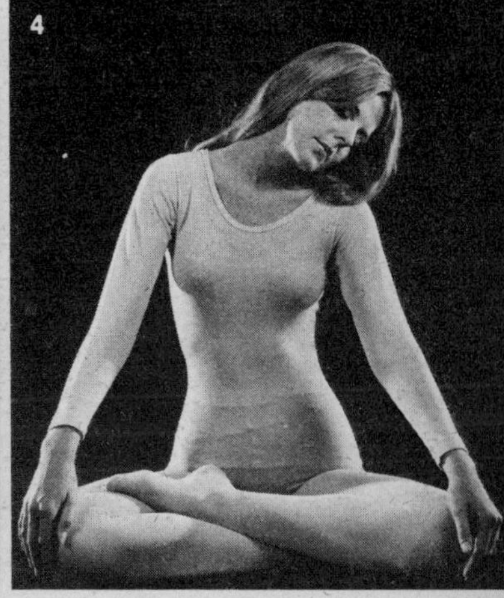
4

shoulder stand

6-7 Perform your extreme position of the Shoulder Stand once as learned on Page 132. Increase the hold of the inverted posture today to a count of 120 (2 minutes). Do not hold longer

Come out of the posture exactly as instructed in the previous directions and relax for one minute

Remember to:

Press chin tightly against chest in the completed posture of Fig. 7. This position brings the blood directly into the thyroid gland

modified head stand

8-9 Attempt to perform the position of Fig. 9 as learned on Page 151. Increase the hold to 20 if possible. Do not hold longer. If this position is not yet possible revert to the position of Fig. 8 and hold for one minute

Relax with head down as previously

Remember to:

Bring the bent knees as close to the chest as possible in Fig. 8
Use a pillow beneath the head if necessary
Keep the elbows close to the body for better balance

Bring the blood into the face, neck and scalp through the Shoulder Stand and the Head Stand is excellent for the health and beauty of these areas.

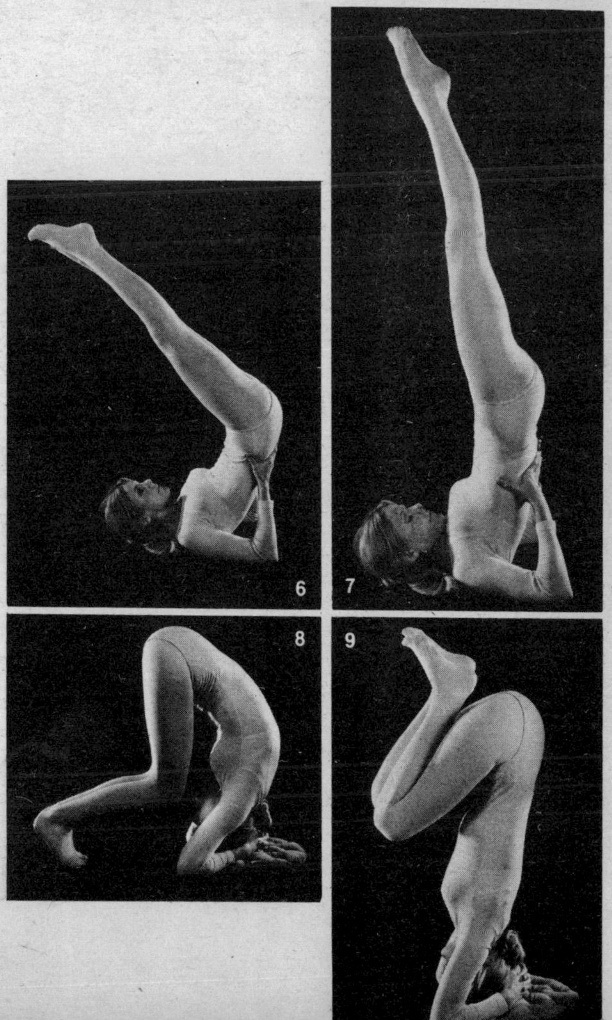

18th DAY

balance posture

THREE MAJOR EXERCISES FOR POISE AND BALANCE

10 Stand with heels together; arms at sides
Raise right arm overhead

11 Shift weight to right leg
Raise left foot behind you
Reach back with left hand and hold left foot
Right arm moves forward to aid in keeping balance

12 Perform the following movements very gently
Bring right arm backward
Pull left foot upward as illustrated

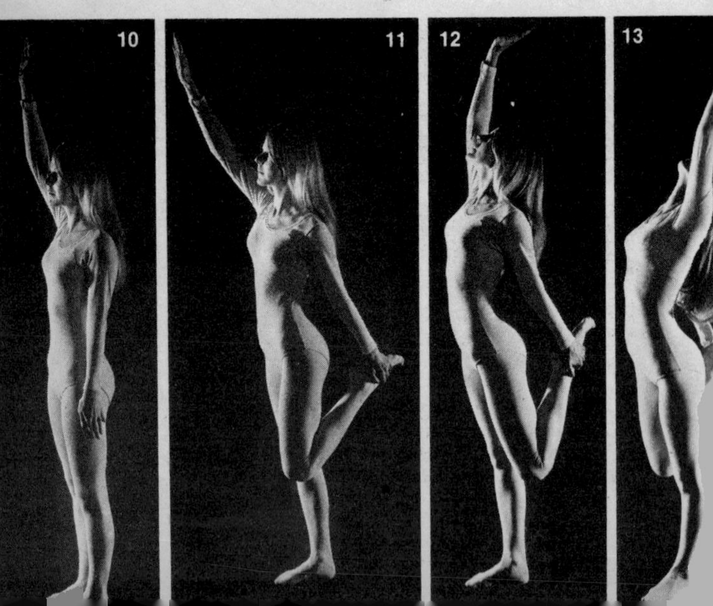

Head drops backward; eyes look upward
Hold as steady as possible for 5

Lower arm and leg gracefully and return to position of Fig. 10
Repeat the above movements twice

13 Perform identical movements three times on opposite side

Relax

Maintaining the balance will undoubtedly be difficult during your initial attempts. Do not laugh at yourself or become discouraged. The moment you begin to lose the balance simply lower your arms and leg. Pause a moment, regain your composure and begin again. At first you may have to attempt the position of Fig. 11 quite a few times before you can steady yourself long enough to execute the stretching movements of Fig. 12. Repeated attempts will result in success

Note the beautiful form and symmetry of the body in the completed posture

Proceed to next exercise

dancer's posture

14 Stand with heels together
Place palms together on top of head
Elbows are parallel with sides

15 In very slow motion bend knees and lower body
Continue to lower into the squatting posture (note position of toes)
Without pause (there is no hold) begin to push up very slowly

16 Straighten into upright position, remaining on toes
Lower soles of feet to floor (Fig. 14)
Without pause repeat four times very slowly

Relax

If you lose your balance at any point, pause a moment and begin again

Proceed to next exercise

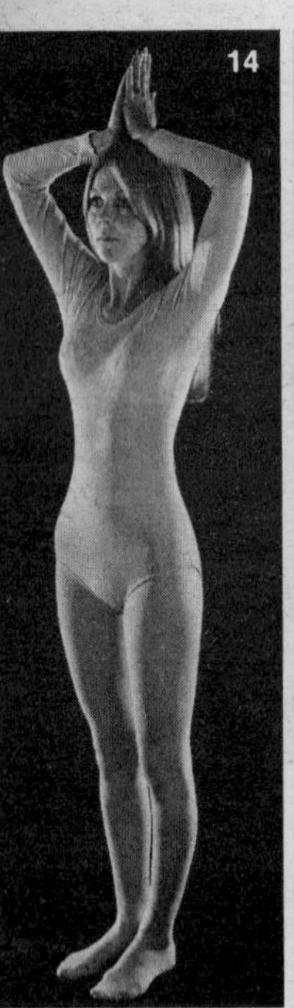
14

15

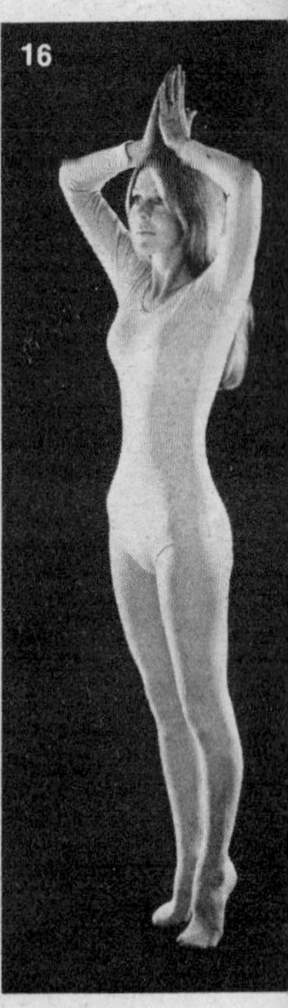
16

rishi's posture

17 Perform twice in each of the two positions as learned on Page 170. Alternate the sides (first left, then
18 right) for each position. Hold each bend for 10. Relax upon completion

You may practice again today if your times permits. The second practice period should consist of attempting to perfect the various postures in which you are weak.

thoughts for the day

YOGA NUTRITION (3)

Let us continue our discussion of the 15th Day.

It is not our intention in this book to treat Yoga Nutrition in detail. To do complete justice to this subject a separate volume is required. But proper nutrition plays a very vital role in our study, so we now offer the following principles as a guide. It has been my experience that if the student will acquaint himself (or herself) with these principles, they will automatically direct him to the life-force foods. He can then select and combine these foods intelligently according to his own needs.

18th DAY

(1) **Learn to live on a minimum of food, eating only what is light, agreeable and fully nourishing.** The less you eat, the better you will look and feel, providing your food is of a high quality. Your meal should always leave you feeling light and energized in body and clear in mind; if this is not the case, you have either overeaten or consumed foods that are rich, heavy or devitalized.

(2) **Eat as many foods as possible in their natural state.** All edible natural foods, i.e., foods that grow and certain milk products, are high in life-force. Natural foods will lose their life-force to the extent they are tampered with. "Tampering" refers to refining, canning, preserving, aging, fumigating, etc., and cooking in a manner that renders them lifeless and indigestible. For example, almost all fruits and many vegetables can be eaten raw or **lightly** steamed or baked. Dairy products with only the lowest possible fat content should be consumed. Canned, frozen and preserved foods should be eaten sparingly. (Check to see how many "devitalized" foods you chose on your imaginary shopping trip that was suggested on the 15th Day.)

(3) **Refined sugar products, coffee, alcoholic beverages and an overabundance of high protein preparations are to be considered as artificial stimulants and will, in the long view, deplete the life-force.**

(4) **Meat, fish and poultry should be consumed moderately.** The Yogi believes that the protein in animal flesh and animal products is of a low quality and actually requires more energy for digestion than it imparts. The protein of cottage cheese, avocados, nut butters, legumes, etc., is preferred.

(5) **Eat as few different types of foods at each meal as possible.** The more simple and homogeneous your foods, the more quickly and completely they will be digested and utilized.

FOR STREAMLINING WAIST AND HIPS

circular motion

1-2-3 Perform once from each of the three positions learned on Page 27. Hold each of the rolling movements for a count of 5 today. Relax upon completion

The circles that we have been making with the trunk are in a counter-clockwise direction (we move to the left first). Now we will perform the entire exercise once, from each of the three positions, in a **clockwise** direction (moving to the right first). Therefore, bend forward a few inches into the small circle position. Roll and twist in a small circle to the right; hold for 5. Roll and twist in a small circle to the backward position, etc.

Relax upon completion

1

2

3

triangle

4-5-6 Perform once in each of the three positions as learned on Pages 18, 30 and 38. Alternate the sides (first left, then right) for each position. Hold each bend for 10. Relax upon completion

Today you should be able to execute the ankle holds in a wide stance with the arm in the 90 degree position as in Fig. 6

abdominal lifts

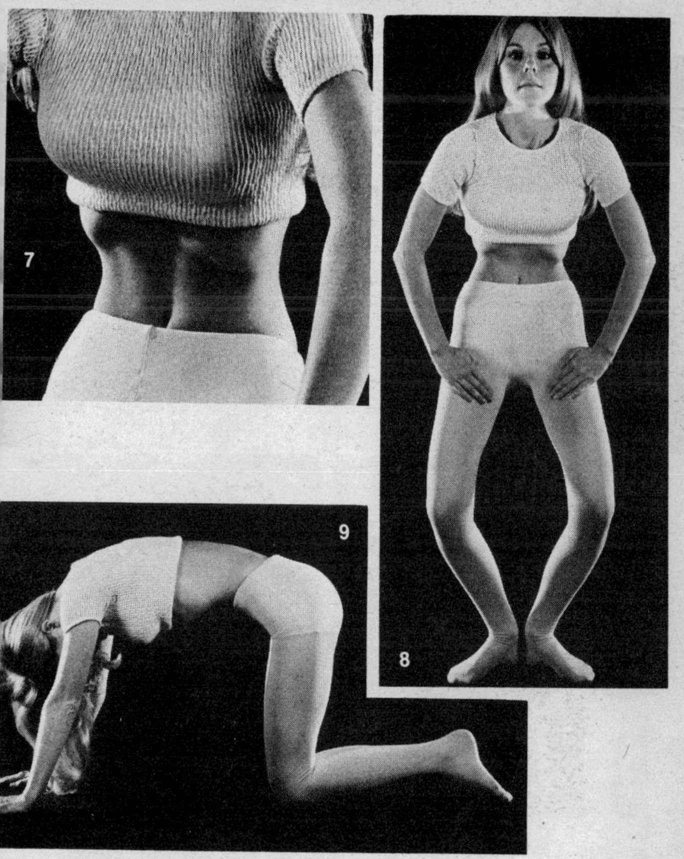

ABDOMINAL LIFTS (16 A, B, C)

7-8-9 These three positions were learned on Pp. 92, 95-96 and 97-98

Today we will attempt to perform between 5-10 rhythmic lifts to each exhalation. (Do less if necessary but not more than 10). Relax briefly after each group

19th DAY

Perform 3 groups in the sitting position of Fig. 7 and 5 groups in both the standing and All Fours position

At this point you should be able to execute a satisfactory lift movement. If not, be patient and continue to practice as deep a contraction as possible

Remember that the movements must be rhythmic

side bend

10-11-12 Perform once in each of the three positions as learned on Pp. 102-103. Alternate the sides (first left, then right) for each position. Hold each bend for 10. Relax upon completion

Remember that the arms must remain parallel in each of the six bends

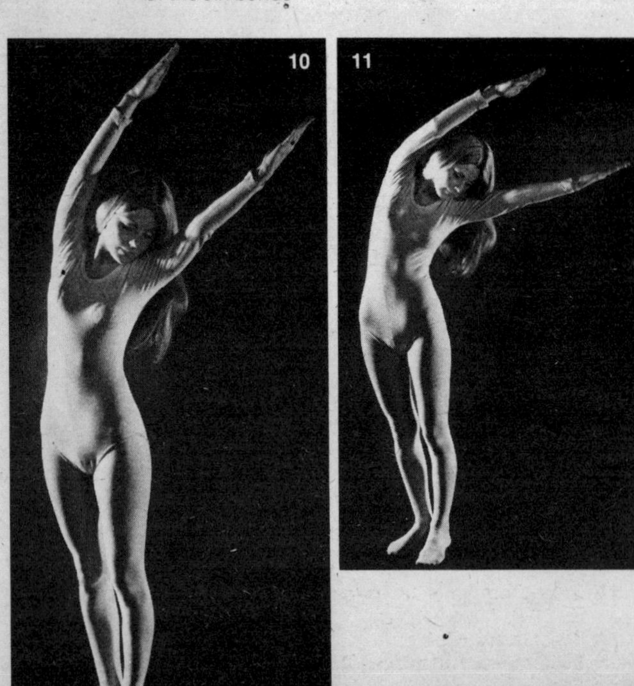
10
11

elbow-to-knee

FOR TRIMMING INCHES FROM THE WAISTLINE

13 Sit in a cross-legged posture
Interlace fingers behind head
Keep elbows back

14 Very slowly bend as far as possible to left
Elbow should touch floor is possible; if not, bend as far as you can without strain
Both knees must remain on floor
Right elbow points upward
Hold for 5

15 Slowly straighten to upright position

16 Twist trunk to left
Lower trunk and bring right elbow down toward left knee

Touch elbow to knee if possible
Both knees must remain on floor
Hold your extreme position for 5

Slowly straighten to upright position

17 Very slowly bend as far as possible to right
Touch elbow to floor if possible
Both knees remain on floor
Left elbow points upward
Hold your extreme position for 5

Slowly straighten to upright position

18 Twist trunk to right
Lower trunk and bring left elbow down toward right knee

Touch elbow to knee if possible
Hold your extreme position for 5

Slowly straighten to upright position

Lower arms and relax

Repeat entire routine once

Proceed to next exercise

14

15

16

17

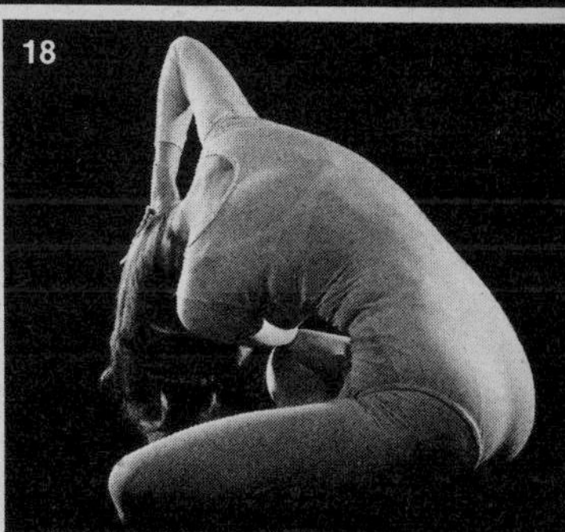

18

19th DAY

side raise

A POWERFUL MOVEMENT FOR THE HIPS AND ABDOMEN

19 Lie on left side as illustrated
Legs together
Head supported by left hand
Right hand firmly on floor

20 Very slowly raise right leg as high as possible
Hold for 10
Lower slowly

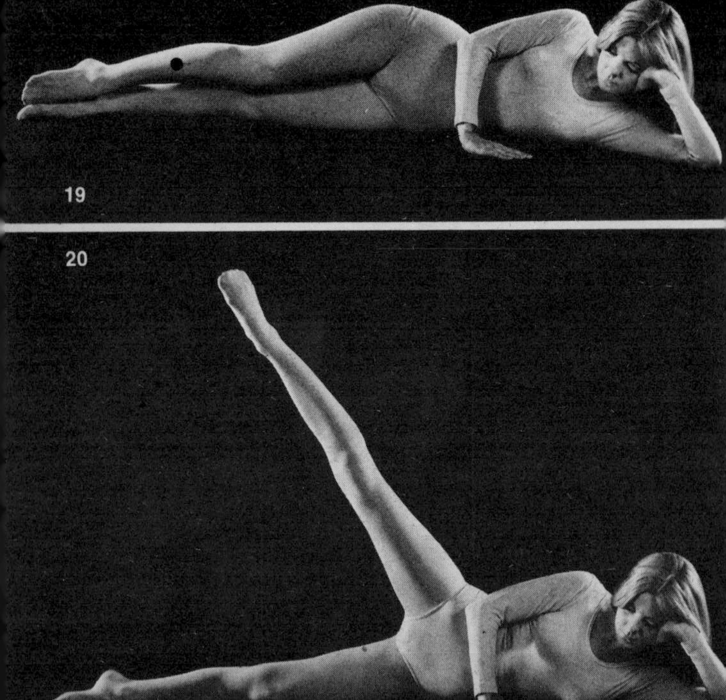

21 Push firmly against floor with hand
Raise both legs a short distance
Do not raise farther than illustrated
Legs must remain together
Legs are raised directly from side; they do not sway to right or left
Hold for 5
Lower slowly to floor
Relax briefly

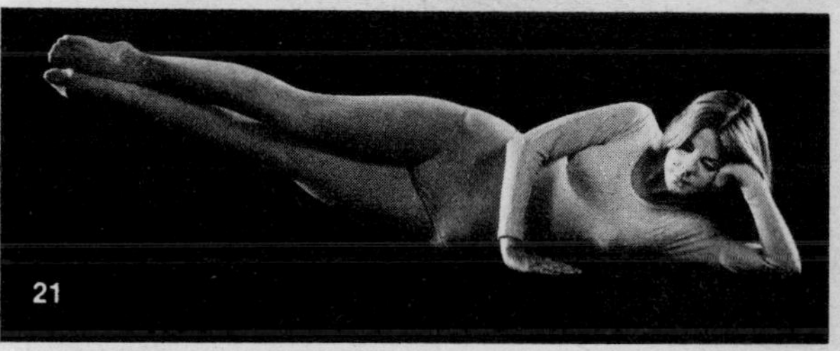
21

22 Push against floor
Raise both legs as high as possible
Legs must remain together
Legs must be raised directly from side
Hold for 5
Lower slowly to floor
Relax
Repeat entire routine once

23 Perform identical movements lying on right side
First, raise only the left leg (Fig. 20)
Next, raise both legs a short distance (Fig. 21)
Finally raise both legs as high as possible
Hold for 5
Lower slowly to floor
Relax

Repeat entire routine once

Proceed to next exercise

22

leg over

24 Perform three times to each side, alternating legs (right leg to left side; left leg to right side, etc.) as learned on Pp. 33-34. Hold each position for 10 Relax

Remember to place the leg high toward the head

practice plan 19th day

To complete our 19th Day of practice we will perform the exercises listed below in our continuous motion routine in which there is no pause either between the exercises or *within each exercise.* We began this procedure at the end of our 16th Day. Once the routine is begun, you do not interrupt the continuous motion from beginning to end. Concentrate deeply on all of your movements and make each posture flow into the next like a slow motion ballet.

Today's routine consists of the following:

Circular Motion (once, *clockwise,* from your extreme position only)

Triangle (to each side, extreme position only; do not hold)

Side Bend (to each side, extreme position only)

Elbow-to-Knee (entire routine, once; do not hold)

Side Raise (each side once, extreme raise only; do not hold)

Leg Over (to each side once; do not hold)

Assume the cross-legged posture and perform three Complete Breaths. Then sit very quietly and listen to your body as we have practiced previously.

thoughts for the day

THE BEAUTIFUL WOMAN

Physical beauty is an external expression of the spirit. It grows and is cultivated internally and without conscious effort it is manifested externally. Therefore, only a woman who has discovered her true nature, her "self," can be truly beautiful. Genuine beauty is all-encompassing and is present not only in physical appearance but in movement, voice, thought and feeling.

A beautiful woman radiates from within; her complexion glows and her eyes shine. Her movements and gestures are poised and graceful, they flow with a natural rhythm. The entire body of a self-realized woman will be beautiful because she is deeply aware of her inner beauty and this awareness is transferred to all who come in contact with her. The humility, compassion and love of a beautiful woman are genuine and a mystical quality is present in her aura.

Each woman who has developed her inner nature is beautiful in her own unique way and no one can ever truly look like her. There are potentially as many different types of beauty as there are women. The "look" of the beautiful woman is never out of style because, without effort and regardless of how she dresses or in what environment she functions, she is continually making the style—the style of her own individual beauty. Since the sensitive woman has perceived that beauty takes the form of a continual inner unfoldment, endlessly changing in color and hue, becoming ever more intense and expressing itself as a unified whole, her quest for beauty becomes a process of discovering and revealing more and more of her inner being, of her true nature, of her real self.

As you awaken and cultivate the great reservoir of life-force that lies within you, indescribable positive changes will occur and you begin to experience an unimagined beauty, not only on the physical level, but in all aspects of your life. Remember also that a woman is at peace with herself only to the extent that she develops her inner beauty. Because she has found herself, she is able to give of her beauty—to her friends, family and husband and it is in this giving that true fulfillment is realized.

review

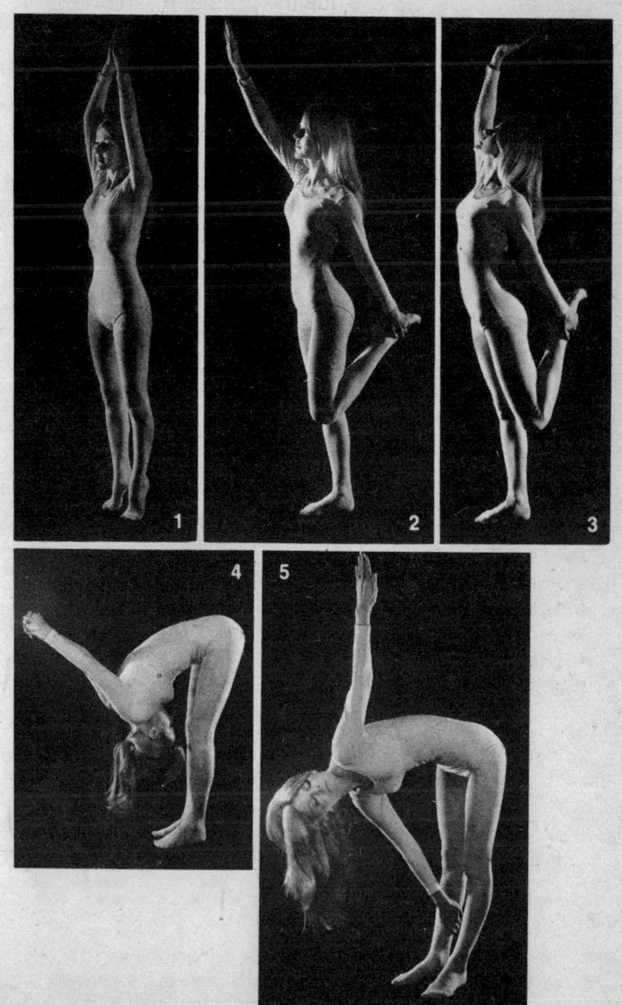

20th DAY

complete breath standing

1 Perform three times as learned on Pp. 53-54. Today, hold each extreme raise for a count of 7. Relax upon completion

balance posture

2 Perform three times with right arm raised, then three times with left arm raised as learned on Page 194.
3 Hold each extreme position for 5 and pause briefly between repetitions. Relax upon completion

Remember to:

Practice with patience; repeated attempts will teach your body the necessary balance technique
Regain your composure and begin again whenever you lose the balance
Bring the raised arm backward and the leg upward as far as possible in the extreme position of Fig. 3. You are not simply attempting to maintain balance; you are performing an **intensive stretch while balancing**

chest expansion

4 Perform once in each of the three positions as learned on Pages 9, 20 and 67. Count 5 in each backward position and 10 in each of the forward positions

Perform the leg movements learned on Page 110 following the extreme position only. Hold the leg positions for 10.
Relax upon completion

rishi's posture

5 Perform once in each of the two positions as learned on Page 155. Alternate the sides (first left, then right) for each position. Hold each bend for 10.
Relax upon completion

dancer's posture

6

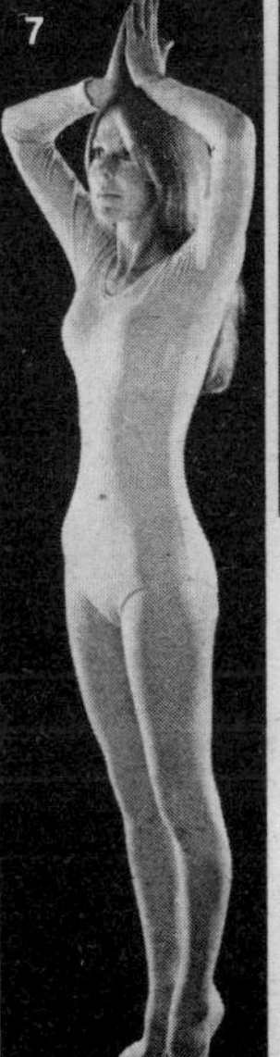

7

8

6 Perform three times as learned on Pp. 195-196. The movements are done in continuous motion; there are no holds. Relax upon completion

Remember to:

7 Lower and raise in very slow motion
Keep the knees as close together as possible throughout the exercise
Begin again from the starting position whenever you lose your balance. **Do not laugh at yourself** (very important)

knee and thigh stretch

8 Perform three times as learned on Page 21. Hold each extreme position for 5. Relax briefly

bust exercise

9 Perform three times as learned on Page 161. Hold each raise for 5. Relax briefly

9

10

11

full twist

10-11 Perform extreme twist twice to left side, then twice to right side as learned on Page 183. Hold extreme twists for 10.
Relax upon completion

Remember to:

Review the instructions beginning on Page 184 carefully
Sit erect
Turn head so that chin comes close to shoulder

scalp exercise

12 Perform 25 times as learned on Pp. 59-60. Relax briefly

lion

13 Perform three times as learned on Pp. 59-60. Hold each extreme position for 15. Relax briefly

12

13

20th DAY

neck roll

14 This exercise was learned on Page 191. Today we
15 will perform twice counter-clockwise (rolling to left first as we practiced previously) and add two **clockwise** rolls (moving first to right). Hold each position for 5. Relax briefly

Remember to:

Sit erect
Roll head only; trunk does not move
Keep eyes closed

14

15

elbow-to-knee

16 Perform the entire routine twice as learned yesterday
17 on Pp. 203-204. Hold each of the bends and twists for 5.

Relax upon completion

Remember to:

Keep both knees on floor throughout exercise
Point elbow upward where so instructed
Twist trunk first, then lower (as in Fig. 17)

16

17

back stretch

18 Perform once in each of the four positions learned on Pp. 12, 22, 71, 138-139 (knees, calves, ankles, feet). Hold each of the four forward pulls for 15. Relax upon completion

18

backward bend

19 Perform once in each of the two positions learned on Page 61. Hold the backward bends for 15 each

Assume the position of Fig. 21 as learned on Page 174 Hold for 15 if possible, less if necessary. Attempt to place as much pressure on heels as possible. Relax. (Manipulate toes with hands if discomfort is experienced upon completion)

modified head stand

20 Attempt to perform position of Fig. 9 as learned on Page 193. If possible, increase today's hold to a count of 25. Do not hold longer. If this position is not yet possible revert to position of Fig. 8, 18th day and hold for one minute

Relax with head down, knees touching floor

side raise

21-22 Perform entire routine, learned yesterday on Page 206 twice on left side and twice on right side. Hold

position of one leg raised for 10 and positions of Figs. 21-22 for 5 each
Relax briefly between repetitions

Remember to:

Move slowly
Keep legs together in Figs. 21-22
Raise legs directly from side

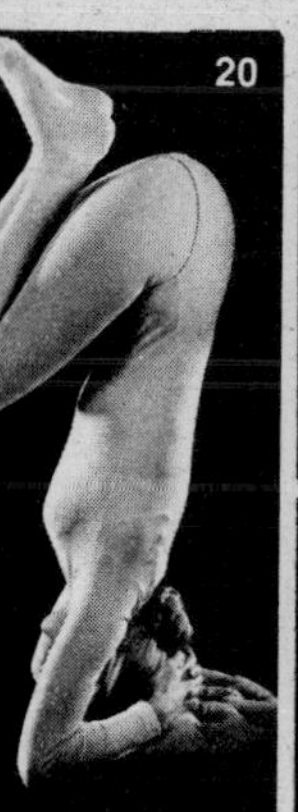
20

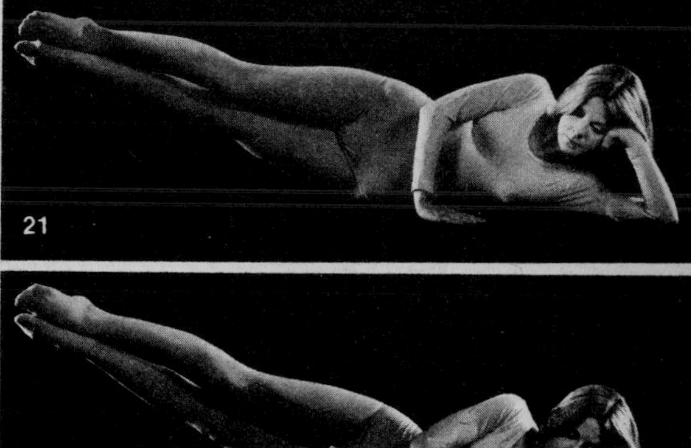
21

22

shoulder stand

23 Perform your extreme position of the Shoulder Stand once as learned on Page 132. Today, increase the hold of the inverted posture to 2:15 (you can count 135 or glance at a watch or clock placed near your head)
Do not hold longer than 2:15

We will pass directly into the Plough upon completion of the count. Therefore, begin to lower legs behind you and lower hands to rest on floor

plough

24 Continue to lower legs until you are in your extreme position of the Plough as learned on Page 135. If you cannot, as yet, touch the floor with your toes, simply go as far as possible without strain. Today we will increase the hold of whatever extreme position you can attain, to a count of 30. Do not hold longer

Come out of the posture exactly as instructed (work for smoothness and keep the head on the floor). Relax deeply, allowing all muscles to go limp, for one minute

cobra

25 Perform the complete routine, including the twisting

movements once as learned on Pp. 72 and 114-115. Hold the extreme raise for 30 and the twisting movements for 10 each. Relax deeply

locust

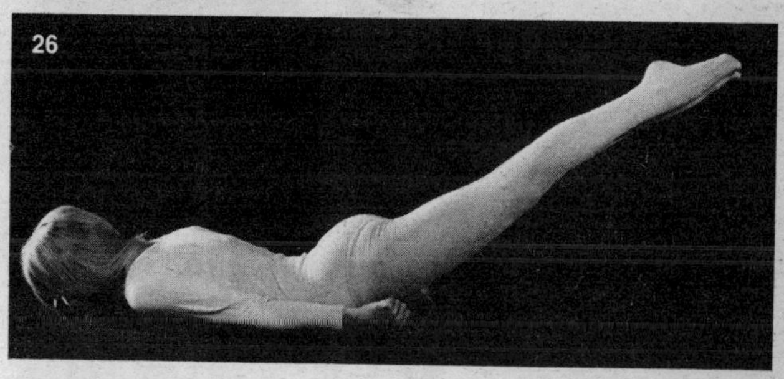
26

26 First, perform once with each leg as learned on Page 105
Hold for 10

Next, perform the moderate position (legs a short distance from the floor as in Fig. 14, P. 106) once. Hold for 10 today

Finally, perform your extreme position (as high as you can raise both legs) twice. Hold each raise for 7. Always raise and lower **slowly.** Relax deeply upon completion

bow

27 Perform your extreme position twice as learned on Page 147. Hold for 10 each. Relax upon completion

Remember to:

Raise and lower very slowly
Keep knees as close together as possible while raising
Lower knees to floor first, then lower trunk and chin
Retain hold on feet between repetitions
Move cautiously without straining; this is a very powerful movement to strengthen the back

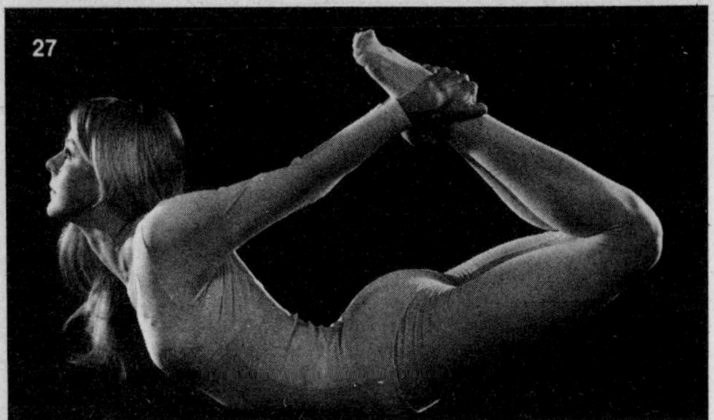
27

practice plan 20th day

To complete today's Review we will perform the exercises listed below in our continuous motion routine, in which there is no pause from beginning to end. You move very slowly with deep concentration on all movements and the postures must be made to flow, one into another, like a slow-motion ballet. Sitting down, lying down, rolling over, etc., all become a part of the routine and are executed in graceful slow motion.

Today's routine consists of the following:

Complete Breath Standing (once; do not hold extreme position)

Balance Posture (once on each side; do not hold)

Chest Expansion (once, your extreme positions only; do not hold backward, forward or leg positions)

Rishi's Posture (once to each side; your extreme position only)

Dancer's Posture

Full Twist (once to each side)

Elbow-to-Knee (the complete routine once; do not hold)

Back Stretch (once, your extreme position only)

Backward Bend (the extreme position only)

Side Raise (once on each side; your extreme position only; do not hold)

Plough (your extreme position; do not hold)

Cobra (the complete routine including twisting; do not hold)

Locust (once, your extreme position only; do not hold)

Bow (once, your extreme position only; do not hold)

complete breath

28 To conclude the routine, assume the cross-legged posture (always the Half Lotus, if possible; if not, continue to practice as in Fig. 8, Page 49 and perform three Complete Breaths. Then sit very quietly for several minutes and become acutely aware of your body. Do not allow the mind to wander

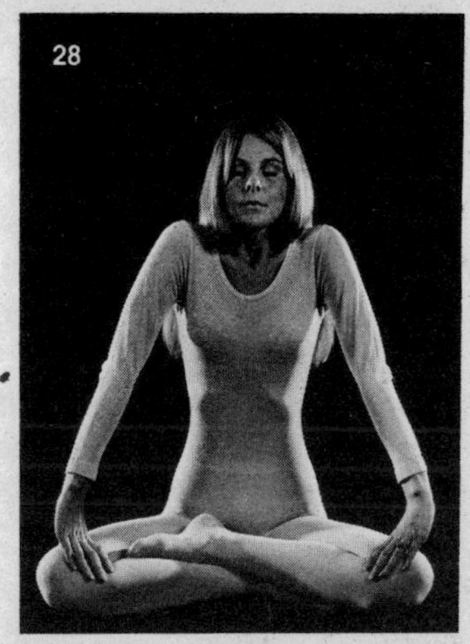

20th DAY

thoughts for the day

WEIGHT REGULATION (1)

Each woman who is overweight has an **individual** problem, since her metabolism and certain other vital factors are different from those of her neighbor. Because of these differences, the amount of food that constitutes "overeating" and the amount of activity that constitutes "adequate exercise" vary with the individual. Among your friends you can observe those who eat heavily at mealtime, pack in several between-meal snacks and perhaps do very little active work or exercising during the day, and yet may be less overweight than yourself or others who are watching their diets carefully and are quite active. What accounts for this apparent discrepancy? The simple fact is: **Bodies function differently** with regard to metabolic processes.

Since no two people are alike (and it is important to understand this statement in its most profound sense), the necessity of learning to truly "Know Thyself" can be appreciated. "Knowing" one's self entails turning away more and more from those outside sources that want to tell you how you should look, what you should weigh, how to make yourself beautiful, etc., and, in place of these, undertaking a perceptive self-examination. For example, you must no longer compute your correct weight from the charts on the scales or those listed in the Sunday supplements (as though millions of people could have identical bone structures).

Rather, you should learn to know at what weight **you** are functioning at **your** best; and, in a similar vein, exactly how the foods **you** are eating affect **you,** as well as the value that various sports, exercise routines and other activities hold for **you.** If a large-boned woman attempts to model her measurement after those of the mannequins in the fashion magazines, she will not only be frustrated in her attempt but she can actually find herself in serious physical trouble. She simply is not meant by nature to resemble a mannequin. However, if this same woman will proportion her weight correctly, improve her muscle tone, make her skin taut and firm, develop an erect posture and move with poise and balance, she will reveal herself as confident, vital and harmonious as was nature's intention. Each woman is beautiful in her own right.

We will continue this discussion tomorrow.

slow motion firming

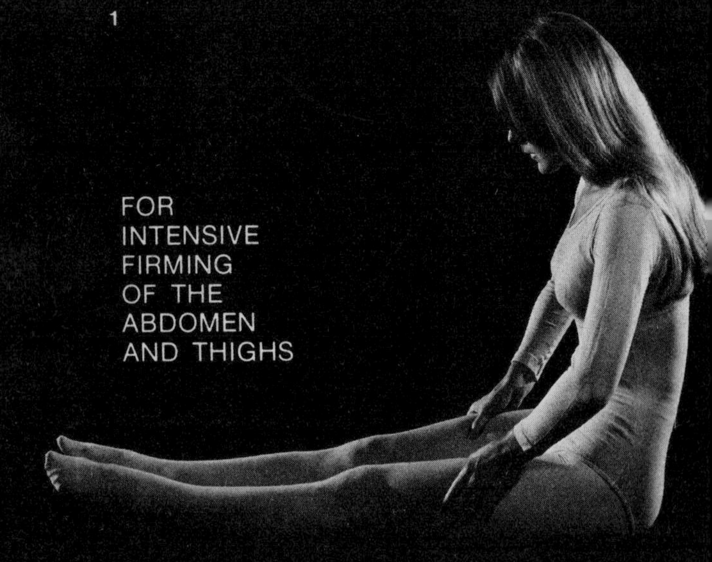

1
FOR
INTENSIVE
FIRMING
OF THE
ABDOMEN
AND THIGHS

1 Sit with hands gripping thighs

2 Hold thighs firmly
Very slowly lower back toward floor

3 Continue slow lowering until back rests on floor
Place palms on floor

4 There is no holding in this exercise
As soon as back touches floor, bring knees slowly into position illustrated

5 Straighten legs
Lower legs to floor as slowly as possible

2

3

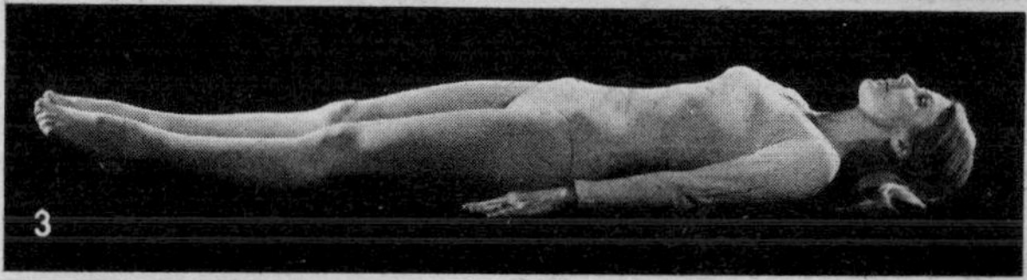

4

5

6 Without pause raise trunk, arms outstretched, to upright position (If this is too difficult, use hands for aid)

7 With arms still outstretched, bend forward slowly
Hold farthermost area of legs possible
Bend forward and down as in Back Stretch exercise
Do not hold
Without pause straighten to upright position and hold thighs (Fig. 1) Relax briefly

Repeat entire routine twice in continuous motion

Proceed to next exercise

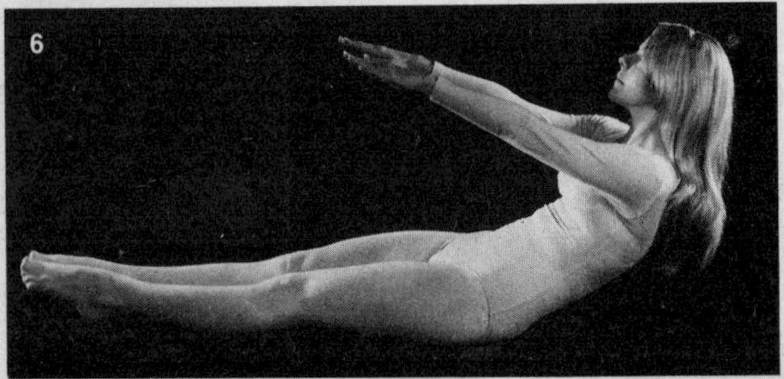
6

7

side raise

8 Perform only your extreme position three times on each side as learned on Page 206. Today, hold each raise for a count of 7. Rest briefly between repetitions. Relax upon completion

Remember to:

Move slowly
Keep legs together throughout movements
Raise legs directly from side

8

back push-up

TO FIRM LOWER BACK, BUTTOCKS AND BACKS OF THIGHS

9 Study illustration
Note that heels are drawn in; knees together
Palms rest firmly on floor, close to head

10 Push against floor with hands and feet
Raise body a moderate distance
Do not raise farther than depicted
Hold without movement for 10
Slowly lower body to floor (Fig. 9)

11 Push against floor again
Arch neck and rest top of head against floor
Raise as far as possible
Keep knees together
Hold for 10
Slowly lower body to floor; relax

Repeat entire routine of moderate raise followed by extreme raise, twice

Proceed to next exercise

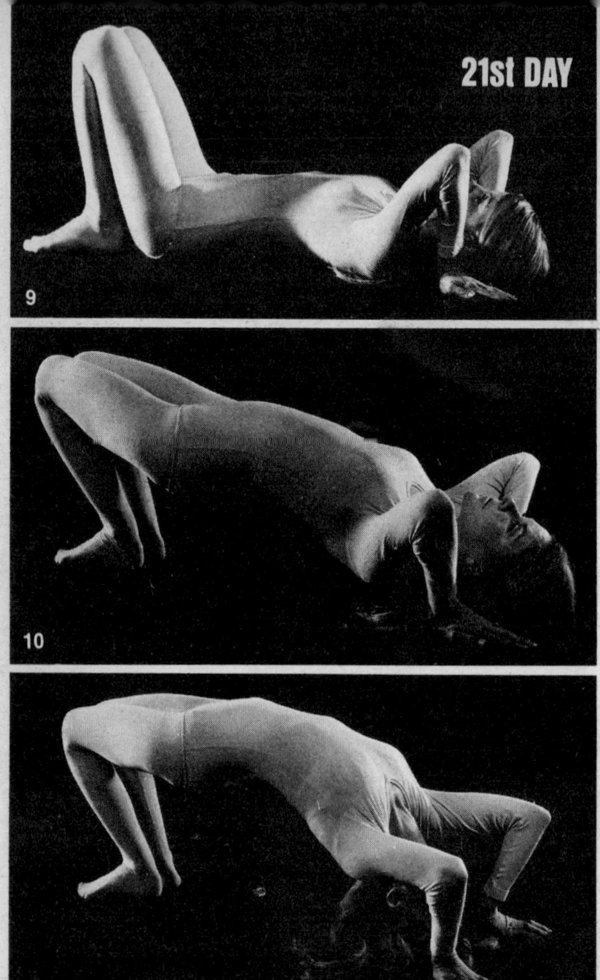

locust

12 First, perform once with each leg as learned on Page 105

Hold for 10

Next, perform the moderate position (legs a short distance from the floor as in Fig. 14, Page 106) once Hold for 10

Finally, perform your extreme position twice. Hold each raise for 7. Rest briefly between repetitions. Relax upon completion

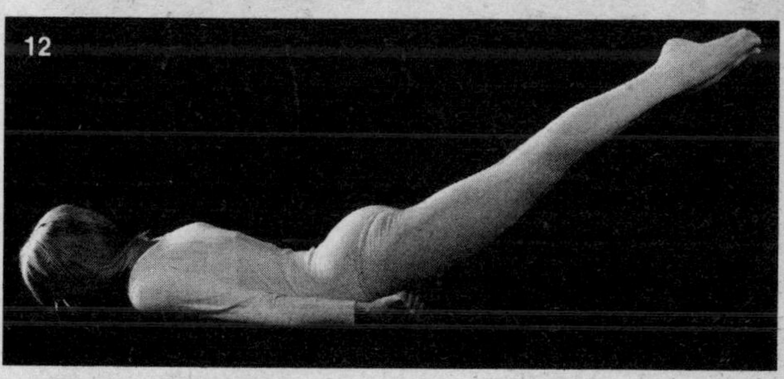

To complete today's practice we will combine three firming exercises into a routine. This routine is to be performed in continuous motion; there is no holding and no pausing between the movements.

side raise —LEFT SIDE

13 Perform your extreme position once. Do not hold. Roll onto your back (gracefully, in continual slow motion)

back push-up

14 Perform your extreme position once as learned today. Do not hold. Roll to your right side (gracefully, in continual slow motion)

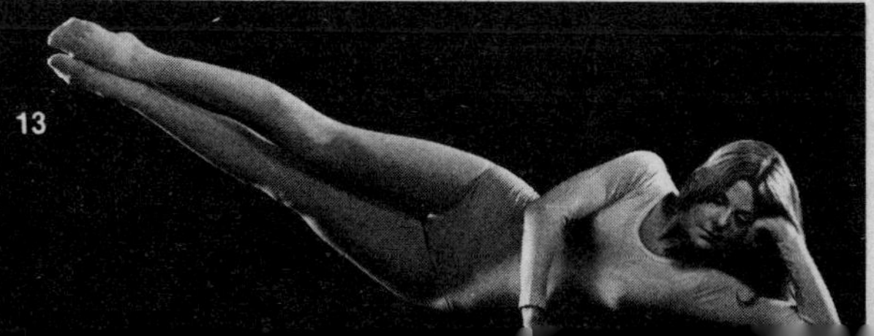

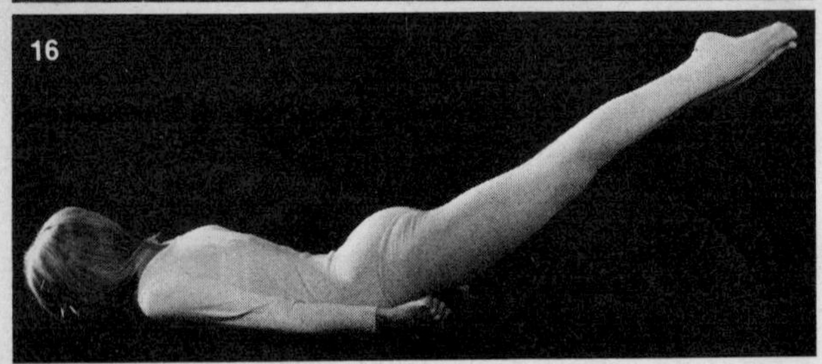

side raise —RIGHT SIDE

15 Perform your extreme position once. Do not hold. Roll gracefully onto your abdomen

locust

16 Perform your extreme position once. Do not hold. Roll gracefully to your left side

Without pause, repeat the entire routine twice

Upon completion relax deeply with cheek resting on floor and become aware of what is transpiring in your organism. Do not allow your mind to wander

thoughts for the day

WEIGHT REGULATION (2)

In Yoga we have a unique and wonderfully **natural** approach to weight regulation. The postures are performed, as you already know, without strain and with minimum effort and are designed to stimulate and promote the correct functioning of the important organs and glands that are weight-control factors and that receive so little conscious attention in the usual systems of exercising or in the use of "reducing" machines. Specifically, you will be working on the thyroid gland, improving blood circulation, breathing in a way designed to help burn excess fat and strengthening many areas where you will find that weight is more easily removed when they are firmed. Each Yoga exercise will, in one way or another, aid you in weight regulation and control. Even those stretching and breathing techniques designed to alleviate tension are helpful since the desire of the compulsive eater can often be diminished if nervous disturbances are reduced.

A word about the dietary aspect of weight regulation is essential here. Unless your physician has specifically placed you on such a diet, the Yogi is not in accord with the principle of the current "high-protein" fad. The increased metabolic activity that results from deliberately setting the body on fire with great quantities of meat, poultry, eggs, powders and wafers is not in accord with the quiet, relaxed and passive state of mind and body that we wish to attain in Yoga. In addition, such things as appetite depressants designed to reduce the normal desire for nourishment, a voluntary coffee and cigarette diet, the synthetic products that are taken in liquid form in the place of food, the various "miracle" diets so generously offered by the women's magazines, are all in conflict with our concept of natural weight regulation.

Weight taken off through these dietary "gimmicks" will return in almost every case when the program is discontinued. Why? Because these various plans are **unnatural;** they do not assist nature's methods but oppose them. Permanent weight regulation can result only by harmonizing with your body, not fighting it. You must turn your attention inward, become sensitive to the true requirements of your organism and learn how to fulfill these needs. Believe it or not, your body **wants** to be at its correct weight level.

We will conclude this discussion tomorrow.

ADDITIONAL MOVEMENTS FOR

rishi's posture

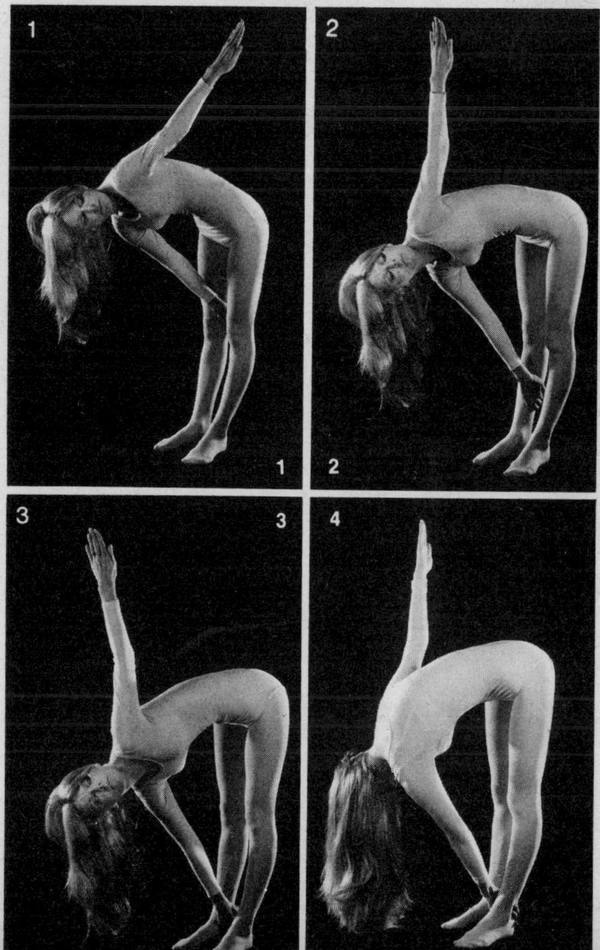

22nd DAY

1 Perform once in each of the two positions as learned on Page 155. Alternate the sides (first left, then right)
2 for each position. Hold each bend for 10

3 Now attempt to move right hand down to right heel
This is the extreme position
Keep knees straight
Eyes must see back of hand
Hold for 10

4 Slowly straighten to upright position
Raise high on toes; hands meet in front
Perform identical movements to right
Remember to move very slowly
Left hand holds left heel for 10

Straighten to upright position
Raise high on toes
Hands meet in front
Very slowly lower arms to sides and soles to floor
Relax

Repeat extreme positions to each side, once

If this extreme position is too difficult today, simply move hand as far down the leg as possible on each side and hold for 10

Remember to come up very high on your toes in all twisting movements to strengthen feet, ankles and toes

Proceed to next exercise

ADDITIONAL MOVEMENTS FOR THE

meditation (lotus) postures

5-6 These are the postures that you have been practicing
Your legs should now be responding positively, in some degree, to the Half-Lotus

7 As an aid to the legs in the Half-Lotus we will now use a pillow of approximately 6 inches in height

Sit as illustrated
The additional height provided by the pillow should now enable knees to be lowered close to the floor
Practice Half-Lotus first with left leg on top; then reverse legs

8 This is the posture we have been practicing to prepare the legs for the more advanced Lotus postures
Sit on pillow
Place left foot high on right thigh

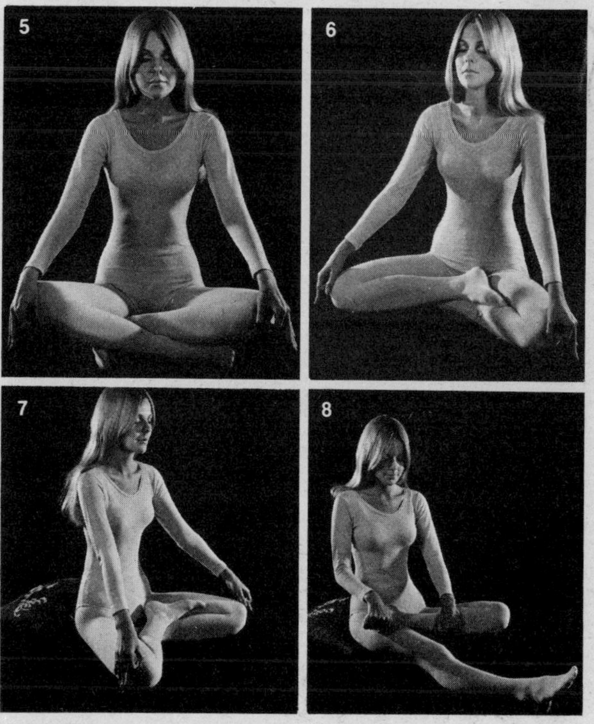

9 The completed Full-Lotus posture
Attempt to place right foot on left thigh
Study the illustration
Spine is straight

22nd DAY

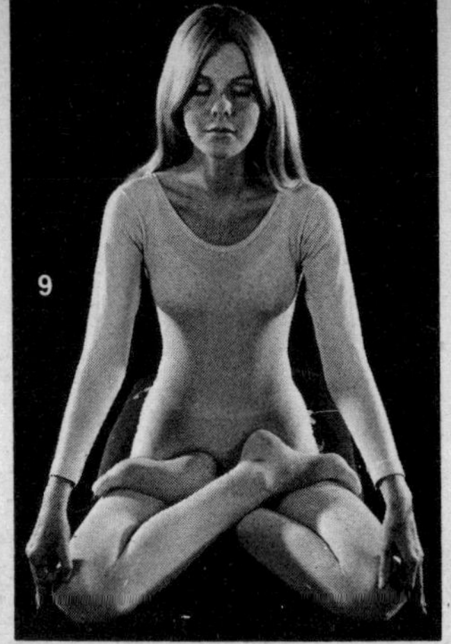

Eyelids lowered
Assume hand and finger position
Hold for a count of 10 only
Uncross legs with hands and stretch legs straight outward
Attempt Full-Lotus with legs reversed (left foot on right thigh)
Hold for 10
Stretch legs outward; relax

The Full-Lotus is an advanced posture and, for most students, a difficult one. It is introduced at this point in our study so that you can attempt it from time to time. Patient practice will, in time, impart the necessary flexibility to the legs, ankles and feet. If you are able to slip into the Full-Lotus today it will become easier in each subsequent attempt.

If the Full-Lotus appears much too difficult revert to the cross-legged or Half-Lotus posture for the various seated exercises. Your success in Yoga is not dependent on being able to assume the Full-Lotus at this time.

EXERCISES FOR THE CHEST, BUST AND POSTURE

chest expansion

10 Perform twice in the extreme position only as learned on Page 67 Count 10 in the backward position and 20 in the forward position. Do not perform the leg

movements today. Keep arms as high as possible throughout exercise for Chest, Bust and Posture. Relax upon completion

bust exercise

11 Perform three times as learned on Page 161. Hold each raise for 10. Sit erect throughout exercise. Relax briefly

10

11

TO IMPROVE POSTURE
FOR LOOSENING SHOULDERS

posture clasp

12 Sit in a cross-legged posture
Place left hand as illustrated

13 Bring right hand over and clasp left hand

14 Pull right arm down an inch or two
Feel intense pull in right shoulder
Hold without movement for 5

15 Pull left arm up
Feel intense pull in left shoulder
Sit erect (do not slump)
Hold for 5

22nd DAY

Repeat up and down movements twice; hold each for 5

Reverse position of arms
Right palm faces away from you
Left hand comes over and holds right
Perform identical up and down movements three times
Hold each pull for 5

Relax

Proceed to next exercise

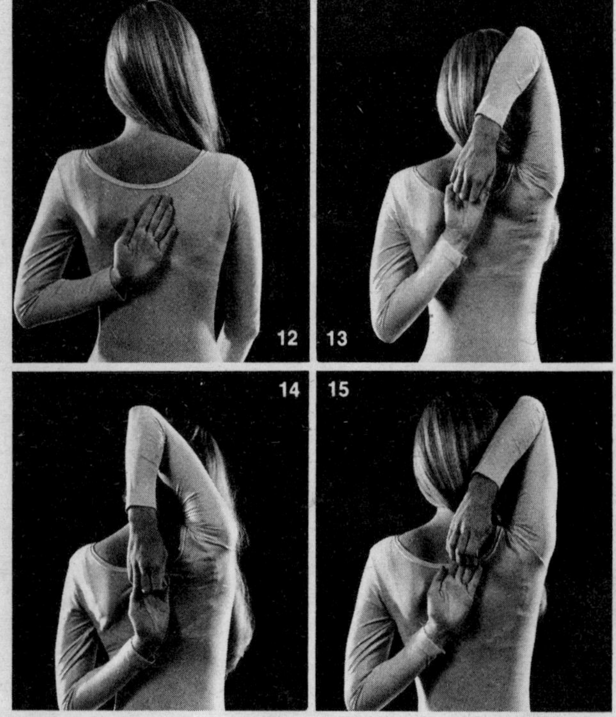

12 13 14 15

cobra

16 Perform the complete routine, including the twisting movements once as learned on Pages 72 and 114.

Hold the extreme raise for 30 (head far back; spine fully arched) and the twisting movements for 10 each. Relax deeply with cheek on floor

ADDITIONAL MOVEMENTS FOR THE

bow

17 Perform your extreme position as learned on Page 147
Hold for 10

We will now increase the benefits of this posture by "rocking" back and forth on the abdomen in a hobby-horse movement.

18 Hold feet firmly
Rock forward bringing chin close to floor

19 Without pause rock backward bringing knees close to floor

Repeat the rocking movements forward and backward three times in continuous motion

Stop all movement for several seconds
Lower knees to floor (do not release feet)
Lower chin to touch floor
Release feet
Rest cheek on floor and relax deeply

Repeat the routine, i.e., holding of the extreme position for 10 and the forward and backward rocking movements in continuous motion three times

22nd DAY

Relax deeply and become aware of what is occurring in your body

Remember that you can practice again today if your time so permits

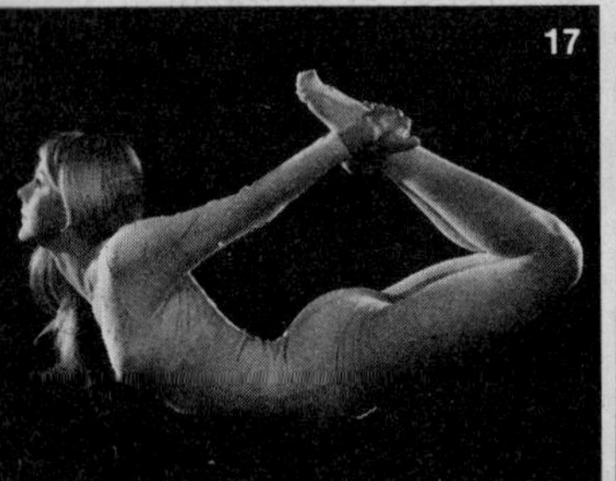

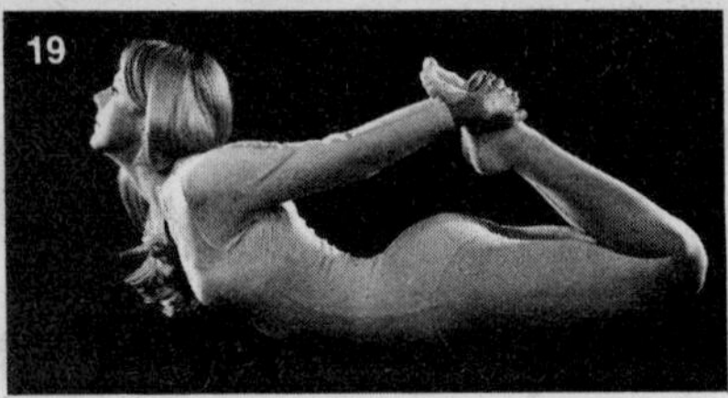

thoughts for the day

WEIGHT REGULATION (3)

In this book you are instructed frequently to become extremely sensitive to what is transpiring within your organism so that you may cater to its real needs intelligently. It is a basic concept of Yoga, with regard to the problem of weight regulation, that the wisdom and intelligence of your own body are much greater than all of the "miracle" diets, the ingenious exercising machines and devices, the calorie-counting charts and various reducing gimmicks. If you will learn to listen to what your body is really telling you, you can accomplish many of your physical objectives, including those of weight regulation and control.

As the life-force is increased through your Yoga practice, the intelligence and wisdom that lie within will make you acutely aware of those things that are of benefit to your organism and those that are harmful. For example, in the discussion of Nutrition (18th Day) you were offered certain guiding principles with regard to the selection, preparation and combination of foods. If you memorize these principles and use them as guides, you will come to know with a very strong **instinct** which foods your body needs to help normalize your weight and which foods to avoid from both the health and weight standpoints. This concept of listening to our inner wisdom extends to all aspects of our lives and we become, with an unshakable conviction of being right, **our own guides.**

The phrase "weight control" may be ill chosen. "Control" usually implies a battle. When you undertake a program of "control" you are prepared for restrictions and denials and this places you at a psychological disadvantage. Since you will have such strong, positive aid in normalizing your weight through Yoga, we prefer to speak in terms of "weight regulation." You **select** the foods you know your body requires rather than **deny** yourself what your taste buds and eyes desire. You practice your Yoga exercises because they are enjoyable and rewarding, rather than forcing yourself to huff and puff away a few pounds as is the case in most other methods of exercising. It is also important and most encouraging to note that among my students who have normalized their weight through the Yoga program, the great majority has **maintained** proper weight. This is because the entire Yoga program becomes a way of life.

leg clasp

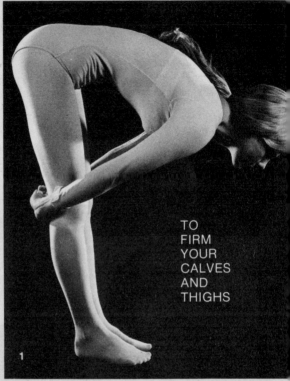

TO FIRM YOUR CALVES AND THIGHS

1

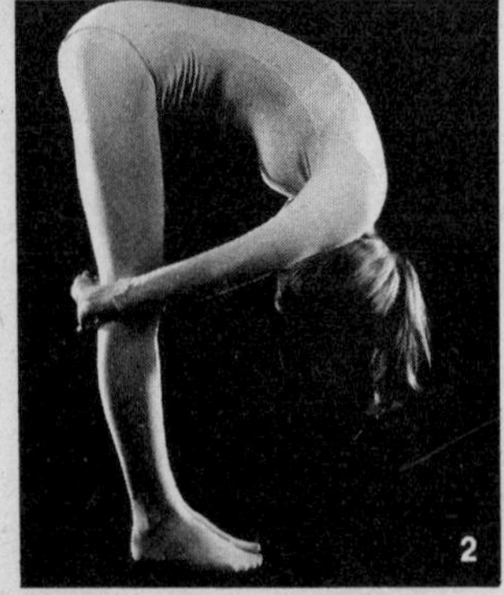

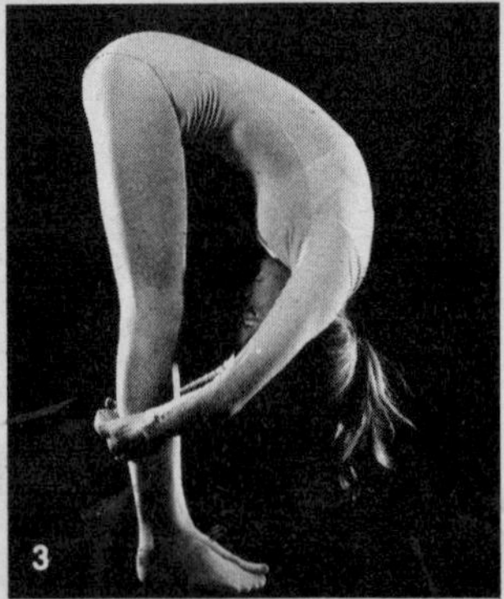

1 Stand with heels together
Slowly bend forward
Bring arms back and clasp hands behind knees

2 Brace hands firmly against knees
Very slowly draw trunk down as far as possible
Aim forehead toward knees
Hold your extreme position for 10

Keep hands clasped but allow trunk to relax by raising it several inches (position of Fig. 1)

3 Now slide hands down to calf position
Do not go farther down than calves
Brace hands against calves
Very slowly draw trunk down as far as possible
Aim forehead toward calves
Hold your extreme position for 10

Unclasp hands
Very slowly straighten to upright position
Relax briefly

Repeat entire routine of knee and calf position once

Proceed to next exercise

triangle

4 Perform once in each of the three positions as learned on Pages 18, 30 and 38. In the extreme position of Fig. 4 assume a very wide stance for intensive firming of the insides of the thighs. Alternate sides (first left, then right) for each of the three positions. Hold each bend for 10.
Relax upon completion

dancer's posture

5 We have practiced this exercise to develop "Balance," as well as to strengthen the feet. It is also an excellent "streamlining" exercise for the legs. Perform five times in continuous motion as learned on Page 213. Move as slowly as possible and keep knees together
Relax upon completion

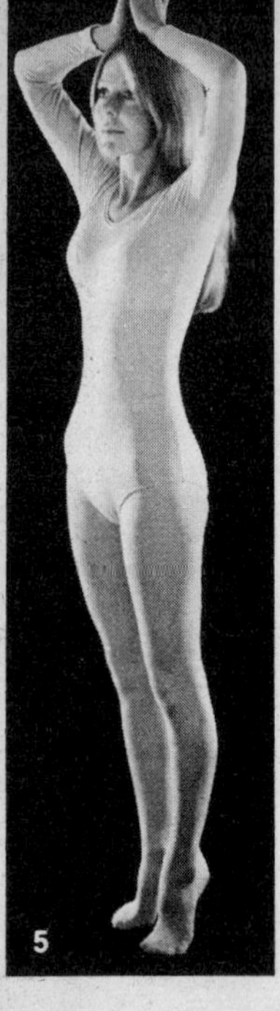

23rd DAY

chest expansion

6 Today we will perform only the leg extension movements learned on Page 110. Make certain to extend each leg far out and bring the head down towards the knees to derive the most benefits for the "hamstrings." Perform the movements twice with the left leg, then twice with the right leg. Hold each bend for 15. Relax upon completion

knee and thigh stretch

7 Perform three times as learned on Page 21. Hold each extreme position for 10. Relax briefly

alternate leg pull

7

8

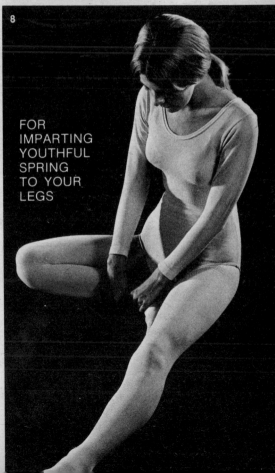

FOR IMPARTING YOUTHFUL SPRING TO YOUR LEGS

23rd DAY

9

10

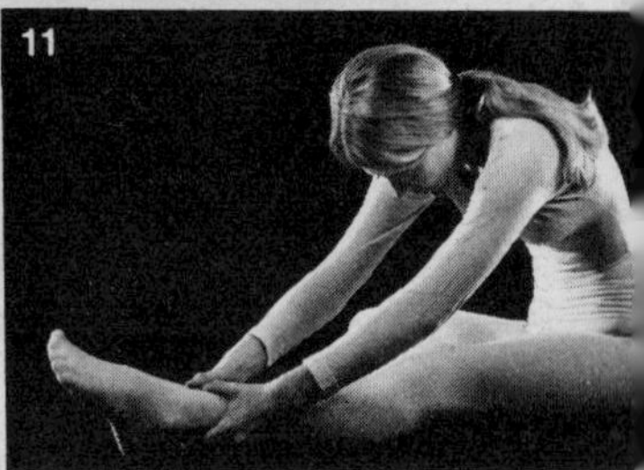
11

8 Sit with legs outstretched before you
Place sole of right foot firmly against upper inside of left thigh

9 Raise arms overhead; lean backward
Reach forward and hold left calf firmly

10 Slowly pull trunk downward as far as possible
Elbows bend outward
Aim forehead toward knee
Relax neck
Hold your extreme position for 10

Release leg and slowly straighten into upright position
Arms are raised overhead; lean backward

11 Reach forward and hold left ankle firmly

12 Pull trunk downward
Elbows bend outward
Relax neck
Hold your extreme position for 10

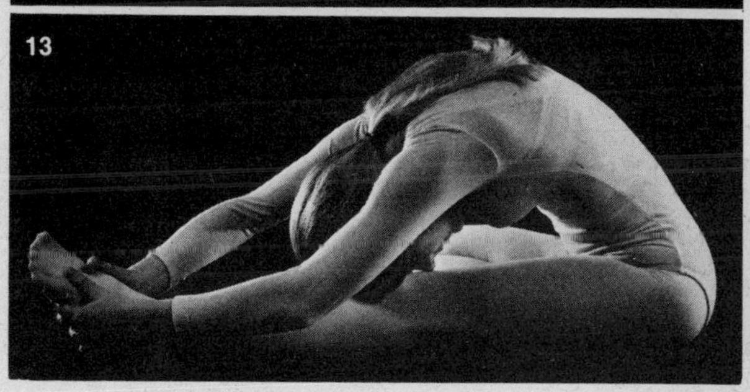

Straighten again into upright position
Arms are raised overhead; lean backward as far as possible

13 Reach forward and hold left foot
Pull trunk downward
Hold for 10
If this position is too difficult, revert to ankle or calf and hold for 10

Straighten to upright position
Rest hands on knees

Extend right leg
Place sole of **left** foot against upper inside of **right** thigh

Perform identical movements to right calf, ankle and foot
Hold each position for 10

Straighten into upright position
Extend left leg
Relax with legs outstretched

Proceed to next exercise

23rd DAY

side raise

14 Perform the entire routine of the three positions, as learned on Pp. 218-219, twice on left side and twice on right side

Hold position of one leg raised for 10
Hold moderate raise of both legs for 5
Hold extreme raise of both legs for 5

Relax upon completion

locust

15 First, perform once with each leg as learned on Page 105
Hold for 10

Next, perform the moderate position with both legs once. Hold for 10

Finally, perform your extreme position with both legs raised as high as possible twice. Today hold each extreme raise for a count of 10 if possible

Relax upon completion

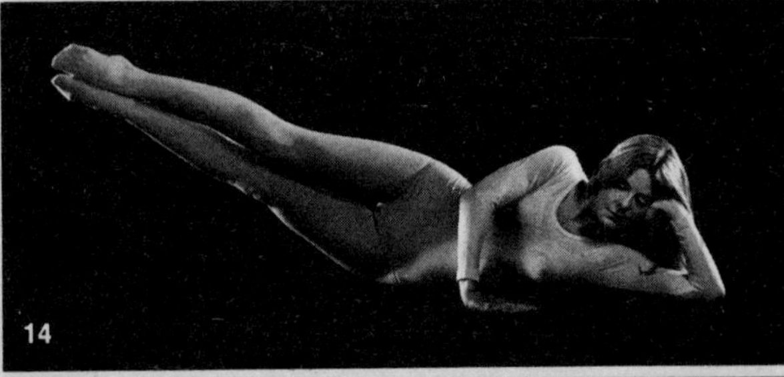

14

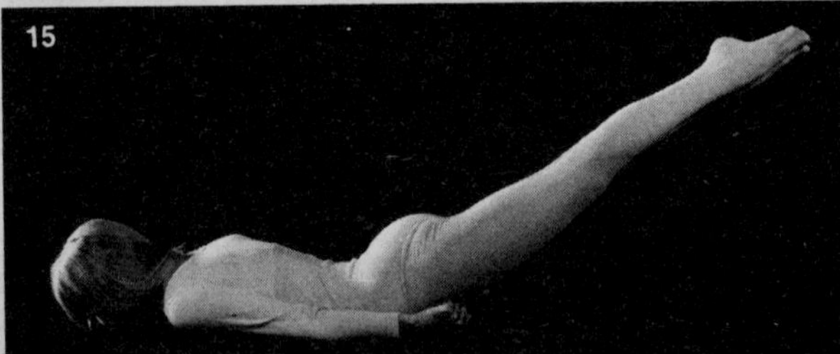

15

practice plan 23rd day

To complete our 23rd Day of practice, we will perform the exercises listed below once in our continuous motion routine; there is no pause from beginning to end.

Leg Clasp (calves position, once only; do not hold)

Triangle (once to each side, extreme position only; do not hold)

Dancer's Posture

Chest Expansion (leg extension only, once to each leg; do not hold)

Alternate Leg Pull (once with each leg, your extreme position only; do not hold)

Side Raise (once on each side, your extreme position only; do not hold)

Locust (once, your extreme position only; do not hold)

Following Locust, rest cheek on floor and relax deeply. Become aware of your body for several minutes. Do not allow your mind to wander.

thoughts for the day

SMOKING

Smoking will inhibit the benefits derived from Yoga practice; indeed, smoking will inhibit your life. However, I have never yet told a student to "stop smoking." I believe this is like saying, "You **must** relax." "Yes, I know I must," is the response. "but **how?"** It is very difficult to overcome any harmful habit through the application of "will power." This approach is fraught with a continual inner conflict and failure usually leaves a person feeling guilty and inadequate.

23rd DAY

The practice of Yoga frequently decreases and eventually eliminates the desire for smoking. This occurs in a natural, subtle manner, often hardly noticed by the student. She finds herself needing to smoke less and less and discovers one day that "I've lost my taste for it." Three principles are involved:

(1) Since we all know very well that smoking holds no value for the human organism, that is, the body certainly does not require nicotine and tar for its well-being, we can classify the habit as largely a **nervous** one. Smoking satisfies a nervous need. In the practice of Yoga the nervous system is greatly strengthened and all manifestations of nervousness and tension can be dissolved. When the nervous system grows calm and steady through the Yoga postures and breathing techniques there is no need to tranquilize it artificially.

(2) Yoga increases the life-force and this means increased energy and power for the entire organism. Your mind, body and emotions know very well what is in their best interests and if you permit your intelligence and wisdom to operate more freely (and this is exactly what happens as you raise your vibrations), you will find yourself increasing those activities that act in a positive manner and automatically decreasing those activities that have a negative effect. **Therefore, an increase in life-force means a decrease in harmful habits.** The wisdom of your organism will not allow you to destroy yourself and it will gradually lessen your desires and appetites to indulge in habits that are against its best interests.

(3) If you follow the **nutritional** suggestions already offered, i.e., the consumption of more natural and organic foods, you will find your smoking need decreasing. Coal tar and nicotine taste good after heavy, rich, devitalized, acid-forming foods. But cigarettes will hold little attraction following a meal that has been composed largely of life-force food.

review

This is an important review session; only four days of exercising remain in which to complete our study. You must practice very seriously today, following the instructions carefully and concentrating deeply on all movements. If you have the slightest doubt regarding any exercise, make certain to refer to the original instructions.

1

2

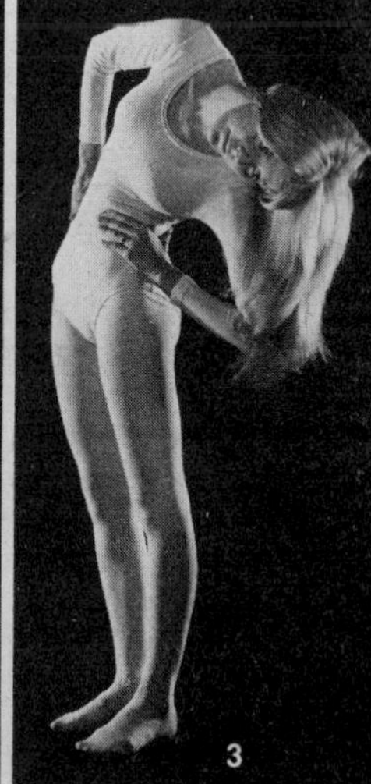

3

side bend

1 Perform once in each of the three positions as learned on Pp. 102-103. Alternate the sides (first left, then right) for each position. Hold each bend for 10. Relax upon completion

balance posture

2 Perform three times with right arm raised, then three times with left arm raised as learned on Page 194. Hold each stretch for 5 and pause briefly between repetitions.
Relax upon completion

At this point your balance should be improving. In the extreme position of Fig. 2 you are not simply maintaining balance; you are performing an intensive **stretch** by moving the raised hand backward and bringing the foot upward

circular motion

3 Perform the three circles once in a counter-clockwise fashion (to the left) and once in clockwise motion. Thus you will be making six circles in all. Hold each of the rolling movements for 3. Relax upon completion

Remember to increase the area of the circle with each repetition. The third circle of both the counter-clockwise and clockwise movements should be very wide

rishi's posture

4 Perform once in each of the three positions as learned on Pages 155 and 235. Alternate the sides (first left, then right) for each position. Hold each bend for 10
Relax upon completion

If the heel position is still too difficult, revert to the calf position. Remember that your eyes must be able to see the back of the upraised hand in each position

Knees remain straight

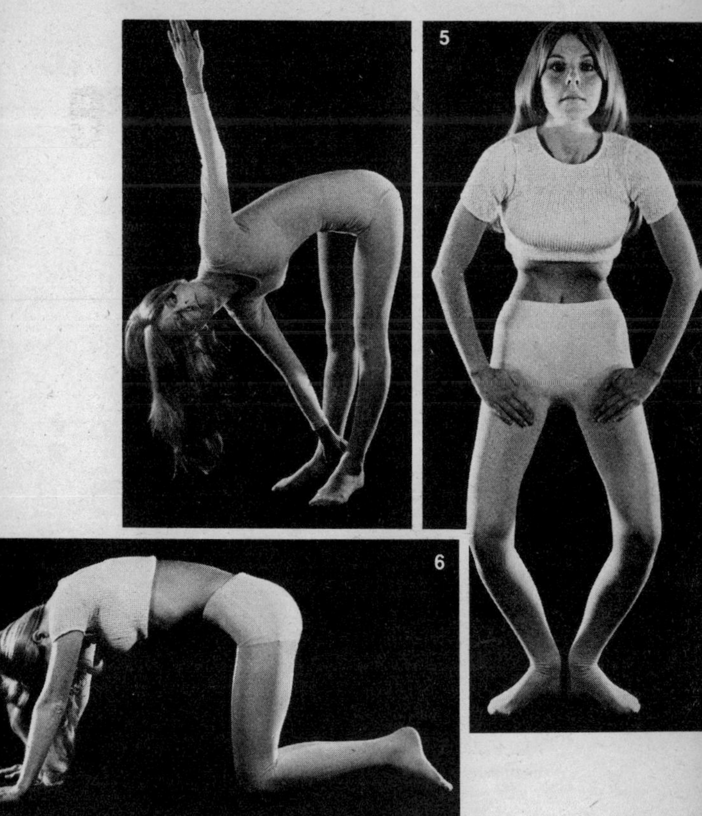

abdominal lifts

ABDOMINAL LIFTS (16 B & C)

5 This exercise was learned on Pp. 95-98. Today
6 we will continue our attempt to perform between 5-10 rhythmic lifts to each exhalation. Perform three

groups in the standing position and three groups in the All-Fours.

Relax briefly after each group

At this point you should be able to execute a satisfactory lift movement. If not, continue to practice as deep a contraction as possible

scalp exercise

7 Perform 25 times as learned on Pp. 59-60. Relax briefly

lion

8 Perform three times as learned on Pp. 59-60. Hold each extreme position for 20. Relax briefly

Make certain your tongue is being extended as far as possible.

neck roll

9 This exercise was learned on Page 191. Today perform the four rolling movements twice counter-clockwise (rolling to the left first), then twice clockwise. Hold each rolling movement for 5. Sit erect and keep eyes closed.

Relax briefly upon completion

7

8

9

posture clasp

10-11 Perform the up and down pulls three times on each side as learned on Pp. 239-240. Hold each of these 12 pulls for a count of 5. Sit erect. Relax briefly

bust exercise

12 Perform five times as learned on Page 161. Hold each raise for 5. Sit erect. Relax briefly

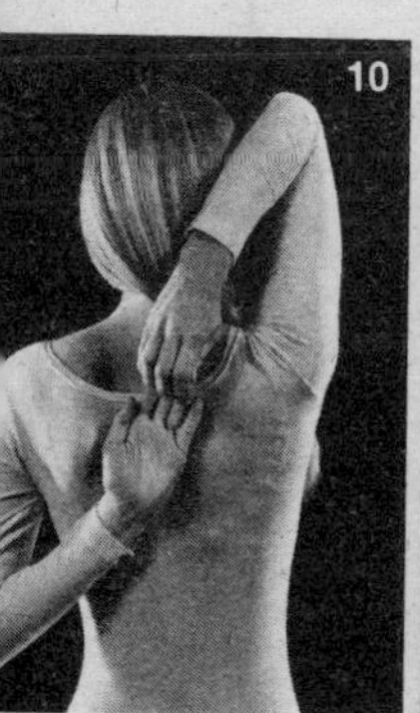
10

11

12

elbow-to-knee

13-14 Perform the entire routine twice as learned on Pp. 203-204 Hold each of the bends and twists for 5 Relax upon completion

13

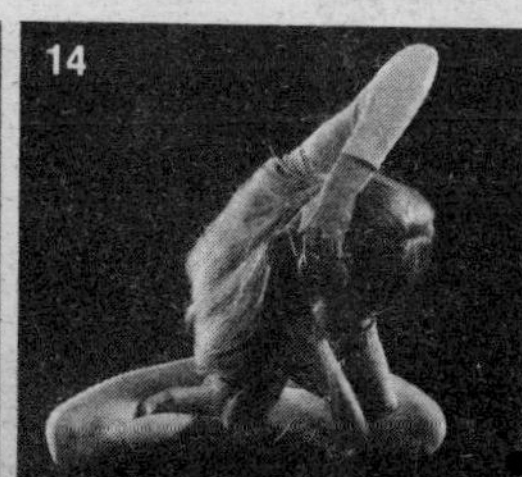
14

15

24th DAY

full twist

15 Perform the extreme twist twice to left side, then twice to right side as learned on Page 183. Hold each twist for 15. Reread the original instructions if you are uncertain of the movements. Relax upon completion

back stretch

16 Today, perform **only your extreme position** three times. This position may be your calves, ankles or feet. Hold first stretch for 10, second stretch for 20 and third stretch for 30. This progressive increase in the counting is important; count accurately. Relax upon completion

alternate leg pull

17 This exercise was learned yesterday on Page 247 Perform the three positions (calf, ankle and foot) once with the left leg, then perform the three positions once with the right leg. Hold each stretch for 15. Relax upon completion. If any of the positions are, as yet, too difficult, revert to a less extreme position and perform that one twice

backward bend

18 Seated on the feet, perform the extreme position once as learned on Page 61. Hold for 15. Next assume the toes position as learned on Page 145. Place as

much pressure as possible without strain on the toes. Hold for 15. Relax briefly

slow motion firming

19-20 Perform the entire routine, as learned on Page 226, twice.

Move in very slow motion. There is no holding in this exercise. Relax upon completion

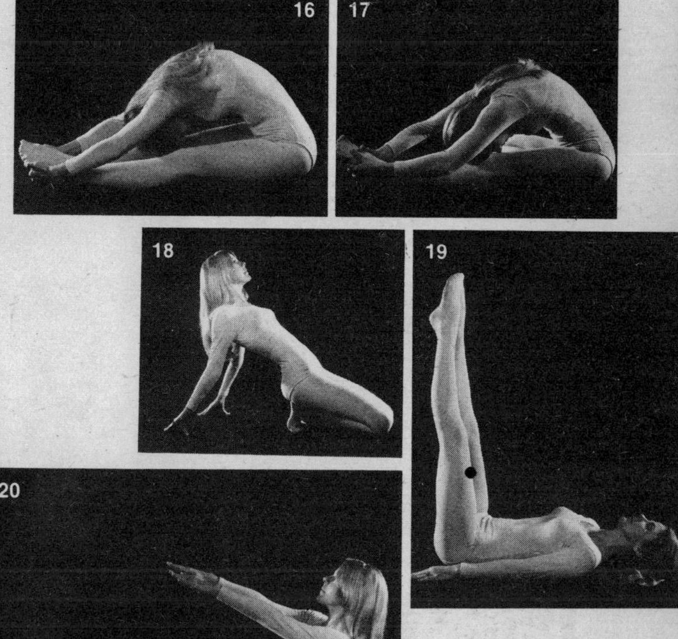

24th DAY

cobra locust bow

21 Today we will again combine these three exercises into a routine as we have done previously on Pp. 187-188

22 Perform the routine as follows:

23 Cobra: the complete routine including the twisting movements, once as learned on Pp. 72-74 and 114-115 Today, hold extreme raise for 30 and twisting movements for 10 each. Relax deeply

Locust: the legs separately (Page 105), then your extreme position once. Today, hold extreme raise for 10 if possible (less, if necessary). Relax

Bow: your extreme position once (Pp. 147-148). Hold for 10 Then perform the "rocking" movements (Page 221) five times in continous motion. Relax:

Repeat the above routine once so that you have performed it twice today.

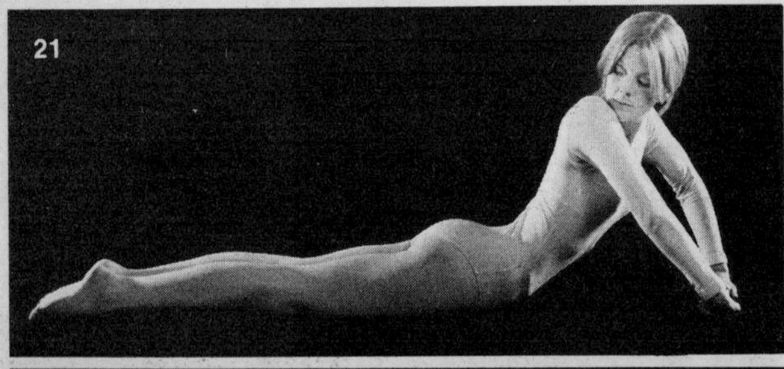

21

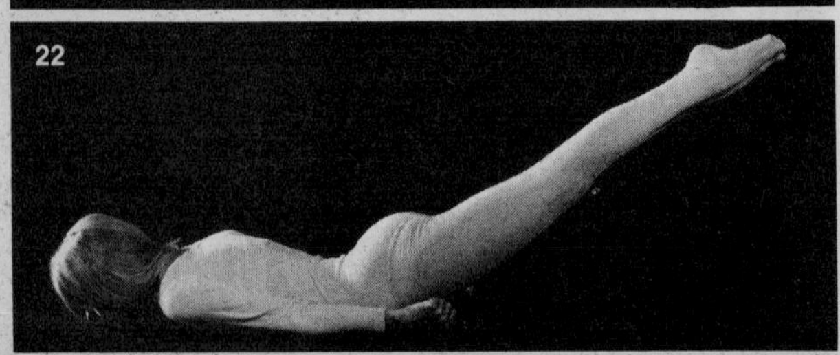

22

23

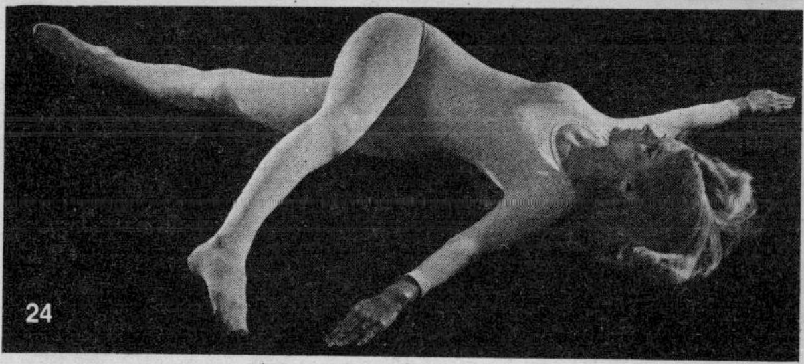
24

leg over

24 Perform three times to each side, alternating legs (right leg to left side; left leg to right side, etc.) as learned on Page 33. Hold each for 10. Relax

back push-up

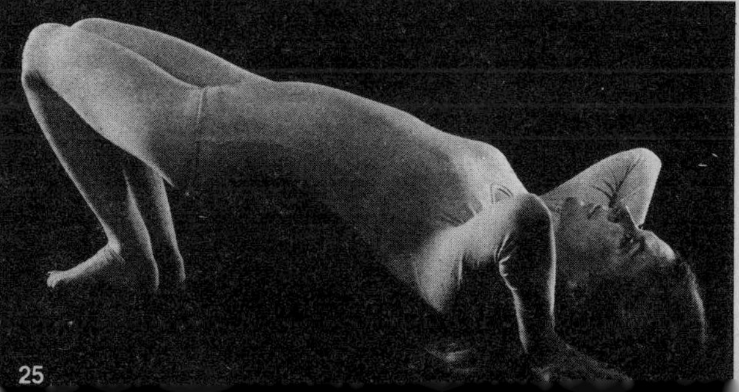
25

24th DAY

25-26 Perform twice in each position as learned on Pp. 231-232
Hold each raise for 10. Keep knees together
Relax upon completion

26

practice plan 24th day

To complete today's Review we will perform the exercises listed below in our continuous-motion routine. In each case perform only your extreme position of the exercise, once. Without pause continue on to the next exercise. There is no stopping of the movement from beginning to end. Remember the slow motion ballet concept.

Side Bend (to both sides)

Balance Posture (on both sides)

Rishi's Posture (to both sides)

Elbow-to-Knee (complete routine)

Full Twist (to both sides)

Back Stretch

Alternate Leg Pull (with each leg)

Slow Motion Firming (complete routine)

Cobra

Locust

Bow (with rocking)

Leg Over (to both sides)

Back Push-Up

complete breath

27 To conclude the routine, assume the cross-legged posture (the Full-Lotus if not uncomfortable, otherwise the Half-Lotus) and perform three Complete Breaths. Then sit very quietly for several minutes and become acutely aware of your body

24th DAY

thoughts for the day

FASTING FOR REGENERATION

To many readers the idea of "fasting" will seem strange. However, it is a technique of such great age that has been used throughout the centuries to achieve so many physical and spiritual objectives that it is certainly worth our serious consideration. **Fasting is not starving.** When you fast you voluntarily give up the eating of food for a certain period of time for a particular objective. From the physical standpoint the fast is undertaken by the Yogi as part of a regeneration program. It is the belief of the Yogi (as well as numerous groups of health-minded people throughout the world) that when the digestive organs are allowed to rest by virtue of having no food introduced into them, a cleansing process is initiated. This process will continue as long as the fast is prolonged. It is when this process has been completed (the completion being designated by certain indications) that the fast is theoretically terminated. At this point, unless food is again introduced into the organism, the body will start to feed upon itself. This marks the end of fasting and the beginning of starvation. But you may be surprised to learn that a long period of time could elapse before this point of starvation is reached.

The complete fast as briefly outlined above is, of course, not practical for the average working woman or housewife. One generally needs long periods of rest during the complete fast. What **is** practical is the "partial" fast and this is accomplished as follows: Select a day during which you can rest and relax; eat nothing at all for that day; simply drink pure water whenever thirsty. You may notice certain negative symptoms such as a temporary headache and some irritability or nervousness. If you busy yourself with activities that you enjoy, these discomforts will be minimized. The next day you would resume eating.

If you fasted in this manner once a week, the Yogi feels you will be doing your organism a great favor. Try it a few times and see. If you find that the fast is of value to you, then after several weeks of fasting one day, you can attempt a two day fast. The fast is always followed by light, natural, nourishing foods as previously suggested.

During the fasting period it is helpful to read inspirational literature, meditate and otherwise relax and revitalize your mind. It is suggested that the fast never exceed two days without the supervision of an authority. (There are a number of fasting institutions in the United States.)

25th DAY

GOOD CIRCULATION FOR HEALTH AND BEAUTY

complete breath standing

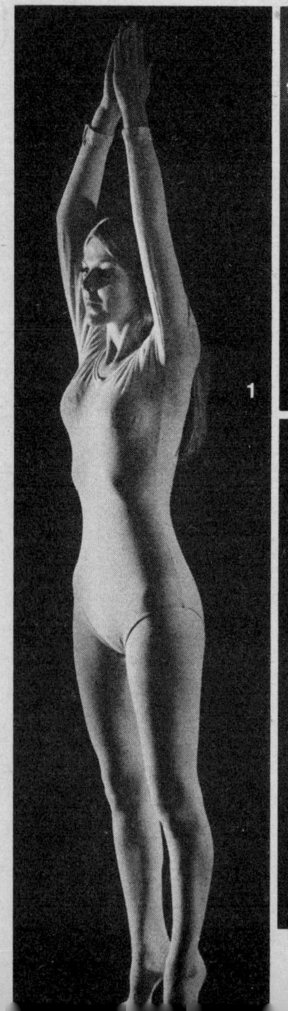

1

2

3

1 Perform three times as learned on Pp. 53-54. Today, hold each extreme raise for a count of 10. Make certain you are performing the correct abdominal and chest movements; move in very slow motion; raise high on toes; hold extreme position steady. Relax upon completion

chest expansion

2 Perform once in each of the three positions as learned on Pages 9, 20 and 67. Count 10 in The backward positions and 20 in each forward position. Keep arms as high as possible throughout the exercise. Do not perform the leg movements today. Relax upon completion

rishi's posture

3 Perform once in each of the three positions as learned on Pages 155 and 235. Alternate the sides (first left, then right) for each position. Hold each of the six bends for 10.
Relax upon completion

ADDITIONAL MOVEMENTS FOR THE

shoulder stand

4 Perform your extreme position once as learned on Page 132. Today, increase the hold of the inverted posture to 2:30 (you can count 150 or glance at a watch or clock placed near your head). Do not hold longer than 2:30

5 Upon completion of the 2:30 count, begin a very slow "split" with legs

6 Continue split until extreme position is achieved
Trunk remains erect
Hold without motion for a count of 20

25th DAY

Bring legs slowly back to Fig. 4
Come out of posture as previously practiced

Relax with back on floor for one minute

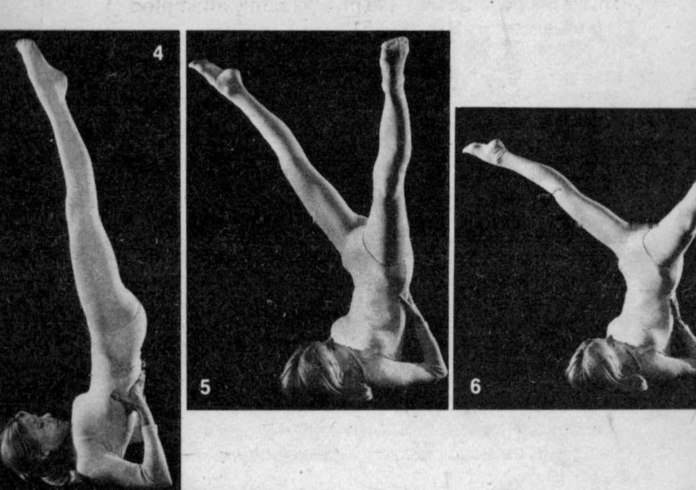

At this point in our study we must introduce the movements for completing the Head Stand posture. If you feel you are ready, attempt the movements cautiously. If you are not as yet prepared, revert to continued practice of the more modified position. The completed Head Stand is to be regarded as an advanced and difficult posture for which patient and sustained practice are necessary. The great benefits of the Head Stand will be commensurate with your effort.

ADDITIONAL MOVEMENTS FOR THE

head stand

7 This is the position we have most recently attempted (as learned on Pp. 150-151)

8 In very slow motion and with complete control we attempt to straighten legs

9 The completed posture. Hold for 10 only

10-11 Come out of the posture by reversing the movements
Keep knees close to chest
Lower legs slowly, with control; do not come "crashing" down with feet banging against floor
Rest in head down position as previously practiced for one minute

Remember to:

Make surrounding area soft with pillows
Perform all movements slowly with control; never attempt to "spring" into completed position
Raise legs only to position that feels secure

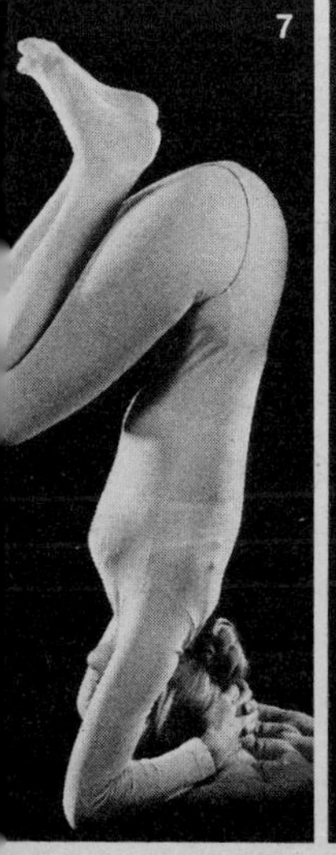

7

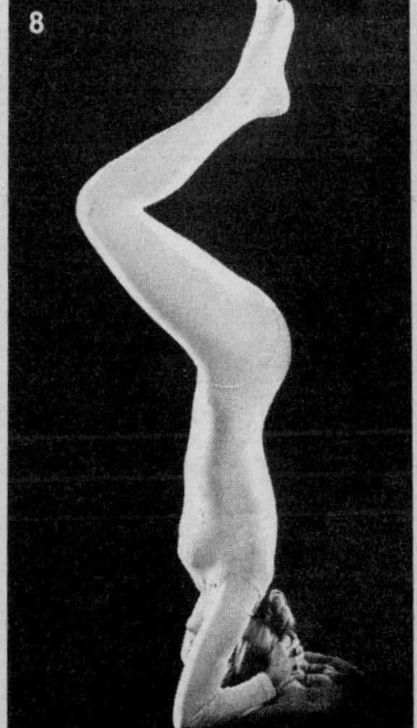

8

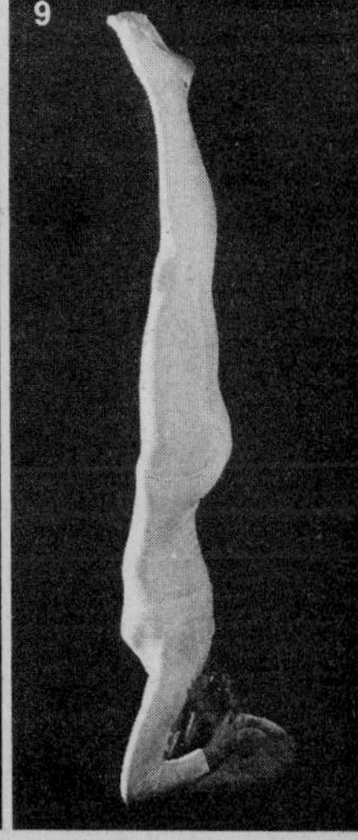

9

25th DAY

Do not make more than three attempts at an advanced position today

back push-up

12 Perform twice in each of the two positions learned on Pp. 231-232. Hold the moderate raises for 10 each and the extreme positions for 20 each. Keep knees together

Pause briefly between repetitions. Relax upon completion

plough

13 Hold your extreme position (as learned on Page 135) for 30. Do not hold longer. Come out of the posture exactly as instructed. Work for smoothness and keep head on floor

Relax with back on floor

locust

14 Perform the moderate position with both legs, once. Hold for 10

Perform your extreme position with both legs raised as high as possible twice. Hold extreme raise for 10 if possible. Pause briefly between repetitions

Upon completion, rest cheek on floor and relax deeply. Allow all muscles to relax. Become aware of what is occurring in your body. Do not allow your mind to wander

25th DAY

thoughts for the day

SLEEP

As yet, we do not fully understand how the organism is recharged during sleep. However, it is clear that a powerful regeneration does occur and if a person is prevented from sleeping for a period of time, there are severe repercussions physically, emotionally and mentally. If you feel tired and irritable on a given day, check back and determine if you've had adequate sleep for the past few nights. It is especially important in the beginning stages of Yoga practice that we conserve, as much as possible, the new life-force that will be available to us. This implies living in a way that does not make excessive demands on our reserves and, toward this end, we have suggested such experiments as "freezing" yourself in action (6th Day) to determine where your energies may be drained unknowingly. There is nothing that can so quickly deplete your life-force as lack of sufficient sleep.

We derive the most benefit from our sleep when it is **deep and restful.** One hour of deep sleep is worth many hours of fitful tossing and turning; therefore, let us suggest the method for deep sleep. From a physical standpoint the Yogi believes the sleeping surface should be as firm as your body will tolerate; the head should be only slightly raised to permit good circulation; the stomach should always be as empty as possible, which means there should be no eating for approximately two hours before retiring. This includes hot milk, cocoa, tea and other concoctions that are supposed to induce sleep; you cannot sleep restfully if the digestive system has to work. Any type of sleeping pill, unless prescribed by your physician, is to be avoided as the plague. The serious student of Yoga will never find it necessary to resort to an artificially induced sleep.

With regard to the mind and emotions: All thoughts must cease when you close your eyes. If there are no thoughts, there will be no restlessness or anxiety and **deep** sleep will result. Because of the concentration techniques we have already practiced, you should now be able to fix your consciousness on one point, with your eyes closed, and permit no distractions. Sleep will follow quickly. If you find yourself particularly tense before retiring, do the Back Stretch, Cobra and Head Twist once and complete the routine with several rounds of Alternate Nostril Breathing that we will learn subsequently (36).

26th DAY

advanced

Today's practice deals with **advanced** positions of certain exercises. If these are, as yet, too difficult, simply execute your most extreme position of the various postures. Proceed cautiously since the advanced work makes intense demands on the organism. However, you will experience increased benefits and a wonderful sense of accomplishment as you gradually sueceed in attaining these advanced positions.

leg clasp

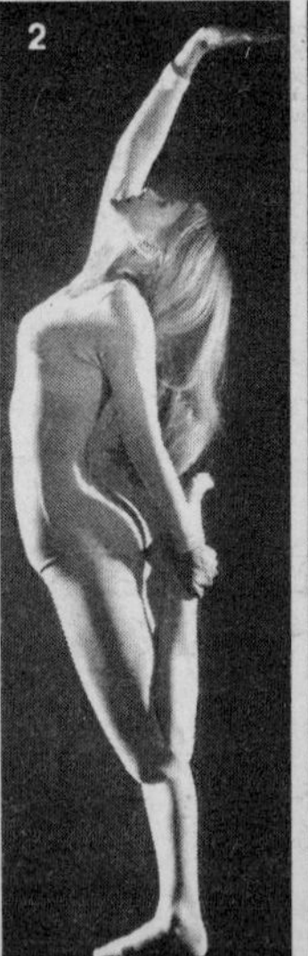

This exercise was learned on Page 244. Perform the knee position once and the calf position twice. Hold each bend for a count of 10

1 Now slide hands down to ankles
Brace hands against ankles
Draw forehead down to calves
Hold for 10

Unclasp hands and slowly straighten to upright position
Relax

Repeat entire routine of knee, calf and ankle position once. Hold each bend for 10

balance posture

Perform twice with right arm raised, then twice with left arm raised as learned on Page 194. Hold each stretch for 5

2 Now bring right arm very far back and left foot up as illustrated. Hold for 10. Relax

Perform identical movements with left arm upraised

3 This is a variation on the extreme position
Perform the movements of Fig. 2 with right arm raised
Hold for 10
Move directly into position illustrated
Hold for 5
Relax
Perform identical movements with left arm raised
Relax

back stretch

4 Perform once in each of the four positions learned on Pages 12, 22, 71 and 138 (knees, calves, ankles, feet)
Hold each of the four forward pulls for 10

5 When the count of 10 is completed in the position of Fig. 4, lower elbows toward floor for ultimate stretch of back and legs. Hold for 10

Straighten to upright position and relax

4

5

alternate leg pull

6 Perform the three positions (calf, ankle, foot) once with the left leg. Hold each stretch for 15

7 When the count of 15 is completed in the position of Fig. 6 lowerelbows toward floor. Hold for 10

Straighten to upright position and relax

Perform identical three positions once with the right leg.
Hold each for 15. Then lower elbows toward floor and hold for 10

Straighten to upright position and relax

backward bend

8 Assume this position on toes as learned on Page 145

9 Very cautiously inch backward a moderate distance on hands (or fingertips if easier)
Do not go farther than illustrated
Drop head backward
Arch spine upward
Remain seated on heels
Bring knees together
Hold for 10

If this position is too difficult today, revert to Fig. 8 or Fig. 7, Page 146 and hold for 15

Inch forward
Return to Fig. 8
Assume a cross-legged posture

Manipulate toes with hands if discomfort is experienced upon completion

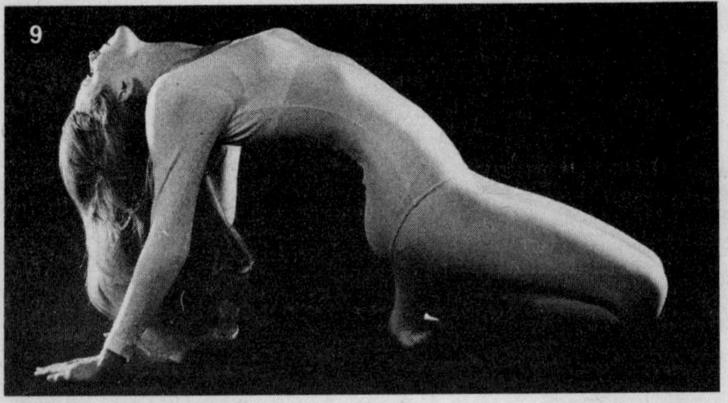

locust

Perform with the legs separately once and then your moderate position once, as learned on Page 105
Hold each raise for 10

10 In the advanced position the knees are bent to enable groin to be raised from floor
Hold for 10
Lower legs and relax with cheek on floor

Attempt the advanced position two more times

plough

11 This advanced position follows that of Fig. 12, Page 137

Clasp hands on top of head
This enables you to inch back several inches farther with toes
Experience the emphasis shifting from lower back (as in Fig. 12, Page 137) to middle area
Hold for 20

12 Lower knees to either side of head
Pressure now shifts from middle to upper back and neck
Hold for 20

Come out of posture by rolling forward as previously learned and relax on back

26th DAY

Now perform all three positions once. Hold each of the extreme positions for 20

12

lotus

13

14

When the Full-Lotus has been accomplished the following two variations should be attempted:

13 The Locked Lotus
Reach behind back with left hand
Hold toes of left foot
Hold for 10 (to help "set" body)
Now attempt to hold right foot with right hand
Hold for 20

A "progressive" posture that becomes easier with each attempt. Excellent for figure and posture improvement

14 The Lotus Shoulder Stand
Assume Full-Lotus
Lie down on back and swing locked legs up
Place hands against hips for support
Slowly straighten legs into position illustrated
Hold for one minute

Return to seated posture and extend legs. Relax

practice plan 26th day

To complete our 26th Day of practice, we will perform the exercises listed below once in our continuous-motion routine; there is no pause from beginning to end. Perform either the advanced positions (as learned today) or your most extreme position of each exercise.

Leg Clasp (heel position—or your extreme position—once; do not hold)

Balance Posture (extreme stretch followed by variation of Fig. 3, once on each side without holding)

Back Stretch (feet position—or your extreme position—followed by lowering of elbows; once without holding)

Alternate Leg Pull (foot position—or your extreme position—followed by lowering of elbows; once with each leg; do not hold)

Locust (extreme raise once only; do not hold)

Plough (perform as much of the three positions routine as possible; move from one position into the next without holding)

Following the Plough rest with back on floor and relax deeply. Focus your consciousness inside your organism and become aware of what is occurring.

thoughts for the day

ADVANCED POSITIONS

You must not feel the slightest discouragement if today's exercises seem beyond your present ability. These are all difficult positions and are offered at this late point in our plan as a **challenge** for the future weeks and months of your practice. If you continue to follow the **Practice Routines** that are presented at the end of this book, all of the movements will soon become second nature, as natural as walking. You will find yourself so limber that you will seek more of a challenge from the various postures and the "advanced positions" will serve this purpose. Increased benefits from the advanced work will be in proportion to your accomplishment. You must never strain to attain a position beyond which your body is comfortable; if you do so, you will actually retard your progress. All intermediate and advanced positions will be achieved with patient practice.

It is necessary to point out that there are hundreds of different Yoga postures. Many of them require astonishing dexterity of the spine and limbs for which long years of practice is necessary. Such advanced postures are sometimes depicted in Hatha Yoga books and demonstrated by visiting Yogis from India. This is often unfortunate, since such postures are not only impractical and unnecessary for the average person of the western world, but they have a discouraging effect and have prevented many people from undertaking the Yoga study. Such people have erroneously believed that these very difficult positions must be an intrinsic part of Yoga and since, for example, they cannot imagine their tired, stiff, tense bodies executing a Head Stand in a Full Lotus, they naturally pursue the idea no further. But it is these very people who could gain so much from simply following the gentle, progressive plan of this book. The 38 techniques offered here are all that need ever be practiced to achieve the many objectives we have discussed. Only those who intend to devote the major part of their lives to Yoga need undertake further study under the competent guidance of a **guru**.

It is important also, for purposes of clarification, to understand that those groups of peoples of the Far and Near East who do strange things such as walking on hot coals, sticking needles into their bodies, allowing themselves to be "buried alive" and so forth are known as **Fakirs** and are never to be confused with Yogis. One who practices Yoga will never permit anything unnatural or harmful to be done to his body or mind. Every movement and aspect of Yoga are completely natural, designed solely for **development of human potential.**

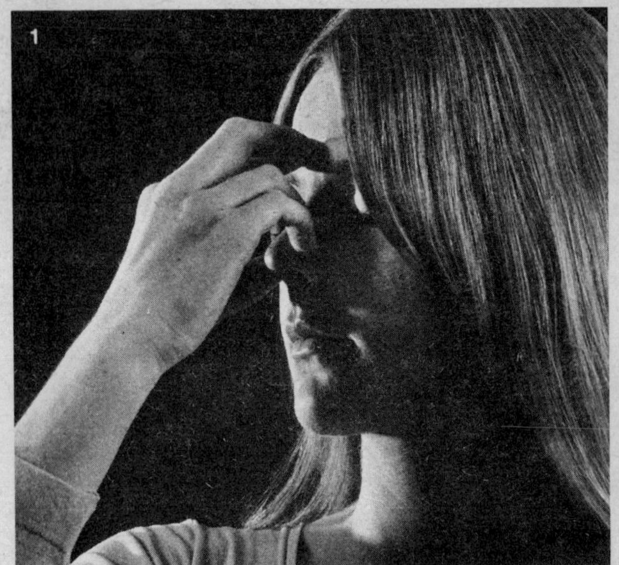

alternate nostril breathing

TO RELIEVE ANXIETY, PROMOTE EMOTIONAL STABILITY

Today we will learn three ancient and highly effective techniques that emphasize the "spiritual" aspect of Yoga. As you practice them today, and in subsequent sessions, you will begin to experience the extraordinary sense of elevation and peace that Yoga has to offer.

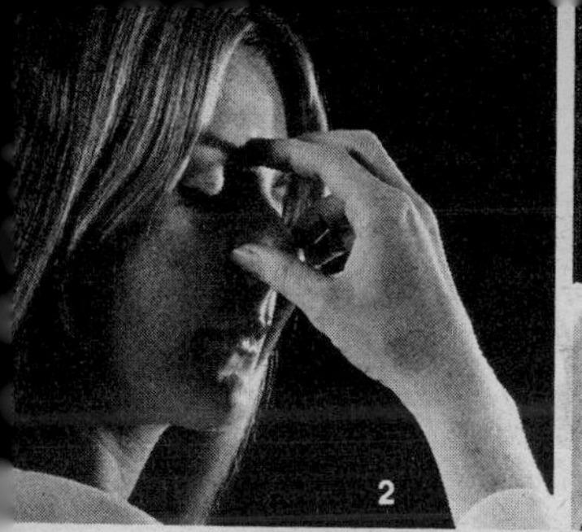

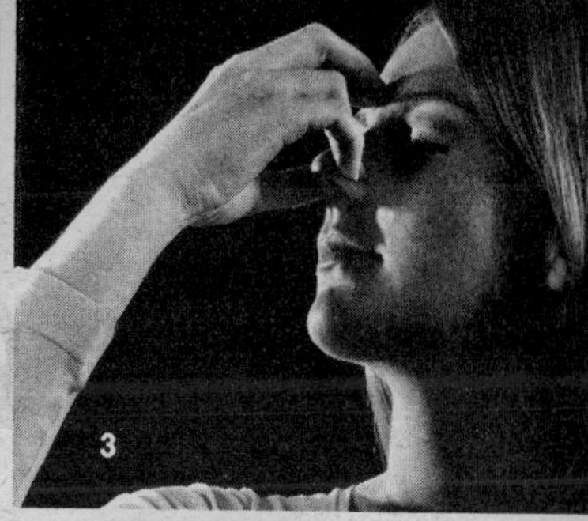

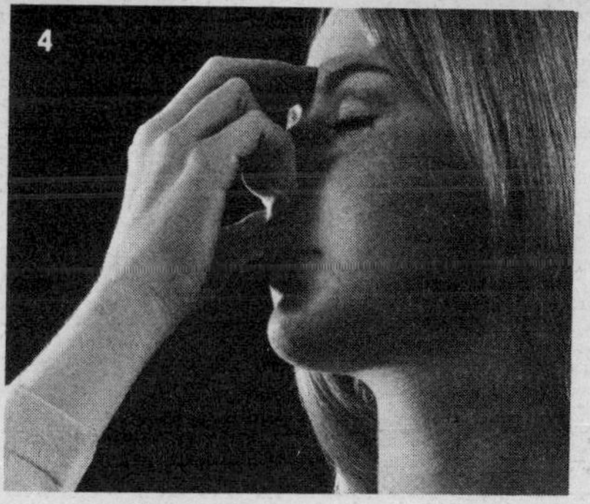

1 Sit in a cross-legged posture
Note position of fingers
Right thumb rests lightly against right nostril
Index and middle fingers are together on forehead
Ring and little fingers rest lightly against left nostril
Exhale slowly and deeply through both nostrils

2 Press right nostril closed with thumb
Slowly and quietly inhale a deep breath through left nostril in a count of 8

3 Keep right nostril closed
Now press left nostril closed with ring finger
Hold air in lungs for a rhythmic count of 8

4 Open right nostril only
Exhale deeply through right nostril in a rhythmic count of 8

Without pause, inhale through right nostril in a rhythmic count of 8 (note: **right nostril, through which you just finished the exhalation)**
Press right nostril closed
Hold air in lungs for rhythmic count of 8

Open left nostril only
Exhale deeply through left nostril in 8

Without pause inhale through **left** nostril in a rhythmic count of 8. This brings you back to the beginning of the exercise. Continue the movements according to the following summary:

- **inhale through left (in 8)**
- **retain (both nostrils closed for 8)**
- **exhale through right (in 8)**

- **inhale through right (in 8)**
- **retain (both nostrils closed for 8)**
- **exhale through left (in 8)**

The above is one complete round

Perform 5 rounds

Counting of the groups of 8 must be very steady and rhythmic
You can beat the groups of 8 with your left hand
Count the 5 rounds with fingers of left hand
Eyelids can be lowered
Breathing must be **deep and quiet**

Upon completion of the fifth round place hands in the classical meditation position as learned on Page 47. Then sit very quietly for several minutes keeping the eyelids lowered.

deep relaxation

FOR IMMEDIATE RELIEF OF TENSION THROUGHOUT THE BODY

5 Lie as illustrated and place fingertips of both hands on solar plexus (top of abdomen)
Close your eyes
Breathe slowly and quietly for several moments
Allow all muscles to relax so that body becomes limp

Now inhale a slow, quiet, deep breath
During the inhalation, visualize in your mind's eye the life-force (prana) in the air passing through your nostrils and lungs and being drawn into your fingertips from the solar plexus. Attempt to visualize this life-force as a brilliant white light similar to that of sunlight

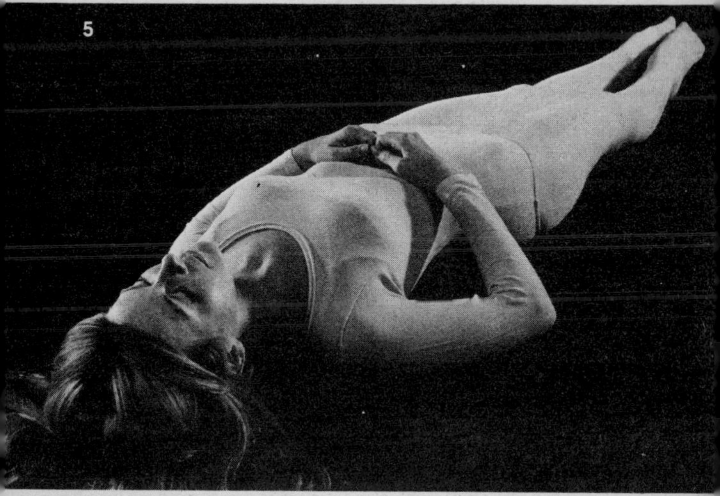

6 Retain the air in your lungs
Hold the image of the white light (your mind must not wander)
Move your fingertips to rest lightly on the forehead
Now begin a slow, quiet, deep exhalation
During the exhalation direct the life-force (visualized as a white light) into your head
Gradually your entire head is flooded with the white light

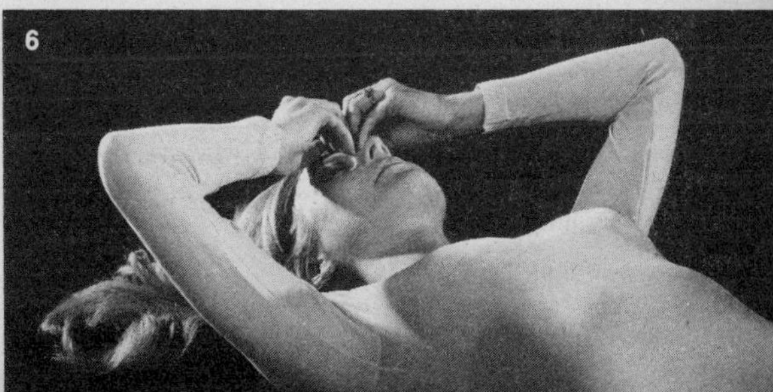
6

When the lungs are once again empty, transfer the fingertips back to the solar plexus
Without pause begin the next inhalation; retain the image of the white light being drawn into your fingertips and repeat the movements described above

Perform 7 times

It is necessary to keep the mind clear of all extraneous thoughts during this exercise so that you can concentrate fully on the white light

Although the imagery of the white light may not be entirely clear or consistent in the beginning, this will come with subsequent practice

Upon completion, rest arms at sides
Allow body to become completely limp and experience the deep relaxation that is occurring throughout your organism

candle concentration

FOR TURNING THE MIND INWARD; DEVELOPING CONCENTRATION

7 Place a lighted candle approximately 3 feet from you
Sit in a cross-legged posture
Gaze directly at flame for approximately 2 minutes

8 Close eyes and gently press palms against them
You will see the image of the flame; concentrate on that image and do not let the flame wander or disappear.
Hold palms against eyes for 1 to 2 minutes

Place hands on knees and relax
This exercise is performed only once

Fix your mind completely on the image of the flame and let no thoughts distract you. If it should disappear, bring it back simply by looking for it (with eyes closed)

You should attempt to retain the image of the flame for the full 1 to 2 minutes

This exercise greatly strengthens the powers of concentration and prepares the mind for the serious practice of meditation

thoughts for the day

MEDITATION

We have suggested that you sit quietly following your day's practice and become aware of what is transpiring within you. Through this technique we temporarily withdraw ourselves from the many superficial activities of the day and turn our attention inward. In so doing we gradually come to perceive the **source** of our existence and automatically integrate ourselves with this source. We allow ourselves, more and more, to become expressions, sounding boards as it were, of the Absolute, of God. As this begins to occur, the individual is freed from the terribly confining limitations of what she has heretofore conceived of as "me" or "I" and the necessity of protecting the phantom known as the "ego." The implications of this cannot be overstated. Energies released from the carrying of the ego burden are tremendous and affect, in an indescribable manner, every aspect of our lives. The consciousness is greatly elevated and the resulting state of existence can only be hinted at with words such as "joy," "bliss" and "true peace."

A comprehensive discussion of the various aspects of Yoga philosophy and meditation may be found in my book **Guide to Meditation.** For our purposes here we shall define meditation as **a profound state of quietude for the entire organism.** In quietude, and **only** in quietude, self-realization or **Yoga** is attained. Today, we have learned three important techniques that will be of immense value in preparing the organism to experience this deep quiescence. Let us now review the principles involved in the actual meditative state. Meditation can be practiced whenever you feel the need for renewal or following your Yoga practice as has been suggested. You assume a cross-legged posture, using your pillow if necessary. The Lotus postures are the result of painstaking experiments by the great Yogis of the past to perfect a position in which frequent movement of the legs would not be required (as the body moves, the mind is distracted). The Lotus also enables the spine to be erect and body firmly rooted. The eyelids are lowered, not closed. The fingers assume the circle position. Breathing will be slowed automatically. Having resolved, gently but firmly, not to be distracted, you remain motionless in this position for as long as is comfortable, becoming acutely aware of what is occurring within.

Review

Because of the extent of our final review (24 exercises), a slightly longer practice session will be necessary. The repetitions of each exercise will be held to a minimum. This is an extremely important session, so practice carefully and patiently.

complete breath standing

1 Perform twice as learned on Pp. 53-54
Hold each extreme raise for 10

chest expansion

2 Perform the extreme positions only as learned on Page 67
Count 10 in the backward and 20 in the forward positions.
Perform the leg movements once as learned on Page 110 and hold them for 10 each

dancer's posture

3 Perform three times in continuous slow motion as learned on Pp. 195-196

28th DAY

triangle

4 Perform once on each side in the extreme position only
Hold each bend for 15

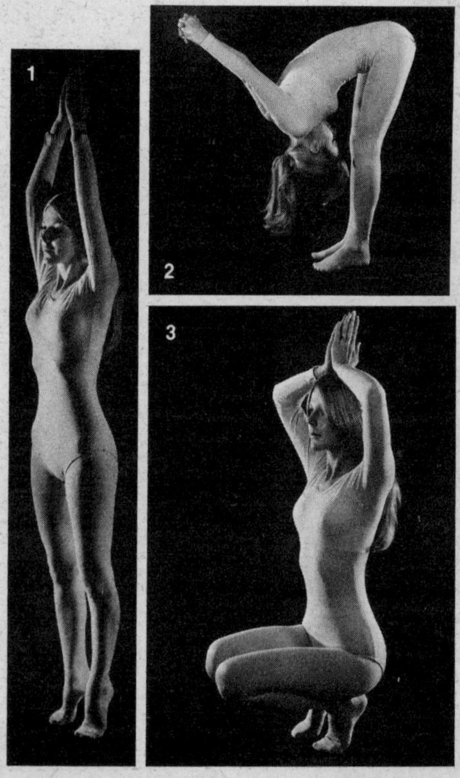

balance posture

5 Perform once with right arm raised and hold for 5
Repeat with right arm raised; hold for 5 and then move

directly into the variation of Fig. 5 learned on Page 274

Hold for 5. Relax a moment and perform identical movements with left arm raised

4

5

6

circular motion

6 Perform once counter-clockwise and once clockwise in the extreme circle only. Hold each rolling movement for 3

rishi's posture

7 Perform once in your extreme position on each side as learned on pages 155 and 235. Hold each bend for 15

leg clasp

8 Perform once in the knee position and once in your extreme position as learned on Pages 244 and 274 Hold each stretch for 10

abdominal lifts

ABDOMINAL LIFTS (16 B & C)

9-10 Perform two groups of between 5-10 rhythmic lifts in each of the positions

7

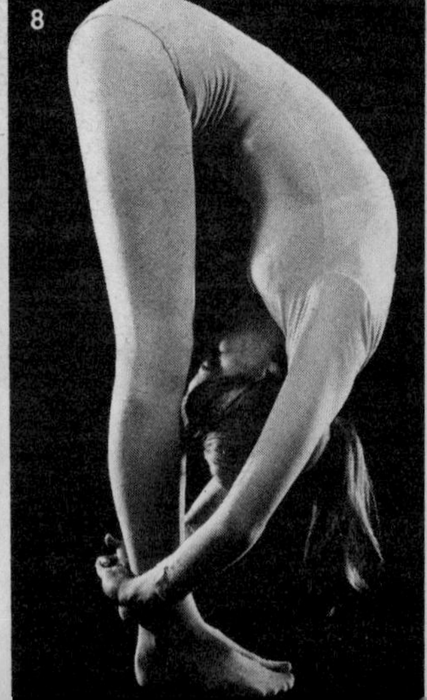
8

elbow-to-knee

11 Perform the entire routine twice as learned on Pp. 203-204
Hold each of the bends and twists for 5

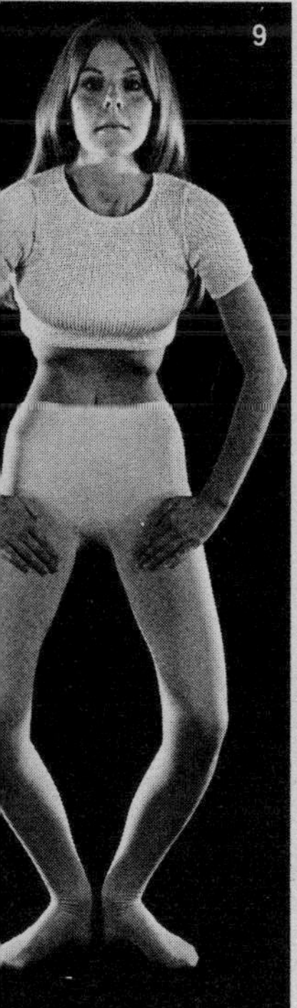

full twist

12 Perform the extreme twist twice to left side, then twice to right side as learned on Page 183. Hold each twist for 15

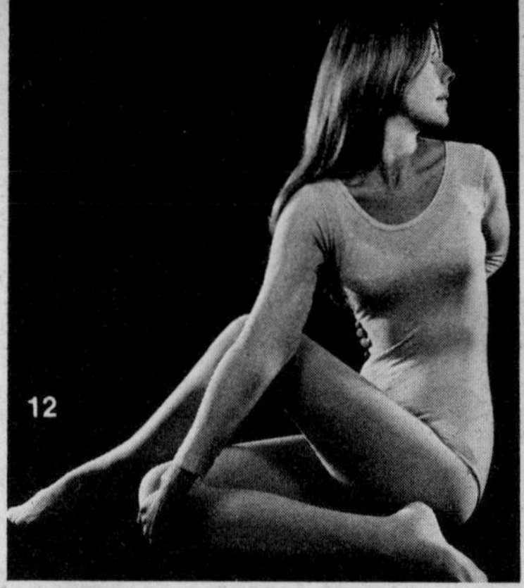

back stretch

13 Perform only your extreme position twice (if possible execute the advanced stretch of Fig. 5 learned on Page 276). Hold each stretch for 20

alternate leg pull

14 Perform only your extreme position twice with each leg (if possible execute the advanced stretch learned on Page 276). Hold each stretch for 10

backward bend

15 Perform only your extreme position once (if ready, attempt the advanced position learned on Page 278). Hold for 20

side raise

16 Perform your extreme position twice on each side Hold each raise for 7

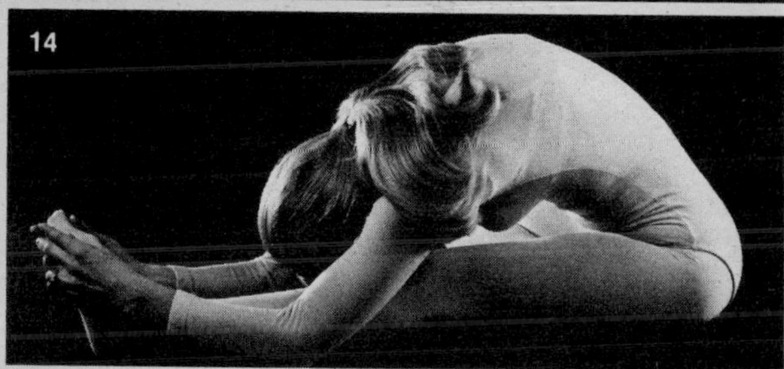

back push-up

17 Perform your extreme position twice. Hold each raise for 10

28th DAY

shoulder stand

18 Perform your extreme position once as learned on Page 132. Hold for 2:30 (a count of 150) and then execute the "split" learned on Page 268. Hold for 20. Bring the legs together and move directly into the Plough

plough

19 Perform as many of the three Plough positions as possible.
Hold each for 10

leg over

20 Perform twice to each side, alternating the legs. Hold each extreme position for 10

head stand

21 Perform your extreme position once. (The completed posture was learned on Page 269.) Hold for a count of 30 today

cobra

22 Perform the complete routine including the twisting movements once as learned on Pp. 72-73 and 114-115. Hold extreme raise for 30 and twisting movements for 10 each

locust

23 Perform your moderate position once, then your extreme position once. Hold each raise for 10

22

23

24

28th DAY

bow

24 Perform your extreme position once; hold for 10. Then move directly into the "rocking" movements learned on Pp. 221-222 and perform five times in continuous motion

alternate nostril breathing

25 Conclude today's practice by performing five rounds of this breathing exercise as learned yesterday

Upon completion, place hands in the classical meditation position and sit very quietly for several minutes keeping the eyelids lowered and listening to your body

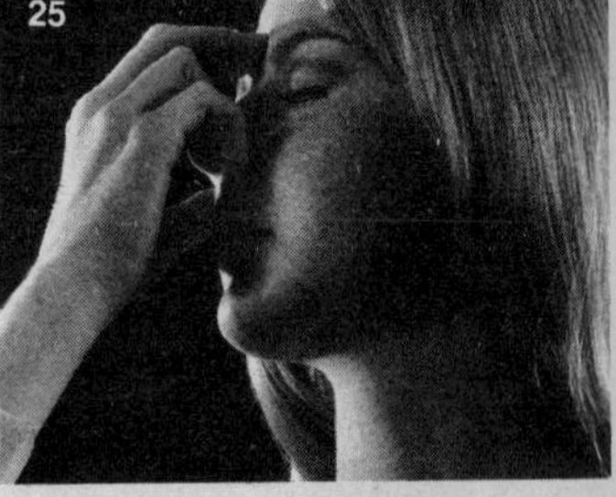
25

thoughts for the day

EVALUATING YOUR ACCOMPLISHMENTS

Today we have completed our 28-Day plan. Let us evaluate what has been accomplished and review our objectives, both those already achieved and those of the future. In a relatively brief period you have gained a working knowledge of 38 Yoga techniques. At this point your proficiency in the exercises, that is, how far you have advanced with the various movements, is of secondary concern. Of primary importance is the fact that you have assimilated the **principles** of execution. You now have the **feeling** of slow motion, of the holding positions, of rhythmic counting, of continuous, flowing movements, of deep concentration. This **feeling** of what is involved in the correct performance will enable you to eventually master each of the exercises, including its advanced positions. You understand the **progressive** concept of Yoga in which your body "sets" itself by passing through various stages of first drawing back and then moving forward. Therefore, you are aware of the value of patient, sustained practice and you know you need never strain or become discouraged in any phase of the study. From these first 28 days you have begun to experience an unparalleled sense of well-being in your body (a number of physical problems may be in the process of solution) and an elevated state of consciousness that has a strong, positive influence on all aspects of your life. This will continue to grow through your future practice.

The most difficult phase of your Hatha Yoga study—the assimilation of the principles of execution and the learning of 38 exercises—is completed. Now, rapid progress and pronounced benefits will result from regular periods of practice. A plan for lifetime practice is offered in the following pages and the first routine should be undertaken **tomorrow.** Do not interrupt the daily routine to which you have become accustomed. If you will continue to practice on a daily basis for another month, you will pass through a second, crucial phase during which an extremely firm Yogic foundation will be established. You will then discover that your body will never allow you to go for more than a few days without performing the exercises, because it will know intuitively that this is what is required for you to feel you are functioning at your best. At the end of this second month you will find yourself looking forward to your daily Yoga practice as one of the most enjoyable, beneficial, stimulating activities of your day.

practice routines

Practice the exercises in each routine consecutively: i.e., 1-A, 1-B, 1-C etc.

All of the exercises we have learned may now be practiced within a period of each three days by using the three routines of the following pages. One routine is to be used for each day's practice session and the three routines are to be continually rotated. For example, Monday, Routine 1, Tuesday, Routine 2, Wednesday, Routine 3, Thursday, Routine 1, etc. Keep a record of your practice so that you always know the correct routine for any given day. Each routine should require 20-30 minutes.

The more advanced positions shown in the routines will be accomplished with patient practice. There is no rush. If an exercise calls for a position that is still too difficult, revert to an easier position. For example, if in the Back Stretch you cannot as yet hold your feet, revert to the ankle position and perform that position twice. The same procedure applies to all exercises in which any position is too difficult. If an entire exercise is difficult, perform it cautiously, as best you can, but do not neglect it.

If you are working on a particular problem, you can practice the group of exercises for this problem as listed in Days 17 through 25. However, this should be done *apart* (at a different time of the day) from the regular routine of that day.

If you have the slightest doubt regarding the correct execution of any of the movements, make certain to review the exercise according to the pages indicated under "references."

These routines may be used as a lifetime plan for practice.

1-A

RISHI's POSTURE

References
Page 155; 235

Repetitions:
Once in each of the three positions; alternate the sides (first left, then right) for each position

Count:
10 for each of the six bends

1-B

TRIANGLE

References:
19; 30-31; 38-39

Repetitions:
Once in each of the three positions; alternate the sides (first left, then right) for each position

Count:
10 for each of the six bends

1-C

BALANCE POSTURE

References:
Pages 194; 274-275

Repetitions:
Three times with right arm upraised; upon completion of third time, move directly into variation
Three times with left arm upraised; upon completion of third time, move directly into variation

Count:
5 for each stretch; 5 for each variation

1-D

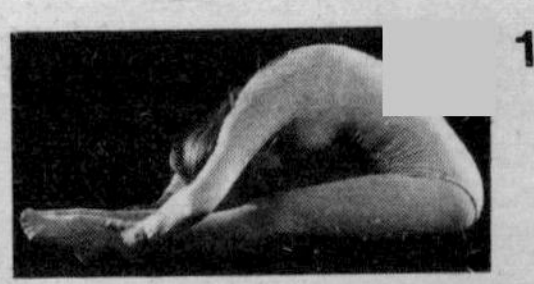

BACK STRETCH

References:
Pages 12; 22; 71; 138-139; 275-276

Repetitions:
Once in each of the knee and calf positions; twice in each of the ankle and foot positions (perform the advanced stretch following the foot position)

Count:
10 for each of first two positions
20 for second two positions
10 for advanced stretch

1-E

BUST EXERCISE

References:
Page 161

Repetitions:
Five times

Count:
5 for each raise

1-F

HEAD TWIST

References:
Page 116

Repetitions:
Once in each of the three positions

Count:
20 in each position

1-G

COBRA

References:
Pages 14-15; 24; 72;
114-115

ROUTINE 1 (Cont.)

Repetitions:
Entire routine, including twisting movements, twice

Count:
30 for extreme raise; 10 for twisting movements

LOCUST

References:
Pages 105-106; 278-279

Repetitions:
Legs separately, once
Moderate position, once
Extreme position, twice

Count:
10 for each raise

1-I

BOW

References:
Pages 147-148; 241-242

Repetitions:
Routine consists of extreme raise, followed by 5 rocking movements. Perform routine twice

Count:
10 for extreme raise; rocking is done in continuous motion

1-J

BACKWARD BEND

References:
Pages 61-62; 145-146; 277-278

Repetitions:
Twice on feet
Once on toes
Once in advanced position

Count:
20 on feet; 10 on toes; 10 in advanced

1-K

LEG OVER

References:
Pages 33-34

Repetitions:
Three times to each side, alternating legs

Count:
10 for each extreme position

At this point in the practice, if your time permits return to the beginning of Routine 1 and perform each exercise once in the continuous slow-motion movement we have practiced previously. Conclude the routine with Alternate Nostril Breathing which follows.

ROUTINE 1 (Cont.)

1-L

ALTERNATE NOSTRIL BREATHING

References:
Page 284

Repetitions:
5 rounds

Count:
Groups of 8 as described in instructions

Upon completion remain seated in cross-legged posture for several minutes and become aware of what is occurring throughout your organism

---

ROUTINE 2 (A-K)

2-A

COMPLETE BREATH STANDING

References:
Pages 53-54

Repetitions:
Five times

Count:
5 in each extreme position

2-B

CIRCULAR MOTION

References:
Page 27

Repetitions:
The three circles twice counter-clockwise;
Then the three circles twice clockwise

Count:
3 in each of the rolling movements

2-C

SIDE BEND

References:
Pages 102-103

Repetitions:
Once in each of the three positions, alternate the sides (left first) for each position

Count:
10 for each of the six bends

2-D

LEG CLASP

References:
Pages 244; 274

Repetitions:
Routine consists of knee, calf and heel positions
Perform entire routine twice. Straighten to upright position and relax briefly between repetitions

Count:
10 for each of the six stretches

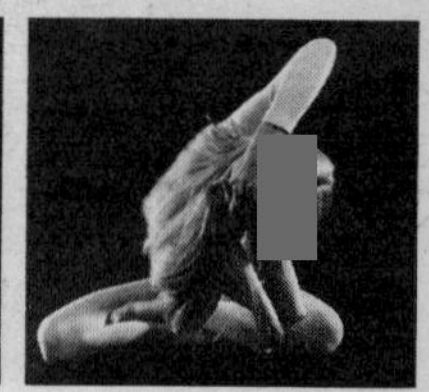

2-E

ELBOW-to-KNEE

References:
Pages 203-204

Repetitions:
Entire routine twice

Count:
5 for each of the bends and twists

2-F

ALTERNATE LEG PULL

References:
Pages 247; 276-277

Repetitions:
Begin with left leg. Perform once in the calf position and twice in each of the ankle and foot positions (perform the advanced stretch following the foot position)
Execute identical movements with right leg

Count:
10 for the calf position
20 for the ankle and foot positions
10 for advanced stretch

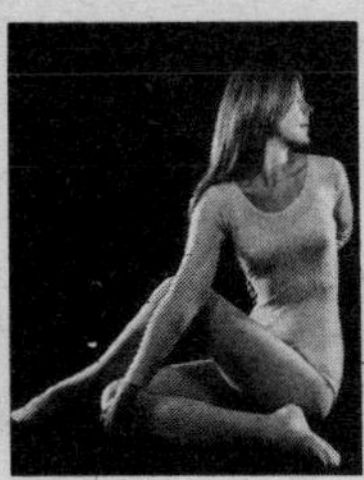

2-G

FULL TWIST

References:
Page 183

Repetitions:
Twice to left side; twice to right side

Count:
20 in each extreme twist

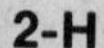

2-H

SIDE RAISE

References:
Page 206

Repetitions:
Begin on left side. Raise right leg once; raise both legs moderate distance once; raise to extreme position twice
Perform identical movements on right side

Count:
10 for each raise

2-I

COMPLETE BREATH

References:
Page 50

Repetitions:
Five times

Count:
Retain breath for 10

2-J

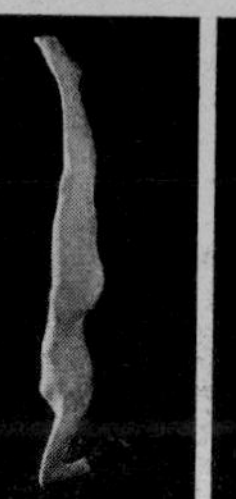

HEAD STAND

References:
Pages 64; 150-152; 269

Repetitions:
Your extreme position, once

Count:
Begin with 30 in your extreme position. Add 15 each time you practice the Head Stand until 3 minutes (a count of 180) is reached. Then continue to hold your extreme position for 3 minutes

At this point, if your time permits, return to the beginning of Routine 2 and perform each exercise once in the continuous slow-motion movement. Eliminate the Complete Breath and Head Stand exercises for the continuous motion routine. Conclude with Deep Relaxation.

2-K

DEEP RELAXATION

References:
Page 287

Repetitions:
Seven times

Count:
In continuous motion as directed

Upon completion, rest quietly on back for several minutes

ROUTINE 3

(A-M)

3-A

CHEST EXPANSION

References:
Pages 9; 20; 67; 110

Repetitions:
Once in each of the three positions. Perform the leg movements following the third position

Count:
10 in the backward and 20 in the forward positions; hold each leg stretch for 10

3-B

DANCER'S POSTURE

References:
Pages 195-196

Repetitions:
Five times

Count:
In continuous motion

3-C

ABDOMINAL LIFTS (B & C)

References:
Pages 96; 97

Repetitions:
Three groups in each of the two positions

Count:
5-10 rhythmic lifts in each group (this will make a total of 30-60 lifts)

3-D

SCALP

References:
Pages 59-60

Repetitions:
25-50 movements

Count:
In continuous motion

3-E

LION

References:
Pages 59-60

Repetitions:
Three times

Count:
20 each extreme position

3-F

NECK ROLL

References:
Page 191

Repetitions:
Twice counter-clockwise; twice clockwise

Count:
5 in each rolling movement

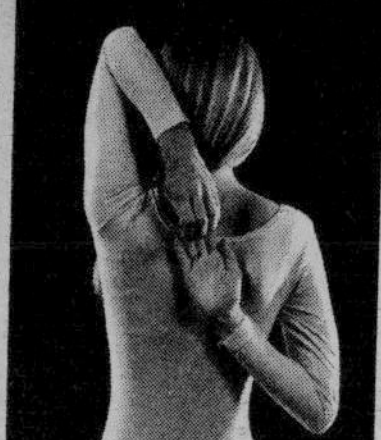

POSTURE CLASP

References:
Pages 239-240

Repetitions:
Five times each side

3-G

Count:
3 for each pull

KNEE and THIGH STRETCH

References:
Page 21

Repetitions:
Three times

3-H

Count:
15 each stretch

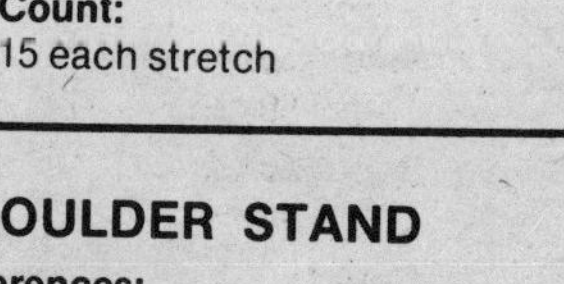

SHOULDER STAND

References:
Page 132

3-I

Repetitions:
Your extreme position, once

Count:
3 minutes (count of 180) is adequate
Advanced students can hold up to 10 minutes

3-J

PLOUGH

References:
Pages 135; 279-280

Repetitions:
Routine consists of the three positions. Perform as many of them as you can Rest on back briefly and repeat the entire routine once more

Count:
20 in each of your extreme positions

3-K

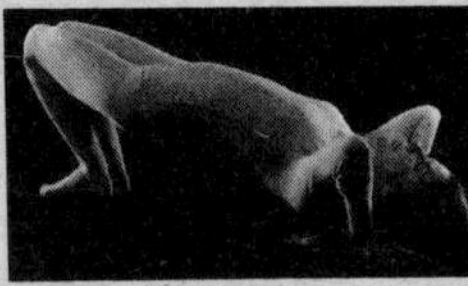

BACK PUSH-UP

References:
Pages 230-231

Repetitions:
Once in moderate position;
Twice in extreme position

Count:
10 for each raise

3-L

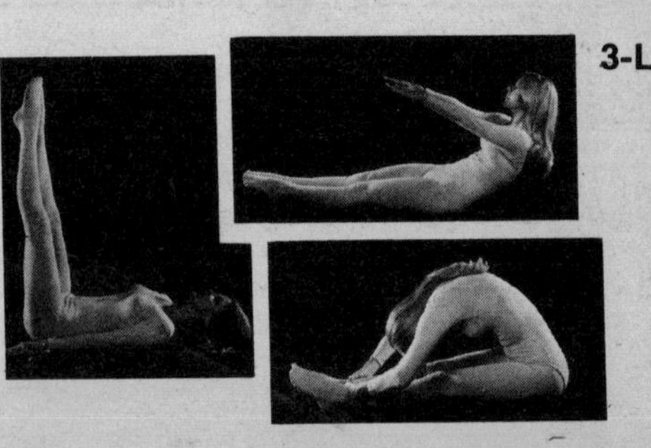

SLOW MOTION FIRMING

References:
Page 226

Repetitions:
Entire routine twice

Count:
In continuous motion

At this point, if your time permits, return to the beginning of Routine 3 and perform each exercise once in the continuous slow-motion movement. Eliminate the Abdominal Lifts, Scalp, Lion and Neck Roll exercises. Conclude with Candle Concentration.

3-M

CANDLE CONCENTRATION

References:
Pages 288-289

Repetitions:
Once

Count:
Gaze at flame for 2 minutes; palm eyes for 1-2 minutes
Relax in seated posture for several minutes

---

sanskrit names for yoga exercises

1. Chest Expansion ....**Ardha Chakrasana**
2. Back Stretch ....**Paschimottanasana**
3. Cobra ....**Bhujangasana**

4. Triangle .... **Trikonasana**
5. Knee and Thigh Stretch **Bhadrasana**
6. Simple Twist .... **Ardha Matsyendrasana**
7. Circular Motion .... —
8. Leg Over .... —
9. Lotus Postures .... **Sukhasana—Siddhasana—Padmasana**
10. Complete Breath .... **Pranayama**
11. Complete Breath Standing .... —
12. Lion .... **Simhasana**
13. Scalp Exercise .... —
14. Backward Bend .... **Supta-Vajrasana**
15. Modified Head Stand **Sirshasana**
16. Abdominal Lifts .... **Uddiyana**
17. Side Bend .... **Nitambasana**
18. Locust .... **Salabhasana**
19. Head Twist .... —
20. Shoulder Stand .... **Sarvangasana**
21. Plough .... **Halasana**
22. Bow .... **Dhanurasana**
23. Rishi's Posture .... —
24. Bust Exercise .... —
25. Full Twist .... **Ardha Matsyendrasana**
26. Neck Roll .... —
27. Balance Posture .... **Natarajasana**
28. Dancer's Posture .... **Urvasana**
29. Elbow-to-Knee .... —
30. Side Raise .... **Uttitha Merudandasana**
31. Slow Motion Firming ..... —
32. Back Push-Up .... **Kamdharasana**
33. Posture Clasp .... **Gomukhasana**
34. Leg Clasp .... **Padahastasana**
35. Alternate Leg Pull .... **Janusirasana**
36. Alternate Nostril Breathing .... **Sukh Purvak**
37. Deep Relaxation .... **Savasana**
38. Candle Relaxation .... **Tratak**

YOGA FOR HEALTH, Mr. Hittleman's television series can be seen in many areas of the country. For a free newsletter and information regarding his various publications and record albums, write to: